AA

ORDNANCE SURVEY
LEISURE GUIDE

NORTHUMBRIA

Produced jointly by the Publishing Division of the
Automobile Association and the Ordnance Survey

Cover: Hadrian's Wall looking east towards Housesteads
Back cover: mid 19th-century engraving of Newcastle
Title page: Alnwick Castle
Contents page: Cauldron Snout on the River Tees
Introductory page: Smailholm Tower west of Kelso

Editors: Rebecca Snelling, Valerie Wenham

Art Editor: Bob Johnson

Design Assistant: John Breeze

Consultant: Tony Hopkins

Editorial contributors: Roland Bibby (A Remote
Kingdom); Carol Bond (A to Z Gazetteer); Jim Crow
(The Romans in Northumbria); Durham County
Council Planning Department (A to Z Gazetteer and
Walks in Durham); Tony Hopkins (The Wildlife of
Northumbria); Liz McIntosh (Farming and Forestry);
Lesley Silvera (Walks in Northumberland); Geoffrey
Wright (The Landscape, Border Strife and Strongholds,
Northumbria's Christian Heritage and the Gazetteer
short features)

Picture researcher: Wyn Voysey
Original photography: S & O Mathews

Typeset by Avonset, Midsomer Norton, Bath.
Printed in Great Britain by Purnell Book Production
Limited. Member of the BPCC Group.

Maps extracted from the Ordnance Survey's 1:625,000
Routeplanner Map, 1:25,000 Pathfinder Series and
1:250,000 Routemaster Series, with the permission of
Her Majesty's Stationery Office. Crown Copyright
reserved.

Additions to the maps by the Cartographic Dept of the
Automobile Association and the Ordnance Survey.

Produced by the Publishing Division of the Automobile
Association.

Distributed in the United Kingdom by the Ordnance
Survey, Southampton, and the Publishing Division of
the Automobile Association, Fanum House,
Basingstoke, Hampshire RG21 2EA.

The contents of this publication are believed correct at
the time of printing. Nevertheless, the Publishers cannot
accept responsibility for errors or omissions, or for
changes in details given.

© The Automobile Association 1987
   The Ordnance Survey 1987

AA ISBN 0 86145 495 2 (hardback)
AA ISBN 0 86145 494 4 (softback)
OS ISBN 0 31900 111 3 (hardback)
OS ISBN 0 31900 110 5 (softback)

Published by the Automobile Association and the
Ordnance Survey.

AA ref: 53934 (hardback)
AA ref: 53921 (softback)

NORTHUMBRIA

Contents

Using this Book

The entries in the Gazetteer have been carefully selected to reflect the interest and variety of Northumbria although for reasons of space it has not been possible to include every community in the region. A number of small villages are described under the entry for a larger neighbour, and these can be found by using the index.

Each entry in the A to Z Gazetteer has the atlas page number on which the place can be found and its National Grid reference included under the heading. An explanation of how to use the National Grid is given on page 84.

Beneath many of the entries in the Gazetteer are listed AA-recommended hotels, guesthouses, camp sites, garages and self-catering accommodation in the immediate vicinity of the place described. Hotels and camp sites are also given an AA classification.

HOTELS

1-star	Good hotels and inns, generally of small scale and with good furnishings and facilities.
2-star	Hotels with a higher standard of accommodation. There should be 20% with private bathrooms or showers.
3-star	Well-appointed hotels. Two-thirds of the bedrooms should have private bathrooms or showers.
4-star	Exceptionally well-appointed hotels offering high standards of comfort and service. All bedrooms should have private bathrooms or showers.
5-star	Luxury hotels offering the highest international standards.

Hotels often satisfy *some* of the requirements for higher classifications than that awarded.

Red-star	Red stars denote hotels which are considered to be of outstanding merit within their classification.
Country House Hotel	A hotel where a relaxed informal atmosphere prevails. Some of the facilities may differ from those at urban hotels of the same classification.

SELF CATERING

These establishments, which are all inspected on a regular basis, have to meet minimum standards in accommodation, furniture, fixtures and fittings, services and linen.

Details are to be found in the AA *Holiday Homes, Cottages and Apartments in Britain* annual guide.

GUESTHOUSES

These are different from, but not necessarily inferior to, AA-appointed hotels, and they offer an alternative for those who prefer inexpensive and not too elaborate accommodation. They all provide clean, comfortable accommodation in homely surroundings. Each establishment must usually offer at least six bedrooms and there should be a general bathroom and a general toilet for every six bedrooms without private facilities.

Parking facilities should be reasonably close.

Other requirements include:
Well maintained exterior; clean and hygienic kitchens; good standard of furnishing; friendly and courteous service; access at reasonable times; the use of a telephone and full English breakfast.

CAMP SITES

1-pennant	Site licence; 10% of pitches for touring units; site density not more than 30 per acre; 2 separate toilets for each sex per 30 pitches; good quality tapwater; efficient waste disposal; regular cleaning of ablutions block; fire precautions; well-drained ground.
2-pennant	All one-pennant facilities plus: 2 washbasins with hot and cold water for each sex per 30 pitches in separate washrooms; warden available at certain times of the day.
3-pennant	All two-pennant facilities plus: one shower or bath for each sex per 30 pitches, with hot and cold water; electric shaver points and mirrors; all-night lighting of toilet blocks; deep sinks for washing clothes; facilities for buying milk, bread and gas; warden in attendance by day, on call by night.
4-pennant	All three-pennant facilities plus: a higher degree of organisation than one–three pennant sites; attention to landscaping; reception office; late-arrivals enclosure; first aid hut; shop; routes to essential facilities lit after dark; play area; bad weather shelter; hard standing for touring vans.
5-pennant	A comprehensive range of services and equipment; careful landscaping; automatic laundry; public telephone; indoor play facilities for children; extra facilities for recreation; warden in attendance 24 hours per day.

WALKS

The walks in this book have been carefully planned to suit families but a few need particular care if young children are in the party. Potential hazards are highlighted in the text.

It is always advisable to go well-equipped with suitable clothing and refreshment, and, as an extra precaution, a compass.

Please observe The Country Code at all times.

NORTHUMBRIA ·

Introduction

*For centuries this was the most isolated region in
England and the sense of remoteness still evident
today is the key to its charm. Breathtaking scenery
– waterfalls, forests, golden beaches; legacies of a
fascinating past – Hadrian's Wall, abbeys, castles;
grand gardens; museums; historic cities and tiny
villages are all described here. Walks and drives seek
out the best of the area and there is lots of practical
information too. Backed by the AA's expertise and
the Ordnance Survey's mapping, this guide is as
useful to those who already love the area as it is to
those discovering Northumbria for the first time.*

The Landscape

The Northumbrian landscape, like any other in England, consists of many inter-related features. Rocks have created the skeleton, time has moulded it, wind and weather, water and ice have shaped it, and vegetation has clothed it. However, few areas have been untouched by man: his hands and his endeavours have fashioned so much of what we see today.

Uplands

A small-scale 'physical' map of Northumbria shows the lie of the land, with the line of the A1 from Darlington to Berwick roughly separating the low-lying coastal plain in the east from land which gradually increases in height towards the west, where the northern Pennines shade into the Cheviots to form an upland rim of mountains.

From the Tyne Bridge at Newcastle let vision sweep imaginatively beyond the city's industrial and commercial skyline, in a wide arc reaching to distant lonely heights. These are all about 40 miles away, from Mickle Fell above Teesdale in the south-west, to Cross Fell, then Cold Fell due west, with a leap over the Tyne Gap to Peel Fell above the Border Forest Park. Then the view would bound north-eastwards from one windy summit to the next, to Cheviot itself, thus almost completing a semi-circle. If you walked this upland rim of hills you would be above 2,000ft for much of the way. Beneath your feet would be the oldest rocks of Northumbria; while your vision would range over stunning views.

From Mickle Fell to Cold Fell the proud Pennine peaks reveal wilderness landscapes of heather and peat hags descending eastwards, contrasting with the scarp-face dropping sharply to the fields and hedgerows of the Vale of Eden in the west.

Rivers

The area around Cross Fell sees the birth of great northern rivers, Tees, Wear and South Tyne, with the North Tyne, Rede and Coquet rising on the Cheviots, but all sharing a common desire to flow south or eastwards, down the long dip-slopes of the hills, towards the North Sea. By way of contrast, the Eden's course, west of Pennine, is northwards to the Solway, while in the far north-east the Till, or Breamish as it is called when it rises on Cheviot, wraps itself round the southern and eastern flanks of the hills before swinging north and north-west to join the Tweed.

Viewpoints

From a series of scattered viewpoints much of Northumbria's topography can be appreciated. Ross Castle or Hepburn Wood above Chillingham, both easily reached by short walks, offer superb panoramas across the Vale of Till to the rounded summits of the Cheviots as well as a sight of the sea to the east. Corby's Crags on the Alnwick to Rothbury road are almost as rewarding, while the Simonside Hills above Rothbury show the noble Cheviot skyline..

The view northwards from Hadrian's Wall, particularly in the area between Housesteads and Crag Lough, reveals not only the north-facing scarp of the hard Whin Sill along which the Wall so arrogantly strides, but the parallel wave-like crests in the Carboniferous limestone landscape beyond.

Coastal landscape

Nearer the coast lower viewpoints reveal the intimate scenery of County Durham. Kirk Merrington, near Bishop Auckland, stands about 600ft above sea level. At this height, under ideal conditions, a view to the horizon extends for about 30 miles, encompassing most of the county – a patchwork panorama reaching from the distant Pennines to the glinting sea. This mixture of

agricultural and industrial landscapes reflects the rich soils above the New Red Sandstone and the mineral wealth of the older coal measures. Further north, Penshaw Hill, at about 450ft, shows the more industrialised scene of the Wear basin. There are good views of the coastal plain and the coastline with its castles, its headlands of hard rock and its bays where the sea has eroded softer sandstones.

The Cheviot Hills

The Cheviot massif was once part of a volcano, probably active about 380 million years ago. The granite core and andesite lavas formed conical hills whose smooth tops and rounded shapes are the result of later weathering, especially during glacial times. Only occasionally do outcrops occur, as at the Henhole and Bizzle Burns. The Hanging Stone, Auchope Cairn, Langlee Crags and Long Crags were all formed from metamorphosed lava, but on the broad Cheviot summit a morass of sticky mud and peat hides the pink granite, and it is a determined walker who is prepared to flounder across it to the Ordnance Survey triangulation column. In the surrounding foothill country, especially near Wooler, interesting glacial features occur. Many meltwater channels dating from the Ice Age have left dry valleys, often cutting across hill spurs, as at Monday Cleugh, above Humbleton, while the A697 south of Powburn follows another.

The River Coquet, which rises in the Cheviots, winds its way through the rounded hills near Shillmoor

Most valleys radiating from the Cheviot, including College Valley and Harthope Burn, as well as the Kale Water and the Bowmont on the Scottish side, were widened, deepened, and straightened by glaciers. In the north Pennines too, ice sheets covered the land to a height of about 2,000ft and glaciers flowed down the main valleys – Tees, Wear and Tyne. Smoothing and scouring the sides as they moved slowly eastwards, they deposited boulder-clay and glacial drift over the lower lands towards the coast, yielding good soils suitable for mixed farming.

The Pennines

This range is made of rocks of Carboniferous age, geologically only a little less ancient than the Cheviot volcanics. The Alston Block, as it is often called, is separated from neighbouring areas at its north, south and west by important faults, and is tilted eastwards to sink into the fertile farmlands of the Durham plain. Rocks of the Carboniferous Series comprise limestones, sandstones and shales, capped by gritstone on Cross Fell and the other north Pennine summits. Great earth stresses occurred after these rocks were formed, resulting in mountain ranges, of which the Pennine Chain was one. During these movements a pattern of small fractures in the rocks of the Alston Block resulted in mineral ores of lead, iron and zinc, together with quartz, fluorspar, calcite and barite being forced along openings. These mineral veins were worked for their metal content, particularly in the 18th and 19th centuries, on Alston Moor, in upper Weardale, upper Teesdale, and in the twin Allen valleys. Remains of old workings and spoil heaps add interest and beauty to the landscape, and specimens of ore can still be found in the spoil.

The Whin Sill

At the same time as mineral veins were formed a vast amount of molten magma forced itself between some of the beds of the Yoredale Series and spread as a vast sheet across parts of the northern Pennines and Northumberland. It solidified between existing strata as a dark, hard crystalline rock, usually between 80ft and 100ft thick, but in places over 200ft. Later erosion and faulting has caused it to form impressive, almost vertical crags. The Whin Sill as it is called, gives the most spectacular landscape features in Northumbria: the great waterfalls, High Force and Cauldron Snout in upper Teesdale; the long line of crags forming the thrilling natural foundation for Hadrian's Wall; the coastal crags crowned by the fortresses of Dunstanburgh and Bamburgh and a number of prominent headlands of which Cullernose Point is the most dramatic. The Farne Islands represent a final appearance of the Whin Sill which, more prosaically, is quarried for road metal in Teesdale, Weardale and Northumberland.

Sandstone

The fell sandstone, already referred to, which forms the basis of the heather-covered moorlands of Rothbury, Chillingham and the Kyloe Hills, was deposited by a huge primordial river flowing from great mountain ranges to the north. Afterwards came a succession of rhythmic subsidences and upheavals which allowed vegetation to develop. This, in turn, created the seams of Scremerston coal, worked near Berwick, the North Tyne Valley near Lewisburn and in Redesdale. The main coal measures, however, were laid down considerably later, towards the end of the Carboniferous period.

The characteristic feature of this landscape between the Tyne and the Cheviots is the succession of north-facing, and north-westwards-facing scarps, or edges. Formed of sandstones, they are separated by concentric vales shaped from softer cementstones and shales. Overlaid by glacial deposits of boulder clay forming gently rolling moorlands, they extend in a broad swathe over much of Northumberland, running south-westwards from Elsdon to the Cumbrian border, and beyond it to the Irthing Valley. The Rede and North Tyne flow southwards from these uplands, wide areas of which are now blanketed by extensive plantations of the Border Forest Park. Kielder Water, created by damming the North Tyne above Bellingham, is now an important focus of leisure activity within an otherwise sparsely populated area.

The sandstones are particularly varied and many beds have provided splendid building material. Northumberland is the only English county in which the hard, yellow-grey sandstones of the Lower Carboniferous Series have been used for building, well seen at Wallington, Cambo, Elsdon, Newcastle Central Station and as the major material of Hadrian's Wall. South of the Tyne, and in Weardale, Allendale, the upper Derwent and around Alston, buildings of a dark grey-brown rubble sandstone extracted from nearby Pennine quarries can be seen.

Carboniferous limestones

The Carboniferous limestones formed in warm, shallow seas 300 million years ago, though present over much of Northumberland, show their best features along the coast, particularly between Alnmouth and Berwick. However, commercial use has been made of them over a large area and many limekilns can be seen near the coast and across country as far as Teesdale. Excellent 18th- and 19th-century kilns survive at Beadnell, on Holy Island, and at Crindledykes, south of Housesteads on Hadrian's Wall. Modern limestone-quarrying, leading to the manufacture of cement, occurs in Weardale. Also of commercial importance is the magnesian limestone which runs in a narrow band northwards from Nottinghamshire to Durham. This is dramatically exposed at Marsden Rocks on the Durham coast where weathered sea-stacks provide a fine breeding site for many seabirds. Inland, this rock forms a ridge of low hills stretching across the county and has been quarried in many places.

Ice Age scenery

Reference has already been made to some of the effects of the Ice Age which occurred about two million to 12,000 years ago. Apart from the smoothing and scouring of valleys, and the transport and deposition of boulder clay and glacial drift resulting in the fertile soils of the coastal plain, other important effects on the scenery are worth mentioning. Ice gouged out and deepened rock-basins and hollows, initially filled with melt-waters, some of which survived as lakes, and the group north of Hadrian's Wall – Crag Lough, Broomlee Lough and Greenlee Lough – are well-known examples. Near Wooler, Milfield Plain covers one of England's biggest hollows – once filled by Milfield Lake – while Ford Moss a few miles further north, shows a 25ft depth of peat, mosses and water.

Border Strife and Strongholds

Centuries before England and Scotland were named as individual countries the Romans had created the first border. When they crossed the Tyne at Corbridge in AD70-80 the land to the north was inhabited by Iron Age tribes, the Votadini, colourfully described by Professor I A Richmond as 'Celtic cowboys, footloose and unpredictable, moving with their animals and herds over rough pastures and moorland'. Early settlements were small groups of wooden huts and palisades, probably Bronze Age, succeeded by hill-forts with ramparts of stone and earth, such as Yeavering Bell on the Cheviots, west of Wooler.

Failing to consolidate their intended conquest of Scotland, the Romans built Hadrian's Wall as their northern frontier, thus unknowingly setting the stage for subsequent centuries of argument about the Border line.

Early border country

In the 9th century, the emergent Kingdom of the Scots, under the leadership of Kenneth McAlpin, claimed all the land between the rivers Forth and Tweed, introducing the Tweed as a natural frontier. However, for much of the year, the Tweed is an ineffective barrier, easily fordable in low water at a number of places. As a result, forts were established at Berwick-upon-Tweed, Norham, and Wark for extra protection. At Carham (between Coldstream and Kelso) the eastern March, or division of the Border, ended and the Middle March began, the Border taking a line southwards to the Bowmont Water, on to the Cheviot Hills, and south-westwards along their rounded crests as far as Kershopefoot in Liddesdale. The natural watershed of the hills may have seemed a suitable frontier but it was not clearly defined on the ground, so land on both sides remained disputed territory. For centuries this good grazing country was occupied and squabbled over by local families who were not interested in politics so much as survival.

Bamburgh Castle, ideally positioned for coastal defence, was converted in the 19th century to residential use, but it still retains its imposing grandeur

Border raids

It is likely that for centuries a system of inheritance called 'gavelkind' prevailed in which, at a man's death, his land and property was divided equally among his sons. The result was hardly sufficient to live off, and as this custom continued there was a degree of 'over-population'. To alleviate hardship, livestock-stealing became a way of life among farmers and families on both sides of the Border. Most of the fighting was over cattle and horses, and because the English side of the Border was the richer, it was the Scots who did most of the raiding. The Borderers, who sought quiet, secret ways through the hills, following lonely burns, were known as mosstroopers or reivers – prepared to drive any stock on the hoof, to burn crops and to steal whatever they fancied. The Wardens of the Marches tried to counter these raids by arranging nightly 'township' watches, but these apparently had little effect.

This no man's land territory was a lonely landscape suited to relatively small-scale skirmishing. However, in 1296 the English King, Edward I, began a campaign which heralded another three centuries of larger-scale but intermittent fighting between the two countries in which Northumberland was the frontier-zone.

Fortifications

Particularly after the Scottish victory at Bannockburn in 1314, everybody in Northumberland – and many to the south of the Tyne – felt vulnerable. The nobility built or strengthened their castles; lesser gentry, especially in villages and hamlets, built fortified houses called pele-towers; farmers built smaller pele-houses often called bastles. A list prepared for Henry V in 1415 contains the names of 113 castles and pele-towers in Northumberland alone, others existed in Durham and Cumbria, and to these can be added at least 200 other fortified structures. It is not surprising that one historian claimed that 'Northumberland has more castles, fortalices, peles, bastles and barmkins than any other county in the British Isles'. Today, apart from a few major castles, many of these structures are ruined, but a surprising number have survived, sufficiently intact to justify restoration and improvement, and are now private dwellings, parsonages, and farm or public buildings.

Coastal fortresses

In terms of position and splendour Bamburgh Castle is supreme. The Romans used the same rocky outcrop; it became capital of the ancient Kingdom of Bernicia, and the Anglo-Saxon Chronicle described it as a fortified city – which may not necessarily have implied any great size. Henry II's keep of 1164 survives, and there is Norman work in the gatehouse and angle-towers. Bamburgh was ruinous when Lord Crewe, Bishop of Durham, bought it in 1704, and after his death the ruins were restored to a variety of uses. In about 1890 the industrialist, Lord Armstrong, made more drastic modifications by turning it into a place of residence which has now been converted into flats.

Down the coast, Dunstanburgh Castle captures the imagination, particularly when approached by the coastal footpath from Craster. Its arrogant gatehouse-keep and massive curtain wall crown the dark cliffs of the Whin Sill and form one of the northern coast's most stirring sights. Built as a

Lindisfarne Castle, on Holy Island, further up the coast from Bamburgh, dates from the 16th century

fortress-home by Thomas, Earl of Lancaster, in the 14th century, Dunstanburgh was, however, more a baronial stronghold than a link in the coastal defence chain.

The 'daintie little fort' of Lindisfarne on Holy Island was built by Henry VIII in the 1550s mainly to defend the important anchorage against Scottish invasion. Early this century, Lutyens imaginatively converted it into a remarkable house, and it is now National Trust property.

Castles in County Durham

Durham Castle, Norman partner to the cathedral on the rock above the Wear, was started by William I in 1072, but contains much work of the 12th and 13th centuries, contributed by the successive Prince-Bishops who lived there. Van Mildert, last of the Prince Bishops, who founded the University in 1832, gave the Castle as its first seat, and Salvin rebuilt the late medieval keep in 1840.

In Teesdale the former Neville stronghold of Raby Castle gave important support to the Prince-Bishops' defence of the Palatinate against Scottish raids, and though largely 14th-century in character and appearance, 18th- and 19th-century additions have converted it into a comfortable mansion. Not so at nearby Barnard Castle, whose 12th-century ruins frown gauntly down on the Tees. Edward I seized it in 1296, granted it to the Beauchamp earls of Warwick, from whom it passed to the Duke of Gloucester, later Richard III, who made the last improvements to it in the 15th century.

Baronial castles of Northumbria

Alnwick and Warkworth were the chief baronial castles of Northumberland. Each commanded an important river crossing, thus guarding the coastal route between the Tweed and Newcastle. Both were Percy strongholds of an original Norman plan overlaid by later developments. At Alnwick these are largely 18th-century additions, designed by Paine and Robert Adam at the behest of the 1st Duke of Northumberland (1750-86) whose family continue in residence to the present day. Hotspur Gate in the town was built as part of the walls in the 15th century.

At Warkworth the Percys enlarged the castle in the late 14th century, and despite being plundered for building stone in the 17th and 18th centuries, it remains an example of great military architecture. At the northern end of the village street a bridge over the Coquet incorporates a fortified tower.

Other baronial castles existed at Morpeth and Mitford, both on the Wansbeck and forming the outer defences of Newcastle, whose medieval fortress was largely destroyed in the middle of the last century when the railway-builders devastated it. However, the massive keep (1172-77) survives, together with the Black Gate, the gatehouse built 70 years later.

Guardians of the Tweed

Norham Castle, situated by a bend in the River Tweed a few miles south-west of Berwick, was the most northerly stronghold of the Prince Bishops, as Norhamshire formed part of the County Palatinate, for which they, and not the Kings of England, were responsible. Bishop Hugh de Puiset built most of what survives in about 1160, including the keep, gatehouses and part of the curtain wall. This front-line fortress was frequently besieged, and as frequently repaired, even after its battering by the great cannon, Mons Meg, dragged by James IV's army from Edinburgh on his way to subsequent defeat and death at Flodden in 1513.

During the centuries of strife between England and Scotland, Berwick occupied a strategic position at the mouth of the Tweed, changing hands 13 times. Only fragments of its early walls survive, but the Elizabethan ramparts and bastions, begun by Mary Tudor in about 1555, and completed a few years later, represented a fortification technique introduced to northern Europe for the first time. The best-preserved sections are between Meg's Mount and the Brass Bastion, their construction contrasting sharply with the earlier wall built by Edward I in the northern part of the town. Berwick's castle ruins were swept away by the

The seal of Hugh de Puiset, builder of Norham Castle

coming of the railway even more ruthlessly than those at Newcastle.

At Wark, once a royal stronghold, nothing remains visible apart from some motte-and-bailey earthworks, and these pale into insignificance compared with the massive, grass-covered mound and ditch of the former castle at Elsdon, probably dating from 1080.

Large medieval earthworks also survive at Harbottle, in the Coquet Valley above Rothbury. The castle here was built for Henry II in about 1160, and became the headquarters of the Wardens of the Middle March. Repeatedly sacked and rebuilt, very little remains of its masonry except a grey stone wall on a grassy mound.

A display board at Flodden chronicles the 16th-century battle fought on these now peaceful arable fields

The pele-tower at Belsay is roughly 50ft square, making it one of the larger examples of these defensive tower-houses of the English/Scottish borders

Pele-towers

A pele was originally a defensive enclosure within a ditch or palisade. By the 16th century it had come to refer to the building inside, usually a strong tower of stone. In the 1415 list Northumberland had 78 such towers. Among these of special interest are the 'Vicars' Peles', built primarily for the protection of a Catholic priesthood. Most have been restored to some form of modern use, as at Elsdon. This dates from about 1400 and was used as a rectory until 1962. Now it is a comfortable house retaining its historic character.

The Vicar's Pele at Corbridge, a century older, is constructed of stones from the Roman supply base, Corstopitum, to the west of the town. Standing in the churchyard adjoining the Market Place it has a tunnel-vaulted ground floor now housing a Tourist Information Centre. At the eastern end of Main Street, Low Hall incorporates a small pele-tower probably built in the late 15th century.

To the north of Corbridge, occupying a commanding situation above the Tyne Valley is Halton Tower. This perfect 14th-century pele-tower, four storeys high and built of Roman masonry, had a modest mansion added to it in the 17th century. Aydon Castle nearby originated as a fortified manor house, with an outer and inner bailey but no keep. It is one of the most important architectural and historic buildings in Northumbria, representing as much space and comfort which could be expected in Border country at that early date, about 1300. Belsay Castle, by the main A696 road to the north, is probably the most sophisticated of Northumbrian tower-houses – mid 14th-century with the addition of an early Jacobean house. This is now a shell, but the old tower has been restored and is open to the public, as is Aydon.

Former pele-towers at Embleton and Alnham were used as rectories; that at Alnham was a Youth Hostel for a while, but it now a private dwelling again. Craster Tower is incorporated into a private house, but the pele-towers at Blanchland and Ponteland have a different modern use. The former now forms part of the Lord Crewe Arms, while Ponteland's tower, with handsome 17th-century additions, is the well-known Blackbird Inn. On the Wallington estate, Cambo Tower was heavily restored early last century and has for years served as the village store and post office.

Some church towers were built as defensive structures, like peles, including St Anne's, Ancroft (near Berwick), and St Cuthbert's, Great Salkeld, north-east of Penrith which are both tunnel-vaulted in the lowest stage of their west towers.

Bastle houses

Also known as pele-houses, these were small fortified houses, usually resembling large barns, with accommodation for people on the upper floor and space for livestock below. With very few exceptions they are to be found only in Northumberland, and almost all lie within 20 miles of the border. An Act of 1555 required castles and forts to be repaired within this distance.

North Tynedale and Redesdale, and to a lesser extent the Coquet Valley, were the corridors through which Scottish raiders frequently came, and it is there that most bastle-houses can be identified, often in clusters of two or three as though for mutual help in danger. At Gatehouse, 3 miles up the Tarset Burn beyond Bellingham, two bastles stand on opposite sides of the road. The north one is excellently preserved, probably late 16th-century, with a ground-floor entrance in one gable and an outside stone stair giving access to the upper floor. The 4ft-thick walls have few windows. Black Middens Bastle in the upper reaches of the Tarset Burn has similar dimensions, about 36ft by 24ft. Akeld Bastle, near Wooler, is much longer and retains its tunnel-vaulted ground floor but the upper part has been rebuilt, with an added double stair outside one gable. Between Rothbury and Elsdon, Raw Bastle at Raw Farm is now used as a barn, but possesses unusual carvings on its east side.

The end of Border strife

Eventually the fighting died down. The great families on each side of the Border negotiated, and although small-scale unofficial raids continued into the 1590s, they had ended by 1603 when the English and Scottish crowns were united. A Border line was eventually agreed, peace came to 'Any Man's Kingdom', and sheep could safely graze the quiet Border hills.

A Remote Kingdom

Northumberland's heritage is rich and full of vitality, for this is the surviving heartland of an ancient kingdom – that of the Anglian Beornicas, which escaped significant inroads by other peoples and cultures because of its remarkable isolation after England was united.

Its own language, tradition and values have survived for 14 centuries and although developing and changing with time, they have never lost sight of their Anglian roots.

The region we call Northumberland (Tweed to Tyneside) was the original conquest of a Beornican leader, Ida, nicknamed 'Burner' or 'Flamebearer', whose Angle warrior-sailor-farmers landed in AD547 along the coast between the rivers Tyne and Tweed, and who himself seized the great rock at Bamburgh for his own fortress and capital. In fierce fighting spanning several reigns, his people settled the fertile coastal plain and lower dales, and won peace with the Celtic Britons of the Cheviots. The little kingdom grew until its Angles inhabited all of south-eastern Scotland up to the Firth of Forth; then union with the neighbouring Angle kingdom to the south, Deira, created 'North-of-Humberland' – Northumbria, the land between the Humber and the Forth.

In the 'Golden Age of Northumbria', great saints and kings strode the splendid stage of Holy Island and royal Bamburgh, as the little kingdom welcomed and championed Christianity in pagan England. True, there were wars, religious and dynastic, but not until the Danish conquest of Deira was Northumbria radically altered. Danish settlers swamped Deira and Danish kings ruled in York; but they left Bernicia as a buffer against Scotland. Later, the Scots seized the area between the Tweed and the Forth, establishing the present Border, and Bernicia was reduced to its original area of King Ida's times – but now it alone kept the name Northumberland.

It also kept its heritage and traditions intact, for the region was 300 uncomfortable miles from England's capital, and the scene of constant raiding and feuding. Kings in London, like their predecessors in York, left Northumberland largely to its own devices, and its remoteness – even after peace finally came to the Borderland – was a strong deterrent to settlers.

A language, not a dialect

The Northumbrian language derives from the Angle-Northumbrian speech of King Ida, St Cuthbert, Bede and Harry Hotspur. The visitor may not spot at once its scope and quality, for today many Northumbrians are bi-lingual, and only an unfamiliar accent or odd turn of phrase may be noticed. Acquaintance limited to television's *The Likely Lads* and *Auf Wiedersehen, Pet* suggests that Northumbrian is merely English oddly pronounced; but this is the diluted modern urban 'Geordie' dialect. There is another trap for the unwary: where Northumbrian and English overlap is in short, everyday words. People hear *lang, craa* and *laa* (long, crow, low) and fancy there is little difference between the languages.

The truth is that, while 82 per cent of Northumbrian words are 'Anglo-Saxon' in origin, this applies to only 26 per cent of English words. Moreover, the other 74 per cent are mostly polysyllabic imports from Greek, Latin, French, etc, so alien to Germanic Angle-Northumbrian that the few specimens absorbed into Northumbrian have been modified – 'Northumbrianised' – almost out of recognition. For instance, 'anatomy' becomes *an atomy*, a skeleton, a very thin person.

The Benfieldside Morris Sword, or Rapper, Dancers. This traditional north-eastern dance features short, two-handled swords

By way of genuine contrast between the two vocabularies, try this rural Northumbrian: *'Aa canna thole a bowdikite yin bittock. Sittin aal canny un' bobbersum wi twa-three neebors bi thi lum iv i wintor's neet, wi thi clishmaclavor stotting iboot varry canty un yor byuts faior kizznin i thi fendor, nowt gars ye girn an' flite heff sa much as thi baiorn creepin roond thi brattish an keekin at ye hwin yor nigh dozzint.'*; and a translation:

'I cannot tolerate a mischief one little bit. Sitting all pleasantly and cheerfully with two or three neighbours by the fire on a winter's evening, with lively talk bouncing about very merrily and your boots really scorching in the fender, nothing makes you grimace and cry out half as much as the child, creeping around the screen and peeping at you when you are almost asleep.'

Tongue-twisters
Northumbrian can baffle with tongue-twisters like *'Ifahadnahadnahadnahaddacowped'* (If Aa hadna hadden a haad on 'aa, ha'd a cowped): 'If I hadn't had hold of it, it would have overturned.' It can emphatically reprove, as in *'Ye greet, luggish, lurdy, lorty, little-a-dow, lig-o-bed, lang-nebbed, laidly lordan!'*: 'You great, lumpish, stupid, lazy, dirty, worthless, lie-abed, inquisitive, disgusting blockhead!'; or it can coax a butterfly:

Lee-la-let, me listy hinny,	*Let/Light,* alight;
Light upon the lilly-lea;	*Listy,* energetic;
Mun ye be sa lush-ma-lavey?	*Hinny,* an
Light upon thi ling fo' me.	endearment; *Lilly-*
Divvint be sa lowpy-dikey;	*lea,* turf; *Mun,*
Light an' liarn ti lippen me –	must; *Lush-me-lavey,*
Aa'm thi little lass	time-wasting. *Ling,*
thit luvs ye;	a heather; *Lowpy-*
Lee-la-let, an'	*dikey,* hedge-leaping;
bide wi' me.	*Liarn,* learn; *Lippen,*
	trust; *Bide,* stay.

In the 1745 Jacobite uprising these Northumberland Halflong pipes were carried by a Scot

A long and honourable line of minor Northumbrian poets and wordsmiths is by no means exhausted, and there is a Northumbrian Language Society which researches, records, publishes, and above all seeks to preserve this well-loved language. There is a distinct resemblance between Northumbrian and Border-Scots speech – it is a case of common heritage; in 1018 when the Celtic Scots seized Northern Bernicia its Angle-Northumbrian language spread over the Lowlands.

Songs and Ballads
Northumberland's great treasury of indigenous song and melody is still sung, played and constantly augmented by a host of composers. The language adds character and delight to numerous songs about the lives of shepherds, ploughmen, miners, keelmen and fisherfolk. Ancestors of these songs still survive in quantity. They are the wonderful Border Ballads – strikingly simple, succinct, stark, musical narratives. Unless a personal or place-name appears, their nationalities cannot be distinguished, for the two 'sides' of the Border were of the same race, both moulded in the furnace of Border strife.

G M Trevelyan memorably wrote of them: 'they were cruel, coarse savages, slaying each other as the beasts of the forest; and yet they were also poets who could express in the grand style the inexorable fate of the individual man and woman, the infinite pity for all the cruel things which they none the less inflicted upon one another. It was not one ballad-maker alone, but the whole cut-throat population who felt this magnanimous sorrow, and the consoling charms of the highest poetry.' After the long period of strife, the ballads were treasured and handed down 'among the shepherds and among the farm-girls who, for centuries, sang them to each other at the milking. If the people had not loved the songs, many of the best would have perished. . . .'

Music and instruments
The musical treasury is rich in melodies old and new, and their composers and collectors serve musicians, dancers and appreciative listeners alike. The musical tradition in turn inspires the composers, and fiddle, accordion, concertina, melodion, flute, humble whistle and harmonica unite to serve Northumbrians' devotion to their music. Above all, their own delightful Northumbrian pipes inspire the composers and musicians. These small-pipes were conceived, developed and perfected by Northumbrians. Their tone is wonderfully sweet and they remain largely unknown elsewhere.

Dance
Northumberland has a good quota of country-dance bands and barn dances. Each band has its tireless 'caller', guiding newcomers through the intricacies of the Morpeth Rant, Drops of Brandy and Buttered Peas.

Morris dancing, a relatively recent arrival, is well-established here, and the more traditional North Country clog dancing, in Northumberland and Durham style, is enjoying a considerable revival; but the oldest tradition is sword-dancing. The original wooden, one-handled long-sword has long been replaced by the pitman's preferred variant, the rapper. This is a flat, flexible steel blade with a wooden grip at each end, used to clean pit-ponies' coats. The dancing miners adapted their movements to the narrow confines of their work-

Clog Dancers on Prebends Bridge in Durham. Although the origins of the dance are obscure, it almost certainly came from the mining villages of Durham

places, without diminishing the vigour, speed and intricacy of their steps and the movements of body and sword. Every colliery team had its specialities. The modern rapper teams who perform are no longer exclusively miners, but they still astound the onlooker with their rapid serpentine coilings on a floor the size of a moderately large tablecloth, though the sharp-edged rappers make no allowance for error.

Crafts

Many Northumbrian craftsmen follow with infinite patience the traditional shepherds' art of 'dressing' walking-sticks and crooks. A hazel rod, a ram's horn, simple tools and endless time are the ingredients for these beautiful artefacts, perfected down to the last speckle on a leaping trout, the feathering of a curlew's wing, or the cobweb harness of a tiny coach and horses.

Fishermen's ganzeys (jerseys) are still knitted to the village's own pattern, and worn as the cobles (like Viking long-boats) put out to sea. 'Clippy' and 'proggy' mats are also still made, sometimes from traditional finger-length strips from worn garments and domestic linen, but no longer at neighbourly working parties assembled to help furnish a house.

Corn dollies too have become a hobby, as have stack ornaments – the life-size straw birds and beasts that used to crown completed haystacks, now often seen as an adornment on thatched roofs.

Folk lore

Of course, in its long isolation, Northumberland has accumulated a huge hoard of lore and legend, and a host of bogles and brownies, ghosties and ghoulies.

Toiling Hobthrust, idling Wag-at-the-Wa', dim-witted Dobie, ill-willed, joking Brag; Kilmouly, the miller's unsought assistant, Habretot the spinner; Powrie and Dunter, doting on ruined towers; Blue Cap and Cutty Soames, meddlers in coalmines; wailing Dunnie, sniggering Hedley Kow, tormenting Barghaist; Red Cap brightening his bonnet with travellers' blood, the lethal Broon Man o' the Muir, Deugar luring poor innocents over cliffs – and most of these not individuals but widespread species – in addition to whole communities of fairy folk.

As for the many 'ghaisties', there are the nameless ones dotted about; several White Ladies and several Silkies (unseen – just 'yon sus-sus-sussuration, si-si-sibilant an' slaa', of silken petticoats); and, of course, much-travelled Meg o' Meldon who rushes about everywhere, as the swirls in standing corn plainly show.

Seasonal festivals

Such a community naturally respects its seasonal festivals, significant and enjoyable bonds with its distant past. So the ancient bonfires of early faiths were still common here in the last century, and Whalton village still has its Midsummer Bale (great fire), while Allendale Town keeps up its midwinter fire, fuelled by men in procession with half-barrels of burning tar on their heads. The lingering belief that it is unlucky to 'borrow light' at Hogmanay could recall the Druidic sacred fires from which each household took a burning branch to relight the domestic fire – and no borrowing from neighbours! Such burning branches from village bales were carried around the fields to ward off crop blight and cattle disease, and good Christians leapt the great fires, no longer to propitiate ancient gods, but for good luck.

Ancient spring festivals survive in traditional Easter sports. At Morpeth children gather at the Easter Field to *bool* (bowl) and *jaap* (knock together) their hard-boiled, dyed or painted *pace* (peace) eggs, while at Alnwick two vast football teams gather each Shrovetide to play parish against parish across the castle parkland and the river.

Not so very long ago, every farm turned the last sheaf of corn harvested into a dressed, decorated figure, carried in triumph to preside at the *Kern*

A 'Guyser' dancing round the bonfire at Allenheads' spectacular New Year's Eve fire festival

(corn) Supper. Now the pagan goddess of fertility has become the Kern Babby at Whalton's harvest festivals, but the Christ Child is still traditionally womanly in appearance.

Northumbrian fare

A rare variety of appetising traditional (and new) dishes is met in Northumberland; many meatless from earlier, poorer times. Plum-broth (meat, fruit and spices minced together) and Fromenty (boiled barley, milk and sugar) may have gone, but Hasty Pudding, Leek Pasty, Brawn, Cheviot Cutlets, Pan Hacklety (cheese and vegetables fried), Whitley Goose (onions, cheese and cream – no goose!), Leek-Puddin'-in-a-Cloot, Gordle Cyeks, Singin Hinnies, Stotty Cyeks, are still made and enjoyed, and on Carlin Sunday some pubs continue to provide saucers of strange, hard, fried grey peas, the strictly local Carlins. Yule Babbies are cooked at Christmas – the Babe in pastry and currants. Farmhouse cheese is still made, though only one is a 'named' variety, 'Redesdale', made near Otterburn. Craster kippers, however, are famous – undyed beauties oak-smoked at this tiny Northumberland fishing village.

The Romans in Northumbria

The uplands of the north Pennines and the Cheviots preserve some of the most spectacular and varied traces of the Roman empire in Western Europe. For over three centuries this bleak northern fastness was Rome's north-west frontier. It cannot compare with the sophistication of urban life which flourished in southern Britain and on the Continent, but the military archaeology has its own particular fascination. From the legionary fortresses of York and Chester we can still follow the roads north, built to supply the advancing armies, and we can also trace the temporary camps on the roadsides and see the permanent forts and frontier works which later replaced them.

The Roman advance

The conquest of Britain began with the Emperor Claudius' landing in Kent in AD43, but it was nearly 40 years before the legions penetrated across the Pennines into the Eden Valley. The invading armies passed on either flank of the Pennines, on the east following the line of the A68, Dere Street, up to Corbridge where a supply base was established in AD80, recently exposed during construction work on the A69 dual carriage-way. To the west, where the A66 crosses the Stainmore Pass, the modern road cuts the earthwork camp of Rey Cross, which once held overnight 8,000 men of an invasion force, a legion and its auxiliaries, poised to march north up the Eden Valley towards Carlisle. Along these two routes the legions under their general, Agricola, moved north, into Scotland. But despite Roman victories nearly as far north as Inverness, the Romans failed to conquer the whole island and so over the next 20 years the frontier ebbed southwards. By AD105, a permanent line was established across the narrowest part of England: the 80 miles from the shores of the Solway to the mouth of the Tyne.

The permanent frontier

This was to be the line of Hadrian's Wall, but as yet the frontier was simply a road between the main route-centres of Corbridge and Carlisle, known by its medieval name the Stanegate, or stone road – a reminder of its Roman origin. Along the road were forts, about 16 miles or a day's march apart with some watchtowers or signalling posts between them. This was little more than a lightly held patrolled line, not yet the rigid frontier of Hadrian's time. The best-known fort of the Stanegate system was Vindolanda, where the earliest turf and timber forts have been examined, buried below the later stone-built phases. Waterlogged conditions have preserved timber, leather, fabrics and vegetation which normally perishes in contact with the air, but the most fascinating details come from the rich hoard of writing tablets from the rubbish in the commanding officer's house. These tiny scraps of wood preserve details of life on the northern frontier, from petitions and laundry lists to the copy of an invitation to her birthday party sent by the commanding officer's wife. Life on the northern frontier is shown to have been less grim than is popularly imagined.

From another writing tablet we learn that the soldiers referred disparagingly to the natives as 'Little Britons', but within a few years there was a major uprising of the northern tribes early in the reign of Hadrian. It was serious enough to demand the emperor's personal attention, and following his visit work began on the great wall which bears his name. A Roman author tells us that it was intended to divide Roman from barbarian and as a military solution it was typical of an emperor who sought to regulate and secure the frontiers of the empire rather than advance in uncertain conquest.

Hadrian's Wall, seen here winding its way along the Whin Sill, was constructed by the Romans as their northern frontier

Hadrian's Wall

The work of building the wall was carried out by the three British legions based at York, Chester and Caerleon in South Wales. With extra auxiliary troops the total force may have been about 25,000 men. Construction began from the east at a bridgehead in Newcastle and eventually the wall extended for 80 Roman miles (76 statute miles) from Wallsend to Bowness-on-Solway. It was initially intended to be 10ft wide, but by the time the construction teams were west of the North Tyne, on the rugged scarp of the Whin Sill, the broad wall was replaced by a narrow one 7 to 8ft wide – probably to economise on the materials used. Further west again the wall was built in turf and only later replaced in stone. The work of construction was a massive enterprise which did not progress without mistakes so that in places a broad foundation was laid and later built over by a narrow wall. At Housesteads (now in the care of the National Trust and English Heritage) an example of the change in the building programme can be seen in the way the fort was built over an already existing turret. The work does not appear to have been fully completed until Hadrian's death in AD138. The full system comprised the wall with a wide ditch to the north and at regular intervals were milecastles, or small forts, with a garrison of about 15 men to patrol and maintain a presence along the wall and to man the turrets between them. Some 7 miles apart were the forts garrisoned by auxiliary regiments of infantry or cavalry and connecting these was a road, a military way, running parallel to the wall. At the major river crossings of the North Tyne and the Irthing there were stone bridges, the massive piers of which still survive at Chesters and Willowford.

The Vallum

South of the wall was a great ditch and double bank, the Vallum, with crossings limited to the forts. This last element in the system has aroused the greatest speculation, and none more wild than the 18th-century view that it was a Roman canal. A more likely, if less colourful, explanation is that the Vallum defined a secure zone south of the wall where there were forts for livestock, and where safe movement was possible in what must have remained an uncertain frontier zone.

Once completed it was mostly abandoned as Hadrian's successor, Antoninus Pius chose to emulate his step-father by building a new turf wall between the Firths of Forth and Clyde. But this Scottish venture was shortlived, and by AD165 Hadrian's Wall was re-occupied and Roman armies withdrew, leaving only the forts on Dere Street at Risingham and High Rochester, and to the west the lonely outposts at Bewcastle, Birrens and Netherby. Hadrian's Wall and its forts were repaired and it remained the northern frontier of Britain until about AD400.

The ruins of the fort at Housesteads on Hadrian's Wall. Examples of Roman sculptures can be seen at the museums along the Wall. The sculpture illustrated (inset) from Corbridge dates from the 3rd century and was originally part of a frieze in a temple to Jupiter Dolichenus

The rebuilding of the Wall

A major rebuilding programme began around AD200 and this proved to be more durable than Hadrian's work. In places the wall was narrowed to as little as 6ft but it was built with a hard, white lime mortar to bind the core and face, best seen in the section owned by the National Trust near Castle Nick, west of Housesteads. Recent excavations have shown that this rebuilt wall was whitewashed, so that it stood stark and white on the crags, a harsh reminder of Roman domination to the subject Britons.

Most visitors today will see in the well-ordered forts, the massive stones in the gates and the bridges, and the inexorable sweep of the Wall over the Whin Sill, evidence for the military organisation and power of Rome. But in the museums along the Wall, whether Chesters or Newcastle, the small finds, inscriptions and sculptures all hint at the civil and religious life associated with the forts. The military presence attracted people from far and wide. Taverns and

small workshops grew up to service the soldiers' requirements. At Housesteads, excavations in the settlement south of the fort found a counterfeiter's mould, loaded dice and two murder victims buried beneath a house floor. In the same area was found a shrine to local hooded deities and we also know that German irregular troops worshipped a very German Mars attended by Valkyries a little further down the hill from the fort. More exclusive were the mystery cults from the eastern parts of the empire, especially that of Mithras, whose temple at Carrawburgh is very well preserved. It was not only religions that came westward; from South Shields and Corbridge we know of a merchant from Palmyra, a caravan city in the Syrian desert who sold silk banners for military flags. Silk, which originally came from China, was used for the cavalry standards on Hadrian's Wall.

Dere Street

Hadrian's Wall represents the importance of defence and communications along the east-west axis, but at times during Roman rule the north-south axis was more significant. Dere Street is followed approximately by the modern A68. Forts were located along the road north from Catterick: Piercebridge, Lanchester and Ebchester, up to the crossing of the Tyne at Corbridge. The line was projected north again, followed more closely by the modern road past the outpost forts of Risingham and High Rochester towards the great native stronghold on the Eildon Hills and the Roman fort at Newstead. As Dere Street climbs out of Redesdale over the last of the Cheviot ridges it is a few miles east of the modern A68 and the border at Carter Bar. But here, just in Northumberland, is one of the most remarkable and evocative monuments in the Roman North – Chew Green. All that remains are the banks and ditches of earthworks, left crisp and unploughed in the upland turf. The outline of five camps, compounds and forts can be easily distinguished, especially in the clear light of an autumn evening. This was always a lonely place, where the wagon trains and columns of soldiers could be secure, and from where troops of cavalry could patrol and ensure security to the north and south.

Vindolanda was one of the earliest Roman forts in this area, pre-dating Hadrian's Wall

Maiden Way

The principal roads were either north to south or east to west, but one Roman road cuts diagonally across the Pennines from the Wall fort at Carvoran to the Eden Valley and the fort at Kirkby Thore. It is known as the Maiden Way, and the long-distance footpath, the Pennine Way, follows some of its course. For much of its northern length it follows the valley of the South Tyne, with only one intermediate fort along its course at Whitley Castle, probably the administrative centre for Roman lead and silver mining in the region. The earthworks of the fort, especially of the multiple ditches, are among the best preserved in Britain. South-west of Alston the Maiden Way is crossed by the A686 to Hartside and it begins an easy ascent across empty moorland south of Fiend's Fell. From here, up to the west-facing scarp of the Pennines, only the thinnest turf cover separates the walker from the Roman past. The road is preserved to its full cambered width of 5yds with massive kerbs and stone-built culverts and embankments. The descent to the valley is by a series of hairpin bends, before it is lost under rich arable land. The course of the road continues to Kirkby Thore, past some impressive medieval lynchets with the fanciful name of the Hanging Walls of Mark Anthony.

Our Roman heritage

The Roman conquest radically changed the appearance of Britain's landscape. Hitherto, trackways had followed the contours of the land, and building had been unambitious, using local materials in keeping with the surroundings. After Hadrian and his successors had withdrawn from Britain the country was criss-crossed by a series of long, straight metalled highways (and of course the Wall) which marched inexorably over hill and dale, punctuated by the geometric shapes of mile castles and forts. Nowhere in Britain is our Roman heritage more evident, or better preserved and documented, than in the rolling Northumbrian countryside.

The Wildlife of Northumbria

Shepherds and soldiers cast long shadows over Northumbria. Steeped in a history of Border conflict, the countryside also reflects the struggle of past generations to win a living from the land. The moors are wide and windswept, the mires treacherous, and the rivers fast and unpredictable. Man never quite tamed the North, and the survival of wild places alongside modern farms and forests has ensured a rich heritage of plants and animals, many of which have been lost to other areas of the country.

After the ice

It is possible to spend a day on the moors of the North Pennines or the Cheviots and not see another living soul. Half close your eyes in these remote areas and you can imagine what Britain was like just after the Ice Age when the great ice floes had melted, before trees had tracked their way north across the land bridge from Europe and long before our ancestors had sharpened their spears and followed the herds of deer over unknown territory.

The sense of wilderness is an illusion; Northumbria has been affected by man as much as anywhere else in the country. The moors were created by the clearance of the original primeval forest and subsequent grazing of sheep. But there are places where the late-glacial flora has survived; in Northumberland a small patch of dwarf birch has recently been discovered on a moor above the North Tyne Valley, and Jacob's Ladder, the same tall, blue-flowered herb that now graces our gardens, still graces one of the Cheviot valleys, having arrived there up to 10,000 years ago.

Upper Teesdale, a 'lost world' set in the Durham moors, has a unique selection of botanic jewels. Spring gentian, birdseye primrose, Teesdale violet and bitter milkwort are all late-glacial relict species found on the sugar-limestone of Widdybank Fell close to Cow Green Reservoir, and nearby there are swathes of shrubby cinquefoil together with forests of juniper.

Moors and mires

When early farmers cleared the broadleaf forests from the uplands it was with the intention of growing crops and rearing stock. But heavy rainfall was already turning the highest ground into blanket bog, and arable farming was only possible on the lower slopes. The domes and plateaux of Langdon Fell and the Cheviot are now topped by 'peat hags', and from the black peat the bleached skeletons of pines and oaks still protrude. Between the Pennine and Cheviot massifs bog moss and the fast-developing peat turned shallow glacial lakes into mires; many have been drained and reclaimed but in the Hadrian's Wall area a number have survived and are of special interest. Their names, Haining Head, Hummel Knowe and Coom Rigg, sound evocative but mires are rarely dramatic and from a distance they are indistinguishable from wet moorland. Several are surrounded by recent conifer plantations and this has affected their character.

To appreciate a mire it is best to get as close as possible, taking care to avoid the greenest and wettest ground. The tracery of flowers on the cushions of bog moss includes cranberry, sundew and bog rosemary. Clumps of cotton grass attract the large heath butterfly, one of the first butterflies to recolonise Britain after the Ice Age, and a fast-diminishing species in England today.

Moorland, the rough ground established and maintained by sheep grazing, covers a large part of the Northumbrian hills. There are many fine heather moors, managed for grouse by rotation burning and containing a variety of habitats such as dry rocky outcrops and damp flushes of cross-leaved heath and bog asphodel. Golden plovers like to nest on the recently burnt ground where they

A grey, or Atlantic, seal calf. The young are born between September and December

have a clear all-round view and can see potential predators, while dunlin prefer the damp hollows, their nests hidden in clumps of rush or cotton grass. Birds of prey are never far away. Hen harriers are a possibility, usually seen quartering the moors, ambushing unwary ground-nesting birds, and peregrines are likely wherever there are suitable crags. News of the merlin is hard to come by; the fiery little falcon is decreasing throughout the country but there are more pairs in Northumbria than anywhere else. Pipits are its prey, caught on the wing after a rapid chase. By contrast, short-eared owls glide like ghosts over the hills on silent wings. They feed their young on voles, so their breeding success is dependent on the vole population which fluctuates from year to year. Ethereal and unpredictable, this day-flying owl is nevertheless the most likely large bird of prey to be seen on the moors of Durham and South Northumberland.

Heather attracts many beautiful insects. Expanses of flowers in late summer are alive with bees, and this is also the time to look along moorland paths for tiger beetles and emperor-moth caterpillars. In the spring, when the adult emperor is in flight, large hairy caterpillars of the fox moth, northern

A hen harrier on its nest. These birds can sometimes be seen hunting over the Northumbrian moors

eggar and (in the Cheviots) the dark tussock are to be found. The cuckoo, which lays its eggs in the nests of pipits, is the only bird which has a taste for 'woolly bears'.

In northern Northumberland the finest blocks of heather moorland are found on the wide arc of fell sandstone encircling the Cheviots, but the Cheviot massif itself is composed of volcanic rocks, granite and andesite, and heather has been replaced by rough grassland. In general, this sheep-grazing country is not so rich in wildlife but is exceptionally fine walking country and forms an important part of the Northumberland National Park. In the most remote hills of Cheviot and Kielder, as far from man as it is possible to get in this crowded country, there are herds of wild goats to remind us of distant days on the Borders when our ancestors subsisted on what they could defend from wolves or steal from their neighbour.

Woodland, ancient and modern
Broadleaf woodland, composed of oak and elm, hazel, alder and birch, once carpeted the hills and plains of the north-east. Now only fragments remain. These scraps of the 'wildwood' attract high breeding populations of insectivorous birds. Holes in old trees are always tenanted; most are likely to contain families of starlings, great tits and blue tits,

The large heath butterfly, which belongs to the brown butterfly family, is relatively rare

but redstarts and pied flycatchers also occur. Other possibilities include great spotted and green woodpeckers, and colonies of noctule bats.

Until the 1930s there was little coniferous forest in Northumbria but today many miles of the region are covered by spruce trees. The plantations did not take the place of existing broadleaf woodland. Most of what is now Kielder Forest was once open moorland, and the arguments against more afforestation relate to the loss of traditional farming as much as to the loss of important wildlife habitat. Drives and walks through Forestry Commission land can be enlivened by sightings of red squirrels and roe deer, siskins and crossbills. The scale of the new forests has worried many naturalists, however, and it is important that the

A field of marsh marigolds – also known as kingcups – in County Durham's botanically-rich Teesdale

essential wildness of the landscape, vested in such birds as the merlin, should not be threatened.

Burns, becks and denes

Water that begins as rain over the high hills, moors and forests finds its way to the North Sea via a network of streams and rivers. Most of the feeder streams in Northumberland are called burns, a name derived from Old English, while in the Northern Pennines they are known as becks, a word of Viking origin.

Upland streams are usually cold, clear and fast-flowing. At their headwaters they can be unreliable; in the space of a few hours a storm can transform rivulets and runnels from attractive cascades into dangerous torrents. For this reason, and because most streams are low in nutrients having gathered their waters from thin, leached soils or blankets of peat, aquatic plants are few. The larvae of insects, particularly caddisflies, mayflies and stoneflies, survive by clinging to the undersides of stones and feeding on debris brought downstream on the current. Trout, patrolling the deeper pools below the rapids, rely on a supply of these creatures thoughout the year. Many waterside birds which also feed on semi-aquatic insects need to be more adaptable and have to be able to desert the upper reaches of streams at times of frost and drought. Dippers stay in their territories for most of the year, breeding in the early spring when fully-grown insect larvae are most abundant and easy to catch. Grey wagtails wait for a few weeks and nest when adult insects are emerging from the water. It would be difficult to imagine two birds so closely associated by habitat yet so dissimilar in behaviour and appearance. Wagtails are dainty and slim, and feed in a nervous, fussy manner along the water's edge. Dippers are dumpy, with big feet and a short tail, and are at ease diving among the rocks and boulders in the middle of the rushing stream.

As the headstreams run into each other to form small rivers, so the variety of wildlife increases.

Minnows, loach and lampreys attract fish-feeding birds. Of these, the speciality in the Northumbrian hills is the goosander, a 'sawbill' duck known to most bird-watchers as a winter visitor to reservoirs in North London and the Midlands. It comes as a surprise to see a drake goosander, the size of a small goose, negotiating a narrow, rushing watercourse with its mate prospecting a nest site in a nearby hollow tree.

Most of the rivers in north-east England are fast-flowing and rocky and the banks are often overgrown with tree roots. This makes them especially attractive, mysterious and untamed. Sudden ripples in the water may be caused by a sea trout or salmon, or even by an otter. Searching the silted floodline and tangled roots it is still possible to find the spraints and slots of otters. If you know how to look, tracks are easy to find along many river systems but the animals are so shy that hours of patient watching near a holt at twilight will not guarantee a sighting. Mink, by contrast, are widespread and are far more likely to be seen as they search the banks for birds such as nesting sandpipers and mallards.

In many places the burns and becks descend over steep white-water rapids or by waterfalls, known as

Puffins, with their rather comical appearance, may be seen at close quarters by visitors to the Northumbrian islands

'snouts' or 'forces' in Durham and 'linns' in Northumberland. Usually, these falls are to be found at the head of a deep cleft cut into an open hillside and are shrouded by tall trees. These wooded gorges, beautiful timeless places, are called denes and many have been adopted by adjacent towns and villages and are part of the local heritage. The most famous are Jesmond Dene in Newcastle, Hareshaw Dene near Bellingham, and Castle Eden Dene near Peterlee. Castle Eden Dene has recently been designated a National Nature Reserve, and is of special interest because it cuts its way through magnesian limestone and has a rich and unusual flora. It has a wonderful old yew wood and, where it opens out into grassland on the Durham coast, there are colonies of the Northern Argus butterfly. This species was once thought to be a sub-species of the Brown Argus and was given the name Castle Eden Argus.

Grey seals in the waters off the Farne Islands

The coast

When slow-moving rivers meet the sea they
deposit silt and mud which develops into
saltmarshes. The rivers of north-east England have
a steep gradient and are not carrying so much
sediment as the long meandering rivers of the south
and east. Mudflats are few and most of those at the
mouths of the Wear, Tyne and the Tees have been
reclaimed. Even so, such places as Seal Sands
attract large concentrations of wading birds and are
of considerable importance. They are also exciting
places for bird-watchers during the spring and
autumn migration.

To the north of the region, close to the Scottish
Border, is the Lindisfarne National Nature Reserve
which also has fine expanses of saltmarsh and is the
only wintering ground in England or Scotland for
the pale-bellied brent goose. Between these two
extremes the coast is notable for its beaches and
dunes. From Alnmouth to Holy Island lies one of
the least spoilt and most beautiful shorelines of
Britain, a succession of sandy bays and low
headlands. The dunes that back the shore have
been stabilised by marram grass and are studded
with flowers. Bloody cranesbill and burnet rose are
two of the most attractive, while in some of the
damp hollows between dunes, several species of
orchids and helleborines are to be found.

The Whin Sill, a volcanic intrusion which
stretches from the coast, across Northumberland to
Hadrian's Wall and eventually to Teesdale, makes
an important contribution to the landscape. Several
promontories such as Cullernose Point and
Dunstanburgh, are made up of quartz dolerite,
either part of the Sill itself or from associated
dykes. The grassland contains the scarce flowers
spring squill and purple milk-vetch, and the dark
grey cliffs provide nesting sites for kittiwakes and
fulmars. A few miles off the mainland lie the Farne
Islands, a group of small flat-topped and treeless
islets with a thin covering of campion and scurvy
grass. St Cuthbert lived here in the 7th century but
today the only inhabitants are lighthouse-keepers
and nature reserve wardens. No description can

*The rocky cliffs of the Farne Islands provide ideal nesting
sites for birds such as kittiwakes, shags and fulmars*

prepare visitors for the experience of landing on
Inner Farne or Staple Island and being transported
into a world of birds. Puffins, guillemots, fulmars,
terns, shags, cormorants and kittiwakes nest a
matter of feet or inches away from the paths, and
eider ducks regularly site their downy nests actually
on the paths and sit tight whilst visitors walk over
them. To be so close to wild birds is a privilege.
Notice the incredible emerald of a shag's eye or the
sealing-wax red of a tern's legs, but be careful that
the shag does not peck your camera lens and the
tern does not dive-bomb you as you walk away. A
hat is essential.

The sea around the Farne Islands is famous for
its marine life; everything from jellyfish to killer
whales. Farne boat trips usually include a close
view of the grey seals as well as a short landing on
one of the main islands.

The view from Farne provides a memorable
finale; north-west is Bamburgh and Holy Island,
south-west are the Cheviot Hills, and to the south
are golden bays and the dunes of Monk's House.

Northumbria's Christian Heritage

At opposite ends of one of Northumbria's greatest buildings are the shrines of its most famous saint and the scholar-monk whose writings illuminate the shadows of early English history. Behind the High Altar of Durham Cathedral a simple slab of stone is engraved with the single word 'Cuthbertus' in memory of the saint who died on his beloved Farne Islands in the late 7th century. In the cool, austere dignity of the Galilee Chapel, a huge tomb-chest of local marble holds the remains of the Venerable Bede; his death in St Paul's Monastery, Jarrow, was nearly half a century later, in 735. But Northumbria's Christian heritage has even deeper roots.

Paulinus

A Roman missionary, Paulinus, accompanied Augustine to Kent in 601, subsequently becoming the first Archbishop of York. For 36 days in AD627, he instructed the Northumbrian people in Christianity, baptising many of them in the River Glen, west of Wooler. In York he baptised King Edwin, whose heir, Oswald, won a great victory against Welsh and Mercian invaders in 635, at Heavenfield on the uplands north of Hexham. The battle site is marked by the lonely St Oswald's Chapel. Built in 1737, it stands north of the B6318 a mile east of the Brunton crossroads.

Aidan

Paulinus' missionary successes were surpassed by Celtic evangelists who drew their inspiration, not from Rome, but from the early saints of Britain's western seaboard. It was an austere monk, Aidan, whom King Oswald summoned from Iona to bring the message of Christianity to his kingdom. Created Bishop of Northumbria in 635, and based on Lindisfarne, where he founded a monastery, he travelled throughout the north, visiting the lonely huts among the hills.

Cuthbert

Although the ministry of Aidan probably merits his being described as the truest English apostle, it is his successor, Cuthbert, born in 635, who is generally regarded as the most spiritual of the English saints. Instructed at Melrose Priory, where he became prior, he moved to Lindisfarne in 664, but found even that twice-a-day island too worldly, and in 676 moved to the Farne Islands and the solitude of the Inner Farne. Eight years later he was invited by Ecgfrith, King of Northumbria, to become Bishop of Hexham, but soon exchanged that see for Lindisfarne again, and returned to his tiny cell on Inner Farne, where he remained until his death on 20 March 687.

An illustration from the Life of St Cuthbert, *compiled by Bede, shows the trials of the saint*

It seems likely that during his short bishopric, his monks produced the magnificent Lindisfarne Gospels – written, it is said, 'for God and St Cuthbert', now in the British Museum. Cuthbert's saintliness and kindliness not only witnessed the dawn of Christian faith in Northumbria, but made him an early folk-hero, revered by everybody, including, apparently, the sea birds of the Farnes, where eider duck are known as 'St Cuthbert's chicks', and fossil crinoids as 'St Cuthbert's beads'.

Wilfrid

Parallel to these developments of a Celtic-based mission was the Roman form introduced by Paulinus, and under the leadership of Wilfrid and Benedict Biscop – both of whom had visited Rome – this Roman monasticism challenged the Celtic ritual at the great Synod of Whitby in 663. The following year Wilfrid became Bishop of Ripon and later Archbishop of York, with much of Northumbria under his influence. He established the first Christian church at Hexham in 678 which later became a monastery and the seat of a bishop.

This Saxon stone carving of a horse's head can be seen at the museum in Jarrow which stands on the site of Bede's monastery

According to Wilfrid's biographer his church at Hexham must have been magnificent, for none other north of the Alps was said to compare with it. The present church, at the heart of the town, has some masonry of the Augustinian priory founded in 1113, but most of the building dates from 1180 to 1250, and 1850 to 1910. In the chancel is St Wilfrid's throne, the Frith stool, an uncomfortable-looking, tub-shaped stone chair with solid arms and back of uniform height. Its present position is roughly above the apse of Wilfrid's church of 675 to 680 which it occupied in Saxon times. From the centre of the present nave steps lead down to a fine Anglo-Saxon crypt, where the relics of the saint were formerly displayed.

Benedict Biscop

In 1674 Benedict Biscop, a cultured Northumbrian nobleman, founded a monastery on the north bank of the River Wear, at Monkwearmouth. Its church was completed in 675, and fragments of this survive in a later building. The west wall of the present nave and the lowest stage of the tower are 7th-century, but most of the church is 10th-century, with later additions and rebuildings. Not only did Benedict Biscop build a monastery, but he brought back books from Rome to start a library, together with the Arch-chanter of the Vatican to teach the northern monks to worship in the Roman fashion. Thus a European centre of learning was established at Monkwearmouth.

In 682 Biscop founded a sister monastery at Jarrow, with much of the building work done by Monkwearmouth monks. The church was begun in 684 and completed the following year. In the east wall of the present nave, above the chancel arch, is the oldest surviving church dedicatory inscription in England, recording in Latin the dedication to St Paul, and the date, 23 April 685. The present chancel and the lower stages of the tower are of the original church, the remainder are later buildings.

Bede

That same year, as a boy of 12, Bede entered the priory at Jarrow where he was to spend the remaining 50 years of his life. From his tiny cell in the monastery he wrote a stream of books, on history, theology, poetry, grammar and natural science and became the greatest scholar in Christendom. He wrote the earliest English version of the Gospel, and his *Ecclesiastical History of the English People* told the story of England from Roman times, described by Sir Arthur Bryant as '. . . lucid, just, immensely learned . . . a

monument to his age, his Faith and his country'.

More than 600 monks lived in the twin foundations of Jarrow and Monkwearmouth and for two centuries it was one of two English centres of culture and learning (Wessex was the other). The present surroundings of these monasteries could not be more removed from that Golden Age.

An early church

The same can be said of Northumbria's other great Anglo-Saxon church, that of St John the Evangelist at Escomb, west of Bishop Auckland, in County Durham. With no apparent monastic associations it is probably contemporary with the early buildings at Jarrow and Monkwearmouth, and is one of only three complete surviving Saxon churches in Britain. It is kept locked, as is its near-circular churchyard, but the keys are obtainable from a modern bungalow opposite. Its simple interior, without aisles, transepts or tower (and a chancel arch which may have come from the Roman fort of Binchester nearby), follows a pattern from Roman Gaul. Its cool, austere beauty, hallowed by 13 centuries of worship, is eloquent and moving.

The Congregation of St Cuthbert

The end of the 8th century saw the beginning of a series of Danish raids on the north-east coast. These were more disruptive than overwhelmingly destructive, and it seems likely that during the 830s monks from Lindisfarne transferred their church, and St Cuthbert's body, to Norham. In 875, in the face of a larger-scale Danish invasion, there was a major exodus from Lindisfarne or Norham, and for over a century the 'Congregation of St Cuthbert', as the peripatetic Lindisfarne community was called, wandered far and wide over Northumbria, always carrying the body of their saint.

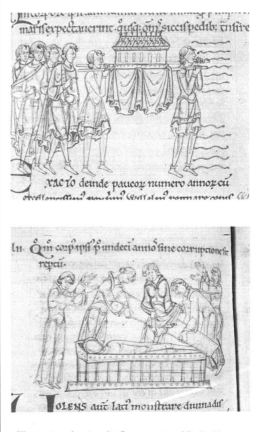

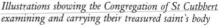

Illustrations showing the Congregation of St Cuthbert examining and carrying their treasured saint's body

The magnificent garnet-studded St Cuthbert's Pectoral Cross in Durham Cathedral dates from the 7th century

St Cuthbert's Cave, near Belford in Glendale, is reputedly one of the resting places of the saint's body

From 934 to 939 King Athelstan of Wessex, grandson of Alfred the Great, was King of All England, including Northumbria. During that time he visited Cuthbert's shrine at Chester-le-Street and presented it with gifts including vestments, parts of which are now preserved in Durham Cathedral. His copy of Bede's *Life of St Cuthbert* is now in the library of Corpus Christi College, Cambridge.

In 995 the Congregation of St Cuthbert evacuated again, this time to Ripon, but stayed only a few months and decided to return to Chester-le-Street. However, they never arrived there as in September 998 they settled on the naturally fortified plateau of land almost encircled by the Wear at Durham. Here they built a wooden church as permanent home for Cuthbert's relics. Almost a century later, in 1093, the foundation stone of the great Romanesque Cathedral was laid by the Norman bishop, William of St Calais. In 1104 St Cuthbert's relics, after 250 years of being carried throughout Northumbria, were solemnly placed in their present position behind the High Altar.

The view through the beautifully carved west door of the priory on the island of Lindisfarne

Priories

But Northumbria's Christian heritage is widespread throughout the region. After the Normans reformed the see, Durham became a monastic cathedral, and it was Durham monks who refounded the Benedictine monastery on Lindisfarne and started to rebuild the priory church there in 1093. Now in ruins, enough of the church still stands to be hauntingly beautiful. Its slender piers support a wonderful 'rainbow' arch across a transept and the west front and doorway show exquisite Norman carving – all in dark red sandstone. Monks from Durham also refounded

Tynemouth's Benedictine Priory, but most of what survives there owes its aesthetic appeal to the late 12th and early 13th centuries, with the exquisite 15th-century Percy Chantry beneath the soaring east wall framing a view of sea and sky beyond the promontory high above the north bank of the Tyne.

Finchale (pronounced Finkle) Priory occupies a sheltered loop of the River Wear north of Durham in a lovely setting overlooked by wooded banks. Although the 13th-century remains are meagre when compared with, say, Fountains or Rievaulx in Yorkshire, they form the most significant group, outside the Cathedral, in the county.

Augustinian canons, who followed a rather less austere rule than Benedictine or Cistercian monks, occupied two beautifully-situated priories at Brinkburn and Lanercost. At Brinkburn, in a delightfully wooded part of the Coquet Valley below Rothbury, only the church survives in the purity of the Early English style. It was restored with exquisite good taste in 1858 and is now in parochial use.

In the moorland landscapes of the upper Derwent, Premonstratensian Canons, following a Rule of austerity similar to Cistercian monks, founded Blanchland Priory. They cultivated riverside haughs, built a mill, and grazed sheep on the neighbouring hills. Part of their 13th-century church survives in the present structure, but the layout of the monastic buildings is recalled by the shape of the present village created on the Lord Crewe estate in 1752.

One more priory merits mention, that at Hulne, near Alnwick. This is one of England's earliest Carmelite monasteries, founded in about 1240, and showing extensive remains within a rare monastic defensive wall. It all stands in the private park of the Duke of Northumberland, with no vehicular access. But you can walk to it and savour the peacefulness of its setting by obtaining a free permit from the Alnwick Castle Estate Office.

The church at Escomb is one of the oldest and least-altered Saxon churches surviving in England

Parish churches

Northumbria's deep roots in the Christian faith are also illustrated in many of its parish churches. Norman lords, Prince-Bishops, abbots and priors may have been the great landowners, but it was peasant families who worked the land, tilled the soil, grazed their stock, and worshipped at small stone churches.

Through that long tunnel of time we can still catch glimpses of Northumbria's Saxon and Norman heritage of Christianity. Along the Tyne Valley, where the Roman Wall and its associated forts were a convenient quarry for good building stone, many churches contain Romanesque work. Corbridge's west tower has 8th-century masonry, but most is of the 10th century. Roman monolithic columns are incorporated into the 12th-century nave at Chollerton, and there are Roman fragments in St Oswald's, Heavenfield. Good Anglo-Saxon masonry is also prominent at Bywell St Andrew, Ovingham, Warden and Bolam north of the Tyne, and Billingham and Staindrop in County Durham.

Durham's influence was widespread, both ecclesiastically and architecturally. In the far north, by the Tweed, the Prince-Bishops owned Norhamshire, and the Norman church at Norham, particularly the exuberant carving of the south chancel wall, was surely Bishop de Puiset's work. Equally sumptuous is his exquisite detail at St Lawrence, Pittington, a former mining village east of Durham. The richness of Durham Cathedral is also echoed in small urban scale in the Norman splendour of St Laurence, Warkworth.

On various places throughout Northumbria lonely churches are evidence of the sparsely-populated countryside of Norman times, symbolised as well as anywhere by that at Thockrington, small and grey on its rocky outcrop, and surrounded by spacious grasslands.

Farming and Forestry

Northumbria supports a surprisingly varied farming and forestry industry. Over a distance of less than 50 miles the traveller can cross from the rich coastal plain, through mixed farming land with interspersed woodland on the undulating intermediate ground, to wide open hills which support extensive hill farming and major forest enterprises. This land use pattern reflects the landform, soil types and local climate and each industry is gradually evolving and responding to the challenge of the market, backed by advances in technology.

Despite this process of change, land use practices of previous eras are still much in evidence. Old settlements and field patterns can be seen by the keen observer, particularly in and around the Cheviots. On lower ground, features in today's landscape were largely created in the last century and earlier, giving rise to the characteristic field boundaries of stone walls and hedges, interspersed by areas of woodland.

Arable farming

The main arable farming area occupies the coastal plain of Northumberland and Durham, which is almost 100 miles long, extending inland along the main valleys of the rivers Tweed, Tyne, Wear and Tees. Here the rainfall is surprisingly low, averaging 23-30in each year, and this means irrigation is a serious consideration for certain of the crops grown.

The major arable crops are cereals, oilseed rape and potatoes, with other lesser crops of importance locally. Farmers are now tending to sow their grain crops in the autumn rather than the spring, which means that harvest begins in July. The harvest of winter varieties is followed by that of grain sown in spring, then farmers start the race against time to sow the new winter crop before the soil becomes too wet or cold.

Cereal growing has expanded rapidly in the last decade into the more traditional livestock fattening areas, such as around Belford. The development of grain storage and drying complexes by both private companies and farming co-operatives is a feature of the coastal plain and these storage facilities play an essential role in the modern farming system.

Hay stacked in fields in Upper Teesdale and (inset) being lifted on to a waggon at the turn of the century

Several centres operate their own transport fleet, and the ports of Berwick-upon-Tweed, Tyneside and Teesside provide important shipping outlets.

Barley, the main cereal, occupies three-quarters of the cereal acreage. It is grown mainly for feeding livestock, but high quality malting barley is produced on the lighter soils of north Northumberland and the Borders. A small proportion of the wheat crop is used for bread-making. With the demise of the farm work horse the small acreage of oats now grown is used for sheep feed.

Oilseed rape has increased dramatically in recent years. Providing brief unexpected splashes of vivid yellow during May, it acts as a break crop in the cereal rotation and the oilseeds are used in animal feedstuffs and as a cooking oil for kitchen use. Potatoes are important on some individual holdings, but their acreage has declined in recent years due to quotas. Other minor crops in the area include combining peas and beans for feed, and linseed; also vegetables for which there is local demand. Soft fruit production on Tweedside and Tyneside provides a new market, mainly operated on pick-your-own systems.

Near this isolated Teesdale farmstead cattle are grazing. The sheep will spend most of the year on the moors

After harvest the stubble is ploughed in readiness for the following year's crop which may be sown in autumn or spring

Industrial and urban fringe farming

In south-east Northumberland and eastern Durham, factors outside of farming have affected the pattern of agriculture. Historically, these areas have produced coal for the past two centuries, supporting the region's industry and main population centres. More recently, open-cast coal working has had a drastic effect. Extensive tracts of land are temporarily taken out of production, but are carefully restored afer coal extraction; attention is paid to drainage, and new hedges and small woodlands are planted to help restore the character of the countryside and provide shelter. This whole process is well illustrated around Acklington.

Farming takes on a new dimensioin in the urban fringe as farmers have to cope not only with the vagaries of weather, the market and their own financial standing, but also with local demand. Various projects have been set up recently on Tyneside, Wearside and Teesside to help to reconcile the difficulties created by vandalism with the need for access, recreation and sites for nature conservation.

Mixed farming

As the land rises in steps away from the river valleys and the coastal plain, mixed farming predominates, adding greater diversity to the landscape. The arable sector has recently expanded into the livestock rearing area, so that cereals can now be seen growing along the hill margins. The Biddlestone edge of the Cheviots, the Coquetside flank of Simonside, the foothills round Jedburgh, Tow Law, Barnard Castle and Great Ayton all show examples. This has led to more intensive livestock production, and cattle are usually wintered in purpose-built accommodation.

Leys (land temporarily under grass) of predominantly rye grass support grazing animals in summer and provide up to three cuts of silage for winter feed. Most of the dairy units are located in the Tyne Valley area, south Durham and Cleveland. Over 1,000 dairy herds have disappeared during the last 12 years and the remaining herds consist mostly of Friesian or Holstein cows, with a few Ayrshire, Shorthorn and Jersey herds.

Sheep grazing also plays a role in the arable system. Highly productive Mule ewes, bred in the hills and uplands, are crossed with sires such as the Suffolk to produce lambs for market, and store lambs may also be bought in to fatten over the winter. The profitability of the lowland sheep industry has an important influence on the well-being of upland and hill flocks.

Permanent pasture occupies land that is too steep, too wet or too stony to cultivate and is also found as parkland round some of the large country houses such as Raby Castle and Wallington Hall. Sheep and cattle are usually a cross between the hardy hill breeds and the rather more productive lowland breeds.

Hill farming

Hill farming provides the greatest contrast of all in the area. The wide open, rolling Northumbrian hills give distant views and an immense feeling of

than in more westerly districts. Hill farms can be relatively isolated and although farmhouses now possess modern amenities, mains electricity has not reached valleys such as the Upper Coquet. The social calendar of such areas centres round events in the farming calendar, and many of the great characters of the farming community are to be found in the hills.

The shepherd's calendar

The hill-farming year starts in November, when the tups are put in with the ewes. Before this are the Tup Sales, and one of the largest in the country is held at Kelso in September. Increasingly, hill farmers are aiming to produce quality lambs. Land improvement is needed to boost lamb production and it also greatly improves the welfare of the hill ewe, allowing the shepherd to spend more time looking *after* his sheep, rather than looking *for* them. The Ministry of Agriculture's Experimental Husbandry Farm in Redesdale and the Hill Farming Research Organisation's station at Sourhope in the Cheviots have pioneered much of this improvement work.

Hill lambing starts in mid-April and is the most hectic time of year for the farmer. After lambing, low-lying fields are cleared of sheep so that winter fodder crops of hay and silage can be made. Pockets of hay meadows rich in wild flowers are a colourful sight until early July.

space, forming an arc which stretches from Wooler in the north through Alston in the west to Barnard Castle. The transition from mixed farming to hill farming is frequently sudden. Cross a rise or turn a bend in the road and you pass from enclosed fields to hills of open heather and rough grass.

Livestock rearing is all important. Most hill farms carry herds of hardy cows such as the Galloway or Blue-Grey and their cross-bred offspring as an additional, but less important, enterprise to sheep rearing.

The hill ewe reigns supreme in the severe conditions of Pennine heather moorland and Cheviot grass heaths. The harsh winter climate, poor soils and short summer growing season lead to an exacting farming system, though the rainfall at a yearly average of around 32in is much lower

Sheep-shearing at Hartside in the Cheviots is now mechanised, but used to be done by hand

The hill ewes are clipped during July and the wool is packed and sent to Wool Marketing Board centres at Hexham and Hawick. About a month after shearing all the sheep are dipped to help control parasites and skin diseases. Late summer is the time for local shows, which may be devoted almost entirely to sheep, as at Rochester Show, and September sees the beginning of the hill lamb sales. Mule ewe lambs (a cross between Blackface or Swaledale ewes and the Bluefaced Leicester tup) are a North of England speciality and buyers from all over the country visit the sales to buy this product of the hills and uplands of Northumberland and Durham.

A track through Kielder provides easy walking – one of the benefits of this man-made forest

Forestry and woodland: the lowlands

About 15 per cent of Northumberland carries forest and woods, and forestry has a great deal to offer the farmer in this county's exacting climate. Northumberland supports the largest man-made forest in Europe, Kielder Forest.

Forestry and woodland is closely interlinked with farming, adding to the delightful mosaic of the landscape and providing shelter, game cover and scope for recreation as well as timber products. On the coastal plain planting is carried out on a small scale, to shelter buildings and the exposed fields.

There are some very attractive broadleaved woodlands in the area, providing ribbons of seasonal variety in the lowlands and sheltered upland valleys. Woodland of semi-natural origin, supporting native tree and shrub species, survives on the banks of the Tweed, Aln, Coquet, Wansbeck, Tyne, Wear and Tees and most of their tributaries. Much of this woodland has received little attention since the felling of the best specimens during the two World Wars and is now a haven for wildlife.

The mixed farming area supports most of the major country estates, whose woodlands were planted to provide shelter, amenity and game cover, and date back to early Victorian times. The National Trust estates at Wallington and Cragside are good examples of woodland replacement.

The hills

Here are some of the greatest contrasts in forestry. Shelter from prevailing westerly winds and cold easterlies is an important issue in hills and uplands and conifer belts are used for this purpose. The climate and soil conditions of Northumberland allow the relatively rapid establishment of conifers, provided the plantations are protected from grazing. During the last century Scots pine was the main species used in shelter plantings. Remnants of these woods, often mixed with sycamore near farm buildings and in the foothills, still exist, but nowadays pine and spruce are more commonly used for shelter belts, with the very attractive larch growing on better soils.

The true forest area is in the hills; the result of planting carried out in the last 60 years. Up to the 1960s, if a hill farm came on the market the land was often purchased by forestry interests and most of the farm would be planted. However, since the 1960s, more account has been taken of the future appearance of woodland, and planting boundaries and the composition of forests has been more carefully planned. Both the State forest service, the Forestry Commission, and private forestry companies have been involved in the expansion of forestry in the area. Constraints imposed by the National Park Authority, the Planning Authorities and the Ministry of Defence mean that expansion of forestry today in Northumbria is more limited than in the past.

The upper reaches of the Coquet (Kidland Forest), Font (Harwood Forest), Derwent (Slaley Forest), Wear and Tees (Hamsterley Forest) all support sizeable areas of forestry.

Kielder Forest

This vast, man-made forest is decried by many as being unsightly, a 'white elephant' – but as it enters its second 60 years, Kielder is proving to be a very productive resource. Most of the trees grown here are Norway and Sitka spruce. The timber, harvested by motor-manual methods and purpose-built harvesting machines, supplies the paper mill at Shotton in North Wales and the chip-board mill at Hexham, in addition to numerous local outlets. Wood production from Kielder Forest is due to double in the next 15 years to 400,000 tonnes a year – providing additional important employment opportunities.

Forestry and recreation

As the forests mature and more felling takes place, the opportunity exists to convert the current vast tracts of even-aged plantations into forest with trees of varying ages and sizes. Most of the forests in the area are now moving into this phase and combined with the introduction of larger numbers of broadleaved trees along watercourses, a more pleasing landscape is being created with greater wildlife interest and recreational potential. The Forestry Commission provides a considerable number of recreation facilities in the area in the form of car parks, picnic sites and walks. Car rallying, orienteering, bird watching, deer stalking and pony trekking are among the other activities enjoyed in the region's forest areas by summer visitors and by the inhabitants of the large industrial conurbations around Tyne and Wear.

NORTHUMBRIA

Gazetteer

Each entry in this Gazetteer has the atlas
page number on which the place can be
found and its National Grid reference
included under the heading.
An explanation of how to use the National
Grid is given on page 84.

*Above: footbridge over the River Wansbeck at Morpeth – an excellent centre
for touring the Cheviot Hills*

The old harbour at Alnmouth is now silted up and covered at high tide

Allendale

Map Ref: 90NY8355

The Victorians called this peaceful dale 'the English Alps'. Situated on the south-western edge of Northumberland, it has many peaty burns that cascade down the high hills to feed two rivers – the West and East Allen – and its scenery is spectacular.

Capital of this district is Allendale Town, which claims to be the geographical centre of Great Britain. Surrounded by moorland, the town stands 1,400ft above sea level. Its attractive large market square, bordered by pleasant stone houses and inns, is the setting for a most unusual festival held every New Year's Eve.

The Allendale Baal Fire, a farewell to the past year, has origins going back to the Dark Ages. It is a celebration that attracts hundreds of visitors, and the town's hotels are usually booked up months ahead. Men, called 'guisers', dress up in quaint costumes with blackened faces and carry barrels of blazing tar around the town. At midnight a huge bonfire is lit as a pyre to the old year.

The church of St Cuthbert, much restored in the last century, had an infamous curate during the 18th century. He was Robert Patten, a supporter of the Stuarts, who became involved in the 1715 Jacobite Rebellion as chaplain to General Tom Forster. However, when he was captured he turned King's evidence to save his life at the expense of his friends, including the Earl of Derwentwater.

The dale was once an important lead-mining area and evidence of the industry can be seen in the remains of tall chimneys on the moors. Allenheads, at the head of the East Allen Valley, once produced one-sixth of Britain's lead.

AA recommends:
Guesthouse: Bishopsfield Farmhouse, tel. (043483) 248

Alnmouth

Map Ref: 89NU2410

Alnmouth, 5 miles east of Alnwick on the A1068, is a charming resort – popular with golfers and those seeking a peaceful holiday. Yet when John Wesley rode into the town in 1748 he called it 'a small sea-port famous for all kinds of wickedness.'

Situated on a narrow spit of land between the River Aln and the North Sea, Alnmouth was originally the port for Alnwick. In the 18th and early 19th centuries it exported large amounts of corn which was stored in tall granaries, and some of these have been converted to houses. The town is completely unspoilt and very picturesque, with little sailing boats bobbing on the River Aln, and a fine stretch of golden beach.

During the war with France in the 18th century several naval encounters took place off Alnmouth, and in 1779 – 30 years after Wesley's observation – the village church was fired on by the American buccaneer John Paul Jones. He missed by a mile – literally.

Alnmouth claims to have been the place where St Cuthbert was elected Bishop of Lindisfarne at the Great Synod of 684. However, this claim is also made by other towns and villages in Northumberland, notably Whittingham.

Saxon remains have been found in the area and in 1789 part of a carved Saxon cross was unearthed on Church Hill. The later Norman church did not survive either; the last remains were blown down on Christmas Day, 1806, when the Aln changed its course and cut off the ruins from the town.

Just north of Alnmouth is Boulmer – a village with a disreputable past. It was once the centre of a major smuggling operation. Northumbrian and Scottish smugglers would collect rum and gin from boats sailing from the Continent and take the illicit liquor back into the heart of the county. Boulmer now enjoys a more respectable reputation and is home to an RAF base, where the Air Sea Rescue Service is stationed.

AA recommends:
Hotel: Saddle, 24/25 Northumberland St, 2-star, *tel.* (0665) 830476
Guesthouse: Marine House Private Hotel, 1 Marine Dr, *tel.* (0665) 830349

Alnwick

Map Ref: 89NU1813

This former county town of Northumberland is dominated by Alnwick Castle, often described as the 'Windsor of the North'. The history of this grey stone border town is intertwined with the castle and the House of Percy – the north's greatest family. Alnwick Castle, once the strongest fortress on the English side of the border, dates back to the 11th century. In 1309 it became the property of the Percy family, and, although it changed hands more than once over the centuries, it is still the home of a Percy – the Duke of Northumberland.

The grey fortress sits above the River Aln, from which the town takes its name. Perched on the battlements are stone figures of soldiers intended as a threat to the advancing enemy. The interior of Alnwick Castle is decorated in the classical style of the Italian Renaissance – carried out last century by the 4th Duke of Northumberland. Paintings by Titian, Van Dyke and Canaletto are among the works of art, and the castle is famed for its collection of Meissen china.

The castle is open to the public during summer and permits can also be obtained to walk in Hulne Park – a part of which was landscaped by Capability Brown, who was born in Northumberland. From Brislee Tower, a folly by Robert Adam, there is a view encompassing seven castles. Also in the park is ruined Hulne Priory. One of the earliest Carmelite monasteries in England, it was built in 1240.

It is impossible to explore

Alnwick without encountering some reminder of the Percy influence, including the family emblem – a proud lion with a straight tail. One stands on the Lion Bridge and another on top of the Tenantry Tower at the southern entrance to the town. This monument is known as Farmers' Folly as it was erected by grateful tenants whose rates were reduced by the third Duke. When he saw their gift, he put the rents up again!

As a border town, Alnwick was the scene of many skirmishes so it was contained within defending walls. Hotspur Tower, the last surviving gateway, was named after the most famous Percy, Harry, who featured in Shakespeare's play *Henry IV*. The tower, built in 1450, was once used as the county jail.

Alnwick's cobbled market square is the setting for the week-long Alnwick Fair, a medieval costumed fair held annually in June. On Shrove Tuesday a football is thrown from the gates of Alnwick Castle which starts an unusual game of soccer, using the Lion and Denwick Bridges as goal posts.

Several of Alnwick's pubs have interesting features, including the Old Cross Inn – known locally as the 'Dirty Bottles' – in Narrowgate. A collection of dusty bottles has

Over 3,000 acres lie within the walls of Alnwick Castle Park

remained in the window for more than 150 years because landlords have been too superstitious to remove them, as they are supposed to carry a death curse. The proprietor who arranged them in the window died before completing the job. The White Swan Hotel has a unique ballroom – a panelled room that was removed intact from the sister ship of the *Titanic*, the ocean liner *Olympic*, when it was scrapped at Wallsend.

AA recommends:
Hotels: White Swan, Bondgate Within, 3-star, *tel.* (0665) 602109
Hotspur, Bondgate Without, 2-star, *tel.* (0665) 602924
Guesthouses: Aln House, South Rd, *tel.* (0665) 602265
Aydon House, South Rd, *tel.* (0665) 602218
Bondgate House Hotel, Bondgate Without, *tel.* (0665) 602025
Hope Rise, The Dunterns, *tel.* (0665) 602930
Alndyke Farmhouse, *tel.* (0665) 602193
Garage: Central (S Jennings Ltd), Lagny St, *tel.* (0665) 602294

Capability Brown

Lancelot 'Capability' Brown

Lancelot Brown was born in 1716 at Kirkharle, a hamlet in the Wansbeck Valley, but very little is known of his family or of his boyhood years in this quiet countryside.

He went to school at Cambo until he was 16 and was later apprenticed as gardener on Sir William Loraine's modest estate at Kirkharle. Here he undoubtedly learned the skills which proved so useful in later life when he was to transform the geometric gardens of the 17th and early 18th centuries into landscaped parklands graced with trees, lakes and hills. Brown soon acquired the ability to speak authoritatively about the suitability of particular trees for different sites, how to drain wet land or shape lakes, how to raise plants or replant existing ones.

Although Sir William Loraine did little to 'improve' his estate, he did say that Kirkharle was 'the first landscape work ever entrusted to his gardener, afterwards known throughout England as Capability Brown'.

During his six years there Brown created the Kirkharle landscape which can be viewed today from the crest of the hill by St Wilfred's Church. The land drops gently to Parson's Burn, rising equally gently to low hills beyond, with plantations of beech, oak and chestnut – a scene which must have formed a strong influence on the great designs for his later work.

Brown worked very little in his native county after his Kirkharle years. He moved away to work for William Kent at Stowe, and helped him to translate new gardening ideas into practice. Brown's expertise soon became widely known, particularly among Kent's influential friends. Brown married a Stowe girl in 1744 and six years later the family moved to Hammersmith. Over the next 30 years he rode extensively about the kingdom, staying at great houses where he designed over 120 of the parks we admire today, having recognised their 'capabilities for improvement'. Only a handful of these were in Northumberland. In 1738 he worked for Sir Robert Shafto at Benwell Tower on the north bank of the Tyne, but only a few of the trees he planted survive round Dobson's later house, now com-

pletely enveloped in suburban development.

Around 1765 Brown worked for Sir Walter Blackett at Wallington Hall, especially in the East Wood around the Garden Pond. Nearer the house he planted a clump of trees between its south front and the River Wansbeck, and rounded off straight lines of existing woodlands. He also designed the lake at Rothley. He may also have advised on new landscapes and gardens at Capheaton, and at Hartburn Vicarage, but these are not proven work. At Hesleyside, west of Bellingham, where Brown is traditionally credited with a survey of the Charlton's estate, it seems more likely that he merely did some landscape work, probably around the Hesleyside Burn.

His most important work in the county was for the Duke of Northumberland's estate at Alnwick. In about 1760 Brown created a terrace walk below the castle walls, regrassed large areas of rough land with fine turf, planted thousands of trees and shrubs, made enormous 'rides' through woodlands, tamed the often turbulent River Aln, 'discovered' the ruins of Hulne Priory and probably added the tower to the Gothic summerhouse. Much of the planned landscape north and west of Alnwick is Northumberland's best monument to Lancelot Brown who died in 1783 but, surprisingly, he is not commemorated in the county, other than by a small sandstone block beside the B6342 at Kirkharle.

Lobster pots being repaired at the small, ancient port of Amble

Amble-By-The-Sea

Map Ref: 89NU2604

The little seaport of Amble at the mouth of the River Coquet grew in importance with the development of Northumberland's coal field. However, its history stretches back much further. A Bronze Age burial ground was found with evidence of 40 graves and the Romans also appear to have settled here.

Amble is on the edge of industrial Northumberland, and, although not as pretty as some of its neighbouring seaside resorts, it

Bamburgh Castle's huge red sandstone keep, with walls 10ft thick, dates from Norman times

marks the start of some of the finest coastal scenery on the east coast of England.

A mile from Amble is Coquet Island where in 684, Elfleda, Abbess of Whitby, persuaded St Cuthbert to accept the bishopric offered to him by her brother Ecgfrith, King of Northumbria. In 1821 the *Catherine* of Sunderland was wrecked on the Steel Rock at the north of the island with the loss of all nine crew members. The poor men had clung to the rigging for hours, watched by a large, but helpless crowd, who had no lifeboat to attempt a rescue. Twenty years later an 80ft-high white lighthouse was built, and at one time the brother of Grace Darling was keeper here (see page 52).

Coquet island is now an RSPB reserve with a large population of terns, puffins and eider ducks. Boat trips around the island can be arranged but landing is not permitted.

Bamburgh

Map Ref: 89NU1834

The sweeping beaches and dramatic fortress set on a promontory of the Great Whin Sill make Bamburgh one of Northumberland's major attractions. Bamburgh Castle, described by Sir Walter Scott as 'King Ida's castle huge and square' can be seen for miles and dominates this part of the beautiful Northumberland coast.

In fact the Angle chieftain Ida had what was probably a modest wooden structure built in about 547, and this was succeeded by a more permanent affair. Ida's grandson Ethelfrith gave the fortress to his wife Bebba, and the settlement was named Bebbanburgh, from which the name Bamburgh is derived. It was once a

royal city, centre of the ancient kingdom of Bernicia, and it was in Bamburgh that the kings of Northumbria were crowned.

The present castle dates from the end of the Norman period when it was rebuilt in stone to resist the Scots. During the Wars of the Roses it was badly damaged by artillery fire. A Bishop of Durham, Lord Crewe, bought the Bamburgh Estate in 1704 and restored the castle. He also formed a charitable trust which included the foundation of a girls' boarding school here.

At the end of the last century the castle was bought by Lord Armstrong, the Victorian inventor and industrialist. His renovations have been condemned by some historians who would have preferred Norman ruins to Victorian adornments. The ceiling of the banqueting hall is a copy of the one in Westminster Hall, London.

The castle is still the home of the Armstrong family and is open to the public. A recent addition is a museum dedicated to the achievements of this remarkable man who founded the famous armaments factory in Newcastle, and who built Cragside House (see page 46).

Bamburgh, a picturesque village with neat grey stone cottages facing a manicured green, has a popular links golf course nearby where the natural hazards are enhanced by a sharp breeze off the North Sea.

Grace Darling was born here in 1815 and is buried in St Aidan's churchyard. A beam above the baptistry is reputed to have been part of an original wooden structure.

AA recommends:
Hotels: Lord Crewe Arms, Front St, 2-star, *tel.* (06684) 243
Victoria, Front St, 2-star, *tel.* (06684) 431
Sunningdale, 1-star, *tel.* (06684) 334
Camp Site: Glororum Caravan Park, Glororum Farm, 2-pennant, *tel.* (06684) 205, 272 & 457

Barnard Castle

Map Ref: 91NZ0516

Barnard Castle is the administrative centre of Teesdale and the most 'country' of County Durham's country towns. For centuries its two broad main streets have served as markets where produce is bought and sold, and on Wednesdays colourful stalls occupy the cobbled street. Farmers crowd the rings of the market to see their stock 'knocked down' to butchers or graziers, and the numerous inns extend their opening hours on market days.

'Barny', as this lively town is affectionately known, has many surprises. The Butter Market stands where Thorngate, Newgate and the Market meet, like the hub of a

three-spoked wheel. Local butter used to be kept cool here and was sold on the lower floor. In later years the Town Council met for heated discussion upstairs.

Oliver Cromwell was entertained at Blagraves House down the Bank, but the mulled ale and cakes he was served are no longer listed on the bill of fare. Now a fashionable restaurant, the menu indicates that diners with more cultivated tastes are catered for.

High above the River Tees, the remains of Bernard Baliol's castle, dating from 1125, stand proud. The town still bears the castle builder's name, and his successors still own much of the land on the north side of the Tees. Guy de Baliol fought alongside William the Conqueror at Hastings in 1066 and was given a vast area of Teesdale as a reward for his services. His descendant, John, was king of Scotland for a while – until he tried to double-cross Edward I. The Parish Church of St Mary is also Norman but this is not apparent from the outside.

Bowes Museum, beyond the church on the opposite side of Newgate, would make any Frenchman feel at home. It was built by John Bowes, an Earl of Strathmore, who made his fortune in the Durham coal industry. He married a French actress, Josephine Benoite, and together they amassed a great art collection and built this outrageously inappropriate château in which to display the treasures. Now owned by Durham County Council, the museum has an international reputation and contains paintings by El Greco, Goya and Canaletto, as well as fine furniture, ceramics and tapestries. No visitor to the town should leave without at least a peep inside – which may become an all day stay.

The town's fine houses and public buildings reflect affluence. In Victorian times it had its spa, railway station and a fair share of famous visitors. Charles Dickens collected material for his novel *Nicholas Nickleby* while staying at the King's Head in the Market Place, and Dotheboys Hall at nearby Bowes is well-known because of his visit.

AA recommends:
Hotel: Kings Head, 12/14 Market Pl, 2-star, *tel.* (0833) 38356

Beadnell and Seahouses

Map Ref: 89NU2229

The coastline between these two small seaside resorts is of unsurpassed natural beauty – much of it owned by the National Trust. Beadnell and Seahouses have both flourished as family resorts, yet manage to retain some of their original atmosphere as traditional fishing villages. Beadnell's tiny harbour is the only one on the east coast facing west!

There is evidence that the village was established in Saxon times and excavations last century revealed the remains of an ancient chapel dedicated to St Ebba, sister of Oswald, King of Northumbria. However, Beadnell's most prominent feature is a group of disused 18th-century limekilns, now owned by the National Trust. A popular inn in the village centre was originally a pele tower. Beadnell Bay has facilities for water sports, including sailing and water-skiing. Newton, further down the coast, provides more sheltered waters and is very popular with wind-surfers.

Just along the coast towards Bamburgh lies Seahouses. As well as a popular holiday spot, Seahouses is

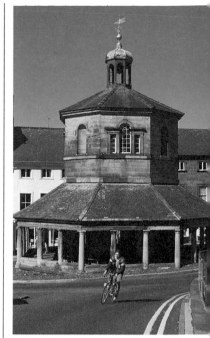

A fire-bell crowns Barnard Castle's butter market which dates from 1747

an active fishing port. The village grew up around the harbour which was built in 1889. Originally it depended on fishing and the lime trade for its livelihood, but now tourism has replaced the latter.

Magnificent sandy beaches stretch out on either side of Seahouses and there are fine views of the Farne Islands and Bamburgh Castle. Seahouses' biggest attraction is a boat trip to the Farnes. Local fishermen take visitors out from the harbour, weather permitting.

AA recommends:
Hotel: Beach House, Sea Front, Seahouses, 2-star, *tel.* (0665) 720337
Camp Site: Beadnell Links, The Chimes, 2-pennant, *tel.* (0665) 720527

Traditional Northumbrian cobles and a fleet of modern fishing boats occupy the harbour at Seahouses

Beamish Open Air Museum. Left: the Co-op Store window. Below: the 'town street' with shops, pubs, stables, houses and a Victorian park. Rides on early electric trams are available

Beamish

Map Ref: 92NZ2253

The village is famous for its museum, known as Beamish Open Air Museum and voted Museum of the Year in 1986. A triumph of co-operation between the local authorities of Northumbria, this is a folk museum, but with a difference. It represents pure nostalgia for north-easterners; trips down memory lane for anyone over 50, and peeps into the past for youngsters. History is very much alive at Beamish. There are steam trains, the Co-op with its 'divi', donkey stones to brighten up cottage steps, a tin bath in front of the fire, gleaming black-leaded kitchen ranges and sparkling brass fenders. There is a colliery to descend and a faithful reconstruction of a Victorian pub in which to spend time and money. Take a tram to the country and visit a 19th-century farm or go to the dentist's, the blacksmith's or the potter of a century ago; there is almost too much to see all in one day.

Beamish Hall and the parkland in which the museum has been created was once the home of the Shaftos, the family of Bonnie Bobby who, as every child once knew, 'had silver buckles on his knee'. At another time it was lived in by the Edens, the family of Sir Anthony, Foreign Secretary and Prime Minister not so long ago.

The estate lies above the most heavily exploited coal deposits of Durham. Even in the 18th century, coal from Tanfield Moor, 2 miles away, was considered to be the best coal in England and was shipped from the Tyne to London in vast quantities.

At Causey Arch, now within one of Durham County Council's picnic areas, you can see the oldest railway bridge in the world. It was built to carry coal in horse-drawn wagons running on wooden rails to the River Tyne before the steam engine was perfected. Replicas of a 1750 wagon and the rails on which they ran have been constructed beside the arch.

AA recommends:
Camp Site: Bobby Shafto Caravan Park, 2-pennant, *tel.* (0385) 701776

Bellingham

Map Ref: 90NY8383

This small market town is the 'capital' of north Tynedale – the very heart of 'raiding' country. Bellingham – pronounced 'Bellingjum' – stands on the east bank of the River North Tyne and lies on the edge of the Northumberland National Park. The nearest town to Kielder Water, Bellingham is surrounded by wild and uncompromising countryside. It is easy to imagine the bloodthirsty deeds performed in the district by the Border Reivers.

St Cuthbert's Church, dating from the 13th century, has an unusual stone roof built as protection against fire after the church was burnt several times by the Scots. In the churchyard there is a mysterious gravestone shaped like a pack which is said to be the tomb of the robber who features in an intriguing local legend.

The story goes that more than 200 years ago the maid at Lee Hall, near Bellingham, allowed a pedlar to leave his curiously-shaped pack at the house. On examining it she saw it move and summoned help from a ploughboy who rushed in and shot the 'pack' – which then groaned and poured blood. It transpired that the pack contained a robber and had been part of a plot to raid the house. In the early hours of the morning the robber's companions were caught and some were killed. It is said that some members of respectable local families were never seen again!

Another famous tale – and the subject of one of the murals at Wallington Hall – is set at Hesleyside, west of Bellingham. Hesleyside Hall has long been the home of the Charlton family – one of the four great families of north Tynedale. In raiding days, when supplies were low in the larder, the lady of the house would place the Charlton Spur on a dish as a subtle hint that a raid on livestock was necessary.

England's most famous long-distance footpath, the Pennine Way, passes through Bellingham. The area is excellent for walking and one of the loveliest walks starts north of the town where Hareshaw Burn joins the River North Tyne, and leads to Hareshaw Linn, a picturesque waterfall, which cascades 30ft into a chasm (see Walk 7).

AA recommends:
Hotel: Riverdale Hall, 2-star, *tel.* (0660) 20254

Belsay

Map Ref: 91NZ1078

Six hundred years of Northumberland's history unfold at Belsay – from the days of bloody border battles to the tranquil era of gracious country house living. Belsay Hall, castle and gardens have recently been restored by English Heritage, and together they show

Grey and pinkish-brown stone houses, cobbled streets and Elizabethan town walls contribute to Berwick's charm

the evolution of border life.

The present village of Belsay was built in the 1830s and 40s by Sir Charles Monck, who used the site of the former village for his neo-Classical mansion, Belsay Hall. Situated on the A696 trunk road to Jedburgh, Belsay is a distinctive village with an arcaded row of brown stone cottages.

Sir Charles, a descendant of the Middleton family, was inspired during a Grecian honeymoon to build Belsay Hall, using the honey-coloured stone taken from the quarry within the estate gardens. By doing so he created a unique rambling garden that is now a highlight of a visit to Belsay. Sir Charles employed the Newcastle architect, John Dobson, to draw up plans for the mansion, which is a perfect square with 100ft-long walls.

Since the building of Belsay Castle in 1370 there has been continuous occupation of the estate by the Middleton family – who lived first in the castle, then in the attached manor house and latterly in the Hall until 1962. The castle has been called the finest English tower house in the north. The construction of the adjoining Jacobean manor house heralded a new era of peace for Belsay; it was one of the first unfortified houses to be built in the area for about 300 years.

Although the buildings at Belsay are of great importance and certainly worth seeing, it is the grounds that make the estate so special. Like the buildings, they reflect a change in fashion over the centuries and include a wooded park with lake, formal terraces and the delightful quarry gardens. Much of the present landscape was created by Sir Charles and his grandson, Sir Arthur Middleton. The gardens are

filled with many rare and exotic plants – all identified with name tags – as well as more traditional shrubs such as rhododendrons. One of the most unusual trees is a magnificent *Davidia involucrata* – known as the pocket handkerchief tree because of its large white bracts.

Two miles north of Belsay is Bolam Lake County Park which has an exceptionally attractive picnic site and is noted for its bird life.

Berwick-upon-Tweed

Map Ref: 89NT9953

As English and Scots fought for control of the Borders, Berwick-upon-Tweed changed hands 14 times. The town, the most northerly in England, was once the capital of the ancient eastern Marches and can claim a rich and romantic history.

During the 12th century the town assumed importance as the most commercial of the four Royal Burghs of Scotland. A town of red-roofed, grey stone houses and quaint, narrow streets enclosed within walls, Berwick has been described as the most exciting town in England. The great Elizabethan walls are regarded as the best-preserved in Europe.

The River Tweed, one of the finest salmon rivers in the country, is straddled by three magnificent bridges, and perhaps the most impressive approach to the town is by rail over the great Royal Border Bridge, designed by Robert Stephenson.

Within Berwick's almost impregnable walls, the narrow streets or 'gates' with their fine Elizabethan and Georgian buildings

bustle with visitors on Wednesdays and Saturdays when the popular open air market is held.

Among Berwick's fine old buildings is the 18th-century guildhall in Marygate, with its 150ft-high steeple where the curfew bell is still rung at 8.00 pm each evening. The oldest purpose-built barracks in the country, designed by Vanbrugh, now houses a museum complex. This features the Borough Museum and Art Gallery, including the King's Own Scottish Borderers Regimental Museum. Another interesting museum, in Palace Green, is the Lindisfarne Wine and Spirit Museum, housed in an old brewery.

Like many other border towns, Berwick has a Riding of the Bounds ceremony – held annually on 1 May – while the Tweedmouth Feast in mid July is a religious festival dating back to 1292. Local schools choose a 'Salmon Queen' and the crowning ceremony marks the start of the Feast Week. This is followed by a traditional salmon supper and a church service.

Fishing, including salmon netting, is a major industry in Berwick and the town has a busy harbour, while its suburbs of Tweedmouth and Spittal have fine beaches popular with holidaymakers.

The Tweed is also alive with sailing boats during the summer.

AA recommends:

Hotels: King's Arms, Hide Hill, 3-star, *tel.* (0289) 307454
Turret House, Etal Rd, Tweedmouth, 3-star, *tel.* (0289) 307344
Browns, Ravensdowne, 2-star, *tel.* (0289) 307170
Queens Head, Sandgate, 1-star, *tel.* (0289) 307852
Camp Site: Ord House Caravan Park, East Ord, 3-pennant, *tel.* (0289) 305288

The Palace at Bishop Auckland has been the official residence of the Bishops of Durham for 800 years

Bishop Auckland

Map Ref: 91NZ2029

Set above the River Wear, Bishop Auckland marks the point where this proud Durham river breaks out of its dale and meanders more freely across the flatter land of central and east Durham. Here too, and perhaps even before the Norman Conquest, the all-powerful Prince Bishops of Durham had a residence. In the 12th century, Bishop Puiset built a more spacious palace as an alternative to his other home, Durham Castle. On the foundation of Durham University and the endowment of Durham Castle, Auckland Palace became the principal residence of the Prince Bishops, and has remained so until the present time.

The town developed little until

Terraces of 18th-century houses flank the north side of Blanchland's pretty L-shaped square

the mid-19th century after many of the Bishop's powers were taken over by the Crown. However, the coming of the railway caused rapid development, and a very ordinary urban sprawl resulted.

The Market Place, with its somewhat Franco-Flemish town hall, a few imposing houses and the Palace Gate, is quite impressive. Since much of the through traffic has been removed it has now taken on a continental air. Bishop's Park is open to the public and its 'mock' Gothic deer shelter, built in 1771 by Bishop Richard Trevor, gives an indication of the lifestyle of the men who held the highest office in the north.

South Church, St Andrew Auckland, St Helen Auckland and West Auckland, almost suburbs of the town, all have buildings of great merit. Now surrounded by modern housing and industrial estates, there are medieval granaries, attractive churches and fine manor houses. West Auckland has two, facing each other across the village green. The old Manor House is now an hotel, so the price of a meal or a pint buys a glimpse of its interior as well as

refreshment.

At nearby Escomb, the Parish Church of St John the Evangelist is the most important Anglo-Saxon survival in Durham – possibly the best in Britain. Its construction dates from the 7th century but the stones and probably the complete chancel arch were acquired from the Roman site at Binchester across the River Wear.

Although surrounded by council houses, the church, unlike most others of its age, has survived almost unchanged, and is as venerable as its contemporary, St Bede, who may well have worshipped here 13 centuries ago.

The Roman Bath House at Binchester (entered through the grounds of Binchester Hall Hotel) is a fine, well-displayed example of a Roman hypocaust.

AA recommends:
Hotels: Kings Arms, 36 Market Place, 2-star, *tel.* (0388) 661296
Park Head, New Coundon (Im N on A688), 2-star, *tel.* (0388) 661727
Queens Head, Market Pl, 2-star, *tel.* (0388) 603477
Garage: Auto Safety Centre, Cockton Hill Rd, *tel.* (0388) 661371

Blanchland

Map Ref: 91NY9650

Romantically situated in a cleft beneath heather-clad moors in the upper Derwent Valley, Blanchland is one of Northumberland's prettiest villages and was designated a perfect village by *Town and Country Planning*. The grey stone houses are grouped around a square which was probably the outer courtyard of Blanchland Abbey, founded in the 12th century. A massive 15th-century gatehouse, once the entrance to the monastery, leads into the square, and houses the village post office with its Victorian post box.

Blanchland Abbey was founded by Walter de Bolbec for Premonstratensian Canons and it is thought the village was named Blanchland – or White Land – after the white habits worn by the monks. The Lord Crewe Arms, named after a former Bishop of Durham, was the abbey guest house and its garden the cloister. It was the home of the Forster family – related by marriage to Lord Crewe, who also owned Bamburgh Castle. This famous family features in Walter Besant's novel *Dorothy Forster*. Dorothy rescued her brother Thomas from gaol and hid him in a priest's hole at the Lord Crewe Arms after his arrest for his involvement in the 1715 Jacobite Rebellion.

Dorothy's ghost is said to haunt a bedroom at the hotel and also to roam the lonely moorland close to Blanchland. The Forster family forfeited their estates to the Crown after the Jacobite Rebellion and the Blanchland Estates were purchased by Lord Crewe. After his death they formed part of a charitable trust. Using this trust fund, the village church was rebuilt during the 18th century.

Smaller than the original 13th-century building, there are several interesting features in the church, including some fine medieval tombstones on the transept floor.

AA recommends:
Hotel: Lord Crewe Arms, 2-star, *tel.* (043 475) 251

Brancepeth

Map Ref: 91NZ2237

Built at right angles across the A690 between Durham City and Crook, Brancepeth has everything. Grand castle, magnificent church, championship golf course, extensive parkland, one or two fine houses and a charming early 19th-century stylised village, almost Tudor in layout but Victorian in reality. The village was recreated by Matthew Russell, a wealthy mine-owner from Sunderland, whose father bought the estate in 1796 for £70,000. Over £100,000 was later spent on rebuilding the present castle.

The church, untouched by the Russells, is a historical delight. Beautifully situated in wooded grounds, it is large and important looking, making one wonder what the original village it served was like before it was cleared to make way for the new one. Nikolaus Pevsner wrote 'There is hardly another church in this country so completely and splendidly furnished'. The rood screen is considered to be the most exceptional piece in the building, but the pews, the pulpit and the ceiling made by Robert Barker in 1638 are a remarkable contribution to the history of architecture in England. There is much more of interest in the church for both expert and layman, and a leaflet is supplied, explaining where to look for what.

Were the castle not sham, it would indeed be the gem it appears to be from a distance. Perhaps it was here, in a 'Neville house', like Raby before the Rising of the North and the subsequent forfeiture of both estates to the Crown, that the liberation of Mary Queen of Scots was planned. The castle is now privately owned and occupied by a publishing company. Access is, however, possible.

The village has hardly been touched by the 20th century. Some modern housing exists but for the most part it is hidden from view. The 18th-century rectory and 17th-century Quarry Hill House at opposite ends of the village are well worth walking between as the journey will take in the whole of beautiful Brancepeth. Holywell Hall lies a mile to the east, between the village and the river. St Cuthbert's body is said to have rested here on its travels.

There are pleasant walks in the area and the opportunity to use one of the disused railway lines which have been converted to footpaths by Durham County Council. From here it is possible to walk to Bishop Auckland, Durham, Consett or even the outskirts of Newcastle. See the Council's leaflet pack – Railway Walks.

Prince Bishops

For almost 1,000 years County Durham was unique, a domain unlike the rest of England, a County Palatine, a Prince Bishopric. The king's writ did not run here, nor was the king's peace kept or threatened here, but the Bishop's. The Bishop of Durham had his own Council and Courts, his own judges, his own army, his own vassals, even his own mint, and rights of admiralty over his own shores. Although these powers were granted by the Norman King William, and confirmed by his son, William II, their origins go back a further two centuries.

The region which was, until a few years ago, the County of Durham, had been known in the past as the 'Patrimony of St Cuthbert', or as 'the Bishopric', or 'the County Palatine of Durham'. Thus, in one important respect, Durham owed its independence to that holy man, Cuthbert, perhaps to his miraculously uncorrupted flesh after death, to the sanctity always associated with him, to the stream of gifts – including land – offered at his shrine, and to the Durham monks responsible for its safe keeping.

The true foundation gift is usually regarded as having been made in 883 by the Christianised King Guthred of Northumbria, who,

A falchion was often presented by the Lord of the Manor to the Bishop as rent. This one can be seen in the cathedral

with the permission of King Alfred, presented to the Church all the land between the Rivers Tyne and Wear, 'freed of all customs and services for ever'. An earlier gift by King Egfrith included land near Crayke, in Yorkshire; later additions included 'North Durham', embracing Norhamshire, Islandshire (with Holy Island) and Bedlingtonshire.

Following the Conquest, William soon recognised the advantages of a quasi-independent power on the northern frontier of his kingdom. It could never be a threat to him since a Bishop could have no legal heirs, and no lay person could rule St Cuthbert's Patrimony. The Bishop and his monks were its spiritual guardians. So William ratified the Saxon gift, granting the Bishop of Durham absolute power within his domain, a spiritual lord and baron of the realm. Only the Bishop governed with crozier and sword, and even today his mitre alone is circled with a coronet, his arms crossed with sword and pastoral staff. The bishops of London, Winchester and Durham take precedence over all other bishops.

The Tudors curtailed the powers of the Prince Bishops, who nevertheless retained most of their independent privileges and revenues which continued to be enjoyed until 1836, four months after the death of the last Prince Bishop, van Mildert. Remarkably, among the long line of formidable, often arrogant, Bishops of Durham, none seriously abused his great powers, and on the whole they governed wisely and well. Some were great scholars, some great builders, some great statesmen; almost all were good men, often with outstanding ability and character. Largely to them we owe the great Cathedral itself, guardian of St Cuthbert's shrine.

In 1632 Lord Baltimore was granted a charter for the government of Maryland, USA. It conferred powers identical to those of the Bishops of Durham, and includes the words '. . . ample rights, jurisdiction, privileges, prerogatives, royalties, liberties, immunities and royal rights . . . as any bishop of Durham . . . in our Kingdom of England . . . hath used or enjoyed.' Thus, alone in the Anglo-Saxon western world, Durham and Maryland have a common political foundation.

Arable crops now cover Branxton Hill – the site of the Battle of Flodden which was fought in 1513

Branxton

Map Ref: 88NT8937

The tiny village of Branxton has an important place in the history of Britain as the site of the Battle of Flodden – the worst of the Anglo-Scottish battles that left thousands dead.

The battle took its name from Flodden Hill, but the actual site where the English defeated the Scots on 9 September 1513 is just west of the A697. A grey stone Celtic cross was erected in 1910 and bears the inscription 'Flodden 1513. To the brave of both nations.'

This last and most bloody battle fought on Northumberland soil was not just a border scuffle, but was linked to greater events in Europe. The English archers proved too much for the Scots under James IV and 10,000 Scotsmen were killed – including James and members of nearly every noble family in Scotland. The body of James IV was taken to St Paul's Church, Branxton, where it rested before it was removed to Berwick. The English, under the Earl of Surrey, lost 5,000 men. The story of the battle has been told many times and was romanticised by Scott in his epic *Marmion.*

Branxton is now a peaceful village, pleasantly situated on a slope and commanding fine views into Scotland. A private garden in the village attracts much attention from visitors for it is filled with large concrete animals. This impressive menagerie was the work of a former owner of the house.

The River Breamish, whose name means 'the bright water' becomes the Till at Bewick Mill further east

Breamish Valley

Map Ref: 89NU0517

One of three remote and beautiful valleys radiating from the Cheviot at the heart of the National Park, the Breamish valley is entered by turning west along the Ingram road, half a mile north of Powburn.

The 'access land' along the valley allows people to park and picnic; a host of footpaths lead more energetic visitors out of the valley and onto the high hills.

The river, clean and gravel-laden, runs north-east to Bewick where it changes its name to the Till. Waterside birds – herons, goosanders, sandpipers, grey wagtails and dippers – are numerous and not too elusive.

Ingram, where there is a National Park Information Centre, is a tiny hamlet with a huge rectory and a small church dating from the 11th century. Its tower appears to have been built for defence. On the surrounding hills are numerous remains of prehistoric settlements and in fact the hamlet's name is thought to mean 'the home of the ancient people of the land'.

Further up the valley is one of the

The grey wagtail hunts for insects on the banks of upland streams

county's loveliest waterfalls – Linhope Spout, which cascades over steep crags into a pool more than 50ft below.

Bywell

Map Ref: 91NZ0461

Just a few miles from the busy A69 lies one of Northumberland's most secluded and picturesque villages. Bywell is no more than a handful of houses, yet it has two churches, a 15th-century castle and a mansion. Situated on one of the loveliest reaches of the River Tyne, Bywell is a true beauty spot.

In the 16th century it was one of the busiest places in Tynedale and had 15 shops, the last of which closed last century. It is famous for its churches, facing each other in a pretty parkland setting. St Andrew's Church, the White Church, was the property of the White Canons of Blanchland. It was rebuilt in the 13th century but has retained its Saxon tower. St Peter's, called the Black Church after the Black Benedictine monks of Durham, is mainly Norman.

The castle, built of Roman stones, stands close to the river and is now in ruins. The grey stone gatehouse was built in about 1430 by Ralph Neville, 2nd Earl of Westmorland, who took part in the ill-fated plot 'The Rising of the North' to release Mary Queen of Scots.

Bywell Estate is now owned by Viscount Allendale who lives in Bywell Hall, built by James Paine and altered by the celebrated Newcastle architect, John Dobson, in 1817. This mansion is set in extensive grounds which are sometimes open to the public under the Northumbria Garden Scheme in aid of the Red Cross.

Chester-le-Street

Map Ref: 91NZ2751

As the name implies, the town stands astride a Roman road. It was the road from Brough on the Humber to the Tyne, where it crossed by the Pons Aelius. Chester-le-Street was *Conganium*, a fort on the road, but there is no longer any visible evidence of the fort or the docks said to be used by Roman ships on the nearby River Wear.

In 883AD, long after the Romans had left, the monks from Lindisfarne arrived here with St Cuthbert's body and made Chester-le-Street the seat of the See of Lindisfarne. Not until 995 was the bishopric transferred to Durham. Only a few stones from the original church survive and these are built into the south wall of the present church of St Mary and St Cuthbert which dates from about 1056. The Anker House or Anchorage, within the church, is now a museum.

From 1383 until the Dissolution of the Monasteries a hermit monk was always resident in the Anchorage, devoting himself to constant prayer and meditation.

The town has one main street and at its northern end an open market operates on Tuesdays and Fridays. The modern Civic Centre in Newcastle Road resembles a 20th-century Crystal Palace. It is not to everyone's taste but, with its sloping, barrel-vaulted, glass-roofed Rates Hall, it is an interesting piece of architecture.

Riverside Park, with its pleasant gardens, offers opportunities for sport and relaxation. Across the river the parklands of both Lambton and Lumley Castles provide an attractive backcloth. Lambton Castle is pure theatre, a mock castle built around the ancient Harraton Hall by the Lambtons between 1794 and 1932, although what remains today is only a fraction of the vast structure which stood here at the turn of the century. The best-known northern architects of the time contributed to the building, including both Joseph and Ignatius Bonomi, John Dobson and Sydney Smirke, and the ruins are extremely attractive.

Lumley Castle, next door, is of a different ilk. It is 14th-century and essentially original. Only the east

Top: Chester-le-Street seen from the south. The spire of St Mary and St Cuthbert dates from about 1400 but the church was built 350 years earlier

Above: Lumley Castle, now a hotel, offers Elizabethan banquets befitting its romantic appearance

front has been altered and even that was done with style. Sir John Vanbrugh was responsible and he created the fine state rooms and the imposing façade. The towers, turrets and bold crenellations of Lumley make it a castle to stir the imagination. It is now a luxurious hotel where banquets and boudoirs are provided for present-day knights of the A1M motorway which passes the end of the drive.

AA recommends:
Hotel: Lumley Castle, 3-star, *tel.* (0385) 891111

Chesters' bath-house was carefully sited above flood level

Chillingham

Map Ref: 89NU0626

The village of Chillingham, set against the dramatic backdrop of the Cheviot Hills, is famous for its unique herd of white cattle.

Chillingham Castle, in a glorious setting overlooking the River Till, became empty in 1933 and fell into decay. However, it was recently purchased by Sir Humphrey Wakefield, Bt, who is restoring it and has opened it to the public. Sir Humphrey is married to a descendant of the original Grey family who owned the castle.

Adjacent to the park is Ross Castle (National Trust), once an important beacon site, standing 1,000ft above sea level. This rocky hilltop has prominent earthworks. The views from this point are far-reaching – to Alnwick, Holy Island and the Scottish hills.

A beautiful tomb of some artistic importance can be found in the tiny church of St Peter. Dated around 1450, it is dedicated to the memory of Sir Ralph Grey and his wife Elizabeth. The exquisite carved figures of the couple still carry traces of the original colouring.

Chollerford

Map Ref: 91NY9170

A stark wooden cross by the roadside near Chollerford marks the beginning of Christianity in Northumbria. It indicates the site of the Battle of Heavenfield in 634, when the young Northumbrian King Oswald defeated the heathen British King Cadwallon. Following his victory, Oswald, later to be canonised, invited Aidan and his monks in Iona to establish a seat of learning in Northumbria. St Oswald's Church stands where Oswald is said to have erected a cross on the eve of this historic battle.

Heavenfield is next to the B6318 Military Road – built by General Wade after the Jacobite Rebellion of 1745 because the roads between

Chillingham, unaffected by agricultural practices, has not changed since medieval times

Wild White Cattle

Five miles south-east of Wooler the 600-acre medieval park of Chillingham Castle is home to the very rare herd of White Cattle, descendants of those trapped within the park when it was enclosed by a wall in 1220. For over seven centuries the breed has thus remained pure, and probably has survived here because it was hunted for sport from medieval times.

The cattle are creamy-white with curved horns which are black-tipped – a feature not likely to be spotted, since close-range inspection is far too risky; the animals are likely to be extremely dangerous, especially when startled or protecting their calves. As with deer, the herd is ruled by a 'king', the only bull allowed to sire calves until he is successfully challenged by a younger male. The resultant fight is rarely to the death, but a badly-injured animal could be doomed; a defeated bull, if not maimed, is likely to be banished by the herd to the hills on the eastern edge of the estate, and not allowed to return for many months.

New-born calves are hidden among the bracken. If human hands touch them their mothers abandon them, and such calves will certainly die. There is a constant fear that, should insufficient numbers of heifer calves be born, the Chillingham strain will die out. Twice within the past 40 years this has almost happened. The severe winter of 1946/47 reduced the size of the herd to just 13 but, by a remarkable extension of the cows' reproductive span, some new calves were born, and in 1966 an outbreak of foot-and-mouth disease caused deep anxiety, but the herd survived. In recent years the numbers have increased to more than 50, and the cattle are protected by a society, The Chillingham Wild Cattle Association Ltd.

Visits to Chillingham Park from April to October, can be made only under the supervision of a warden. There is no guarantee the herd will be seen easily, for the animals may be in the more distant, hilly or wooded areas of the park. In any case it is advisable to have binoculars, since no close approach can be made to the herd. One can all the more admire Thomas Bewick's fine and dramatic engraving of a Chillingham bull.

On one side of the bridge lies Coldstream – in Scotland, and on the other Cornhill – in England

Newcastle and Carlisle were so poor that troop movements had been impossible. Parts of the road, which is like a switchback from Heddon-on-the-Wall to Greenhead, are actually the levelled remains of Hadrian's Wall.

The Military Road crosses the River North Tyne at Chollerford over a lovely arched bridge. Standing by the riverside is one of the most important Roman sites in Britain – Chesters, or *Cilurnum*. Chesters is a country house with the remnants of a Roman cavalry fort in its park, and a museum containing important sculptures and inscribed stones.

The most famous owner of Chesters was John Clayton, a renowned archaeologist and classical scholar who devoted his life to the study of Roman remains in the region.

Clayton, who was born in 1792, acquired five of the wall forts and prevented them from being used as quarries. His work yielded much of what is now preserved at Chesters and the little museum was built in his memory.

Chesters is one of the more accessible forts and also one of the most picturesque, with the relics of an impressive military bath-house standing on a tree-lined terrace above the river. On the far bank are the remains of the bridge abutments which continued the line of Hadrian's Wall over the North Tyne.

AA recommends:
Hotel: George, Humshaugh, 3-star, *tel.* (043 481) 611

Cockfield

Map Ref: 91NZ1224

The Fell, an area of common land to the north of the main street, is where the interest of this historic village is centred. Here history spans the Romano-British to the 19th-century industrial eras, and attached to it is the social history of the early coal mining industry.

Cockfield Fell is real common land where the villagers are still able to enjoy their ancient rights. Nowadays this really only amounts to the right to graze livestock, but may also include the right to collect firewood, quarry stone and even mine coal. Fell Reeves are still appointed, as they have been for centuries, to prevent abuses of the rights, and the commoners' sheep and horses continue to forage on the Fell.

There are public footpaths across the common land and evidence of past industry is plain to see. Saucer-shaped depressions show where coal was dug from early bell pits, and a massive gorge, a fault in the earth's crust once filled with volcanic 'greenstone' has been emptied of its valuable stone.

Cockfield is also the original Dixieland. A brilliant local lad, Jeremiah Dixon who, with a kettle full of coal discovered coal-gas, was eventually sent to American with a certain Mr Mason. Together they surveyed the boundary between Baltimore and Pennsylvania – the Mason/Dixon line from which Dixieland Jazz took its name.

Coldstream

Map Ref: 88NT8439

The world-famous Coldstream Guards Regiment took its name from this Border town on the north bank of the River Tweed. Contrary to popular opinion, the second oldest regiment of Foot Guards in the British Army was not raised in Coldstream. General Monck established his headquarters here in December 1659, having formed the unit out of Fenwick's and Heselrige's Regiments in 1650 to fight Scottish Presbyterians. His men were usually locals who showed great loyalty to their commanding officer despite his tendency to change sides. Having once been aligned to Cromwell, General Monck later captured Newcastle on behalf of the King and was instrumental in returning Charles II to the throne. The regiment, which was given the freedom of the town in 1968, had its headquarters in the Market Square, and the Guards' House is now a museum.

At one time Coldstream rivalled Gretna Green for runaway marriages. A toll house at the Coldstream end of a beautiful seven-arched bridge over the Tweed was the equivalent of Gretna's famous smithy. Three Lords Chancellor of England were married in this hasty way.

The elegant bridge over the river linking the town with Cornhill-on-Tweed on the English side was built by John Smeaton between 1763 and 1766. Robbie Burns crossed it when he made his first entry into England in 1787 and his diary records: 'Coldstream – went over into England. Cornhill – glorious river Tweed, clear, majestic. Fine Bridge.'

West of Coldstream on the A697 is 'The Hirsel', seat of the Earls of Home. The present Earl is the former Conservative Prime Minister, Alec Douglas-Home. His family can trace their family tree back to King Duncan, who murdered Macbeth. The house is a fine Georgian and Victorian mansion standing in beautiful grounds through which flows the Leet Water. One of the features of 'The Hirsel' is the wide range of birds that can be spotted in the grounds – 170 species have been recorded – and the house has nesting boxes for swifts below all the upper floor windows.

AA recommends:
Hotel: Majicado, 7 High St, 1-star, *tel.* (0890) 2112

The splendid Long Gallery of Victorian Cragside House

Corbridge

Map Ref: 91NY9964

The ancient town of Corbridge on the north bank of the River Tyne replaced Bamburgh as capital of Northumbria. It is one of the most attractive places in Northumberland, and its fine houses, some with long gardens reaching down to the river, are highly desirable.

Corbridge today is genteel and quiet, yet it had a violent and troubled past. In 796 Ethelred, King of Northumbria, was killed here and later the Scots paid several unfriendly visits – it was burnt down three times. Two stone towers are reminders of this turbulent history. The oldest, built around 1300, stands next to St Andrew's Church in the Market Place. This was a 'parson's pele', intended to protect the local clergyman and his belongings. It now houses a Tourist Information Centre but is still one of the most authentic and least modernised towers in the county. The younger tower, of about 1600, is attached to Low Hall – an impressive Jacobean house at the east end of Main Street.

St Andrew's Church, one of the oldest in Northumberland, was built with stones from the nearby Roman fort of *Corstopitum*. It has a fine Saxon tower and some of the stonework bears traces of fire as it was frequently a casualty of Scottish raids.

Although no longer a market town, Corbridge has two market crosses – one of 13th-century stone, and the Percy Cross, presented to the town by the Duke of Northumberland in 1807. Also in the Market Place is a fountain called a 'pant' – once used for the village water supply. Corbridge has several pants, the largest one is in Main Street outside the Riverside Hotel.

Dere Street, the Roman road linking York and Edinburgh, runs through the centre of Corbridge. Close to the town, beside the Cor Burn, is the Roman town of *Corstopitum*. This riverside supply base was originally associated with the Stonegate. It developed into a flourishing community and following periods of rebuilding it served as a supply depot for the Wall. The best-preserved Roman granaries in Britain are here and the excellent site museum has a good collection of artefacts, including a remarkable fountainhead – the Corbridge Lion.

Standing above the Cor Burn, a short distance from Corbridge, is Aydon Castle, recently restored and opened to the public by English Heritage. Regarded by many as the best example of a fortified house in the north, it was crenellated in 1305 and sections may even pre-date this.

A museum dedicated to the region's agricultural heritage is based in a typical Northumbrian farmstead at Newton, near Corbridge. The Hunday National Tractor and Farm Museum has Europe's most extensive collection of agricultural machinery.

AA recommends:
Hotels: Angel Inn, Main St, 1-star, *tel.* (043 471) 2119
Riverside, Main St, 1-star, *tel.* (043 471) 2942
Restaurant: Ramblers Country House, Farnley (7m SE on A68), 2-fork, *tel.* (043 471) 2424

Cotherstone

Map Ref: 91NZ0119

The soft, crumbly cheese for which the village is famous is still made locally. Of all the pretty villages beside the beautiful River Tees this is many people's favourite. Here the River Balder joins the Tees and in flood the foaming waters rush along the rocky bed with majestic power; in drier times the cool, clear water sparkles in response to the shafts of sunlight which pierce the trees.

The village stands high above the river, its cottages and grander houses lining the winding main street and the village greens. House styles are varied, belonging to every age and fashion, but they sit so comfortably together that the overall picture is one of complete harmony. The castle is now nothing but a steep mound with some broken stones. Beyond the unmistakably Victorian church a charming lane which once led to the railway station passes pretty gardens before reaching the moors.

The road alongside the River Balder west of the village, leads to Selset, Grassholme, Balderhead, Hury and Blackton reservoirs where sailing, water-skiing and angling facilities are available by arrangement.

Cragside House and Country Park

Map Ref: 89NU0702

Seven million trees and shrubs were planted to create the 900-acre park at Cragside, a mile north of Rothbury. Cragside House and its beautiful grounds, ablaze with rhododendrons in early summer, were built by the first Lord Armstrong, the Victorian industrialist who also restored Bamburgh Castle.

The estate is a magnificent monument to one man and a shrine to Victoriana. Before William Armstrong built his weekend retreat, the scenery north of Rothbury, stretching towards Alnwick, was rough moorland. However, the planting of an enormous park changed not only the landscape, but also the climate of nearby Rothbury which became more sheltered as the trees and shrubs grew.

The great Victorian house and park are now owned by the National Trust who have restored Cragside to its original state – even down to obtaining copies of the original wallpaper.

Cragside was started in 1863 as a hunting lodge, but in 1883 Norman Shaw, the Scottish architect, extended the house. The result was an unusual, Germanic-influenced mansion: not to everyone's taste, but certainly impressive. The house was the first in the world to be lit by electricity – driven by water power, and Armstrong developed his own hydro-electricity system in the grounds with artificial lakes and underground piping.

Lord Armstrong typified the Victorian age of industry and invention. He was knighted for his gun-making and later turned his attentions to building warships. The achievements of this remarkable man, whose Newcastle engineering works became world famous, are featured in an interpretive centre at Cragside.

Craster and Dunstanburgh Castle

Map Ref: 89NU2519

On a warm summer's day you can smell Craster's famous export – kippers! This fishing village, named after the Craster family, is famed for its kippers, cured over oak in a traditional way.

During the kipper-curing season, visitors can peer into the blackened smoking sheds where herrings are suspended from racks above smouldering piles of oak chips. Kippers are on sale and the restaurant attached to the curing sheds does a brisk business in traditional kipper teas. Smoked salmon is also prepared here and can be posted to friends or relatives.

Lobster pots – a familiar sight beside Craster's harbour

The tiny harbour at Craster, often laden with lobster and crab pots, was built in 1906 by the Craster family in memory of a brother who died on active service. Craster Tower is much older – dating from 1415, with Georgian additions.

Between Craster and Embleton one of the most attractive stretches of coastal scenery in the county can be seen. A beautiful grassy path runs between the two villages alongside the sea and past Dunstanburgh Castle – the largest ruined castle in Northumberland. Its dramatic skeleton is perched in a commanding position on steep cliffs over 100ft above the North Sea. Dunstanburgh, built in 1314, was perfectly positioned against attack – the waves dashing against the rocks beneath the castle made invasion from the sea impossible.

The castle was built by the ruthless Thomas, Earl of Lancaster, son of Henry III, who was executed a few years later by Edward II. In the late 14th century, John of Gaunt, lieutenant of the Scottish Marches, extended the castle and later it became a Lancastrian stronghold during the Wars of the Roses.

It is claimed that Queen Margaret was sheltered here on her last night in Northumberland. Eventually the castle was badly damaged by gunfire, and by Tudor times was in ruins. The romantic setting of Dunstanburgh has made the castle a favourite subject of artists, including Turner who painted it three times. It is now owned by the National Trust and administered by English Heritage.

Just south of Craster is Howick Hall, built in 1782 and long associated with the Grey family, who have produced many famous public figures – including Earl Grey, the great social reformer. The gardens at Howick Hall are open during spring and summer and are noted for their beauty. An abundance of daffodils and other narcissi is followed by the glorious blooms of cherries, azaleas and rhododendrons.

AA recommends:
Hotel: Dunstanburgh Castle, Embleton, 2-star, *tel.* (066 576) 203
Camp Site: Dunstan Hill Camping & Caravanning Club Site, 2-pennant, *tel.* (066 576) 310

Strategically placed, Dunstanburgh Castle rambles over 11 acres. Its outline today (top) is much the same as the Victorian engraver's impression (below)

Darlington

Map Ref: 92NZ2914

The nickname of Darlington's football team, 'the Quakers' indicates that this was, and perhaps still is, a Quaker town. The industries here between the 1660s and the present century were created and managed by a properous and powerful Quaker community. Their foresight brought railways to the world and influenced modern banking systems. Edward Pease, the best-known of Darlington's tycoons, backed George Stephenson and created the Stockton and Darlington Railway. Barclays Bank, originally Backhouses, first traded in Darlington and stopped an early run on its funds by piling sovereigns on the counter to give confidence to its worried clients. Backhouse too was a Quaker and almost every one of the numerous mansions in the town's fashionable West End was built for a prosperous Quaker family.

Railways brought business to Darlington, which grew rapidly after 1835. Previously it was a wool and linen town and before that a market town serving the rich agricultural plain alongside the River Tees. Today it succeeds in being all things. The bustling cattle market

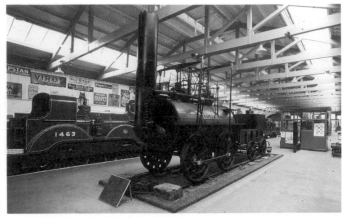

Locomotion No 1, on display in the Darlington Railway Museum

(Monday and Thursday) serves the farming community; wool is still spun in a modern plant here; and heavy industry survives. The Sydney Harbour Bridge and many others around the world were built here and the expertise necessary to design and build even better bridges is still to be found at the Cleveland Bridge and Engineering Works.

As if to prove Darlington's antiquity, the market place is overlooked by St Cuthbert's Church – one of the most important Early English churches in the north of England, and hardly a stick or a stone of the structure was added after 1250. A beautiful

building on a sloping green almost in the centre of the town, surrounded by a green graveyard and mature trees, it looks like a country church. The grey squirrels which scamper up the trees obviously believe it is.

The old town centre still serves the modern populace. Much has been rebuilt but the size has not increased and a few 17th-century fragments and 18th-century buildings remain. The Golden Cock in Tubwell Row is a good example. Almost opposite, No 37 has an ornate cast iron façade built in 1860 – no doubt by an engineer.

The covered market beneath the

The Stephensons

George Stephenson's father was a fireman at Wylam Colliery, one of scores of pits on Tyneside, which by the late 18th century were using steam engines to provide power to pump out water and to lift coal from the seams being worked at an increasing depth. As a boy George worked on a farm before being employed at Black Callerton Pit, driving a gin horse. He soon became a fireman, then a brakesman; in 1798 he was put in charge of Robert Hawthorn's new pumping engines at Water Row Pit, Newburn, and in 1804 transferred as a brakesman to Killingworth, becoming an enginewright at the West Moor Pit of the 'Grand Allies' – the most famous coal-mining partnership in the north-east.

By then the use of steam-power for haulage was in its infancy.

Richard Trevithick had built a steam locomotive for Christopher Blackett at Wylam Colliery, but it was unsuccessful, and in 1815 William Hedley, also of Wylam, built the famous 'Wylam Dilly' which

British engineer George Stephenson was born at Wylam (see page 77)

demonstrated that traction was possible for iron wheels running on iron rails. The engine continued in use on the Wylam waggonway until 1862. At Killingworth, George Stephenson met many of these early pioneers, developed his interest in all things mechanical, and constructed his first locomotive, the *Blucher*, for Sir Charles Liddell, one of the Grand Allies, in 1814. This meant that the days of the colliery waggonway using horse-drawn trucks were numbered.

Cast-iron rails, flanged wheels and improved suspension combined to open the way for George, in partnership with William Losh, to start building locomotives in Losh's works at Newcastle. This eventually led to Stephenson's association with Edward Pease, a Quaker entrepreneur of Darlington, which resulted in great triumph. In September 1825, the world's first passenger railway,

old town hall clock bustles with activity six days a week. It has a wide range of goods for sale but is primarily a food market.

To the north of the centre, an early station of the Stockton and Darlington Railway is now a railway museum. It is not the original building but was built only 17 years after the first passenger train used the line, presumably when the company's finances were in better shape. *Locomotion No 1*, Stephenson's first locomotive built for the Stockton and Darlington Railway, is the main exhibit at the museum and, close by, still carrying the present railway across Northgate, is an original 1825 Stockton and Darlington bridge built by George Stephenson.

AA recommends:
Hotels: Blackwell Grange Moat House, Blackwell Grange, 4-star, *tel.* (0325) 460111
King's Head, Priestgate, 3-star, *tel* (0325) 380222
Stakis White Horse, Harrowgate Hill, 3-star, *tel.* (0325) 487111
Coachman, Victoria Rd, 1-star, *tel.* (0325) 286116
Restaurant: Bishop's House, 38 Coniscliffe Rd, 2-forks, *tel.* (0325) 286666
Guesthouse: Raydale Hotel, Stanhope Road South, *tel.* (0325) 58993
Garages: Auto Safety Centre, 319 North Rd, *tel.* (0325) 58891

Sherwoods, Chestnut St, *tel.* (0325) 466155
Skippers, *tel.* (0325) 467581
Whessoe Service Station (Woodland Rd), Whessoe Rd, *tel.* (0325) 466044

Duns

Map Ref: 88NT7853

Set in the middle of the Merse – the rich agricultural land of the Scottish Borders – Duns was once the county town of Berwickshire. Although it lost that status upon the local government reorganisation in 1973, Duns is still a bustling market town with a rich heritage. James IV made the town a Royal Burgh in 1489 and Duns has several famous 'sons'. This grey Border town retains an old-fashioned atmosphere with several quaint specialist shops that are far removed from today's impersonal supermarkets.

Duns was the birthplace in 1266 of the philosopher John Duns Scotus who is probably best remembered by the word 'dunce' – coined by Cromwell's Puritans to express their disgust at his views.

In 1803 the gardener Joseph Paxton was born in the town. He moved to London, and later became gardener at Chatsworth House, Derbyshire, where he was encouraged to design glass and iron horticultural

buildings. This eventually led him to design the Crystal Palace for the Great Exhibition of 1851.

A museum in Newtown Street commemorates another famous local man – racing driver Jim Clark, who was tragically killed in Germany in 1968. He lived at nearby Chirnside and is buried in the churchyard there. The Jim Clark Room in Duns houses a unique collection of racing trophies and memorabilia.

One-and-a-half miles east of the town is Manderston, Scotland's finest Edwardian country house. The sumptuous mansion has been called the swansong of the great classical house. Set in 56 acres of immaculate grounds, it was designed by the architect, John Kinross. One feature of the house is a splendid silver staircase – a replica of the one in the Petit Trianon in Versailles. Manderston is well known for its sophisticated 'below stairs' arrangements, and a visit to the mansion gives a fascinating glimpse of the domain of the butler and housekeeper. The grounds feature lakeside walks, a woodland garden, stables and a dairy.

AA recommends:
Self Catering: No's 1 & 3 Printonan, *tel.* (089 084) 378
Guesthouse: Black Bull Hotel (Inn), Black Bull St, *tel.* (0361) 83379

powered by *Locomotion*, was opened between Stockton and Darlington. By then, Stephenson had developed a large network of iron-railed tracks from pitheads to riverside and coastal coal-staithes, and his son, Robert, born in 1803, was becoming more and more involved with George's business expansion.

Robert, unlike his father, showed a keen interest in books. George sent him to study privately, first at Longbenton near Killingworth, later at a private academy in Newcastle, where he stayed until he was 16, when he became an apprentice at Killingworth. In 1821 he attended a course of science lectures at Edinburgh University, and eventually became his father's partner as surveyor and engineer for the newly-burgeoning railways. Three years later Robert found himself in charge of mining operations in Colombia, South America, where he stayed

until 1827.

On his return he became manager of the Forth Street works in Newcastle which he used as his working headquarters while he carried out duties as engineer to more railway companies. These included the Canterbury to Whitstable in Kent, two important lines in Lancashire, and the Leicester and Swannington system – the oldest constituent line of the Midland Railway.

In the 1830s the Stephensons were involved in the establishment of the Grand Junction Railway, intended to link London, Birmingham and Liverpool, Robert insisting on being Engineer-in-Chief. The line was opened in 1838, the biggest engineering project the modern world had ever seen. Subsequently meeting the 'Railway King', George Hudson, Robert was commissioned to supervise the construction of the Newcastle and Darlington Junction

Railway, and to close the final links in the London to Edinburgh East Coast route. This included the High Level Bridge over the Tyne and the Royal Border Bridge at Berwick (1849 and 1850). He also opened in 1850 his Britannia Tubular Bridge over the Menai Straits.

Stephenson built two similar structures in Egypt, and a much larger one at Montreal, since replaced. He was a cultured, modest and friendly man; he refused a knighthood, but was the first civil engineer to become a millionaire. After his death in 1859 he was buried beside Thomas Telford in Westminster Abbey. His father had died in 1848, and was buried at Holy Trinity, Chesterfield. Between them, father and son had helped to change the face of civilisation.

Grand opening of the first English railway on September 27 1825

Durham

Map Ref: 92NZ2642

'Half Church of God, half castle 'gainst the Scot'.

The capital of Northumbria and the seat of the Prince Bishops whose throne is higher than any other in Christendom, Durham is dominated by the great cathedral standing on the peninsula high above the city. Flanked on one side by its protective Norman castle and on the other by monastic and collegiate buildings, it presents a skyline that is famous throughout the world.

To experience Durham's full magnificence, approach the cathedral on foot from the west. Climb the steep granite setts of South Street – itself a delight – and gaze across the tree-filled gorge of the River Wear upon one of man's greatest architectural achievements.

From South Street cross Prebends Bridge; pass through the Water Gate and up the South Bailey with its Georgian façades – hiding much older interiors. Before entering the cathedral, enjoy the tranquillity of the cathedral close with its 15th-century College Gate.

Leave the close by the arched tunnel in the top right-hand corner and, by a zig-zag path, follow the west wall of the cathedral to the next path to the right which leads to Palace Green and the great North Door. The best-known door knocker in the world is actually a replica; the original is on view in the library. The interior of St Cuthbert's massive church is breathtaking in its simplicity. Huge pillars, the rose window – best lit by the morning sun – the Neville rood screen, the light graceful ribs of the nave carrying the massive weight of the stone vaulted roof; all combine to spellbind the visitor.

Unfortunately for Durham, the cathedral puts all else in the shade. The castle (University College) is open to the public. It has fine rooms and an enchanting staircase. Its Norman chapel is thought to date from 1070 and the great hall,

The replica of the cathedral's famous 12th-century door knocker

which has a splendid gallery, is used as the students' dining hall.

The city has a wealth of fine buildings; a few are timber-framed but most have Georgian fronts. Durham escaped industrialisation and has remained an administrative centre throughout history. Its university, founded in 1832, is the oldest provincial university in England. Trinity College in Oxford was originally called Durham College and served this city's needs from 1326 until the foundation of its own university by Act of Parliament and the endowment by the Bishop of his Durham Castle and land surrounding the city. In recent years the University has added some splendid examples of modern architecture to the city.

St Nicholas' Church in the Market Place is an elegant Victorian church. So elegant, in fact, that it is on occasion mistaken for the cathedral. The exterior of St Margaret's in Crossgate belies its Norman origins and almost hides the splendid 15th-century clerestory. Also Norman are St Giles and St Oswalds. The latter may be older than the cathedral and the former is beautifully sited high above the river.

Old Elvet was the smart end of the city in the 18th century.

Despite the loss of its south side in 1896 to make way for the construction of the Shire Hall, which in almost a century has refused to mellow, the broad street has elegance and charm.

As a shopping centre Durham serves a large population residing in the former colliery villages which surround it. Saturday is market day.

About 2 miles north of the city the ruins of Finchale Priory occupy a lovely riverside site chosen by St Godric in 1110. The saint lived at Finchale for 60 years in solitude after a pilgrimage to Santiago de Compostella, and died at the age of 105. The priory was begun in 1180 and eventually became a holiday retreat for the monks of Durham. There is a story that a seat in the Douglas tower 'had the virtue of removing sterility and procuring issue for any woman who having performed certain ceremonies sat down thereon'. The seat lost its efficacy as soon as the monks left.

AA recommends:

Hotels: Royal County, Old Elvet, 4-star, *tel.* (0385) 66821

Bowburn Hall, Bowburn (3m SE junc A177/A1(M)), 3-star, *tel.* (0385) 770311

Bridge, Croxdale (2½m S off A167), 3-star, *tel.* (0385) 780524

Ramside Hall, Belmont (3m NE A690), 3-star, *tel.* (0385) 65282

Three Tuns, New Elvet, 3-star, *tel.* (0385) 64326

Redhills, Redhills Ln, Crossgate Moor, 1-star, *tel.* (0385) 64331

Restaurant: Squire Trelawny, 80 Front St, Sherburn Village (3m E off A181), 1-fork, *tel.* (0385) 720613

Guesthouse: Croxdale (Inn), Croxdale (3m S A167), *tel.* (0388) 815727
Garages: Fred Henderson, Ainsley St, *tel.* (0385) 46319
Minories, Alma Place, Gilesgate Moor, *tel.* (0385) 67215

Ebchester

Map Ref: 91NZ1055

The village takes its name from St Ebba, to whom the pretty, totally rebuilt 12th-century church is dedicated. That St Ebba's name was chosen was perhaps a mistake, based on the belief that the remains of the Roman Fort *Vindomara* were the 7th-century ruins of a monastery founded by that particular saint.

The fort which lay to the north-east of the church no doubt guarded the crossing of the River Derwent by Dere Street and an altar from the fort can be seen in the church tower, where other Roman fragments are built into the walls.

The riverside woods, owned by the National Trust, are both attractive and of botanical interest. To the south of the village is part of the Derwent Walk which connects Ebchester with several good footpaths.

Edmundbyers

Map Ref: 91NZ0150

The village is close to the Derwent Reservoir which lies on the boundary between Durham and Northumberland. The houses of Edmundbyers are scattered around large greens which slope towards the church. In the centre, the

Punchbowl Inn is popular with caravanners who spend weekends and holidays on nearby sites. The reservoir, the largest stretch of fresh water in the area, is popular with both anglers and yachtsmen. Visitors are able to launch their craft at the clubhouse and day permits to fish in the reservoir are available from the Water Company's offices.

Several picnic areas and Pow Hill Country Park ring this 3½-mile-long lake, which is managed to provide domestic water supplies for Sunderland and South Shields, good sailing and productive angling.

St Edmunds Church has some very interesting interior woodwork which has come from churches throughout the country. Beyond the church there is a bypassed turnpike bridge and the remains of a lead-smelting mill whose partly collapsed flue can be seen on the hillside. There is a Youth Hostel in the village and at Muggleswick, 1½ miles east of Edmundbyers, the ruins of a 13th-century refugium built by the monks of Durham Cathedral can be seen.

Elsdon

Map Ref: 88NY9393

Elsdon, 3 miles from Otterburn, is a village of great historical importance. It was once the capital

Durham Cathedral on its bluff high above the River Wear

of Redesdale – the most lawless place in Northumberland and scene of some of the worst border fighting.

One of the most important pele-towers (fortified houses) in the county is in Elsdon. Formerly used as a rectory, Elsdon Tower is a prominent feature of the village and is open to the public by arrangement. Built in 1400, it has one room with walls 9ft thick.

Next to the tower is the notable 14th-century church where some of the dead from the Battle of Otterburn were brought for burial.

To the north-east of the village a great pair of grass-covered mounds known as the Mote Hills are evidence of Elsdon's great antiquity. They are not natural hills, but the earthworks of a Norman motte-and-bailey castle, described by Pevsner as 'the best in Northumberland'.

The moorland around Elsdon is inhabited by thousands of sheep. Milking sheep for cheese was a traditional Northumbrian craft, which has recently been revived at Soppitt Farm, just west of the village. The Redesdale Sheep Dairy is open to the public, who can watch the unusual sight of sheep being milked at 4pm daily from April to November.

AA recommends:
Self Catering: Billsmoor Foot Farm, *tel.* (0669) 40219
Guesthouse: Dunns Farmhouse, *tel.* (0669) 40219

Etal

Map Ref: 88NT9239

A thatched roof in the once turbulent English border lands may seem incongruous. Yet in the tiny village of Etal beside the River Till there are thatched cottages and a thatched pub in one of the prettiest streets in the county. At the end of the street are the imposing ruins of Etal Castle that bear witness to the fact that this idyllic village was once the scene of a border conflict. The castle, crenellated in 1342, was destroyed by the Scots on their way to the Battle of Flodden. The ruins are beautifully situated on the edge of a steep bank above the Till with superb views of the Cheviot Hills.

At the opposite end of the village is the 18th-century Etal Manor, home of Lord and Lady Joicey who own the impressive Ford and Etal Estates. In the grounds of the house is St Mary's Church, built in the middle of the last century by William Butterfield. The grounds of Etal Manor are usually open on certain Sundays during early summer and again in the autumn when they are renowned for their autumn crocus.

Northumberland is currently undergoing a revival of traditional crafts, and several have mushroomed in and around the Ford and Etal Estates. Beautiful hand-made furniture is manufactured in the Old Power House next to the River Till and at Errol Hut Smithy and Workshop at Letham Hill visitors can see a working smithy, and spinning wheels being made by hand.

Across the River Till is Crookham, scene of the last of all the border skirmishes. It was in this hamlet in September 1678 that the Crookham Affray was fought between mounted parties of Scots and English.

A few miles north east of Etal is Duddo, a tiny village famous for the Duddo Stones, one of the best preserved stone monuments in Northumberland. Five stones – 5-10ft high – are all that remain of a stone circle which may have formed part of a burial place. Several Bronze Age relics have been found nearby.

Farne Islands

Map Ref: 89NU2337

This small group of 28 islands off the Northumberland coast forms part of the most easterly section of the Great Whin Sill. The largest island is Inner Farne, nearest to the mainland. Further out are Brownsman, Staple, the Wamses and Longstone. Most of the others are simply bare rock, some rarely visible above the water.

The Farne Islands are world famous as a bird sanctuary and are the only east coast breeding ground of the grey seal. However, the islands are also of great historical importance as centuries ago they were used as a retreat by St Aidan and St Cuthbert. Although St Aidan often visited the Farnes for prayer and meditation, it was the gentle Cuthbert who really belonged here. He spent his final years here as a hermit, having built a cell of earth and stone with help from angels – if the Venerable Bede is to be believed.

St Cuthbert loved animals so it seems fitting that the islands with

Grace Darling

The best-known English name for a courageous act of rescue at sea is that of Grace Darling, daughter of the lighthouse keeper on the Longstone, one of the largest and outermost of the Farne Islands. Still painted in red and white the Longstone lighthouse dates from 1826. Just before dawn on 7 September 1838, Grace, then a young woman of 23, looking through the window of her small circular room, observed a ship aground on Big Harcar, half a mile to the west. It turned out to be the 400-ton *Forfarshire*, bound from Hull to Dundee, and although, when sighted, it was too dark to see if there were any survivors, within a couple of hours figures could be identified, either clinging to, or moving about on the rocks. The passenger-carrying luxury steamer may have foundered because her master could have mistaken the Longstone light for one closer inshore.

Grace's younger brother was away on the mainland, so she, her mother and father were the lighthouse's only occupants. A northerly gale was blowing, but it seems likely that the seas were much less mountainous than contemporary artists depicted. Had they been really severe there would have been no possibility of Grace and her father launching their coble to try to rescue survivors.

One woman and eight men were saved. Nine other people had earlier put off in one of the ship's boats and were picked up by a Montrose sloop, but 43 passengers and crew members of the *Forfarshire* were

Grace Darling and her father struggling to reach the 'Forfarshire'

lost in the tragedy. When the newspapers gave details of the rescue Grace Darling immediately became a national heroine. *The Times* wondered whether such female heroism had ever previously been recorded, a comment which apparently caused some jealousy in the Northumberland fishing village of Seahouses. The lifeboat there, with Grace's brother on board, had also gone to the *Forfarshire*, only to discover the nine survivors had already been taken away by Grace Darling and her father in their coble. Ironically, the lighthouse keeper's log of the rescue has no mention of his daughter's part in it – presumably it

was neither more nor less than was expected.

Four years later Grace died, probably of consumption, and was buried in the churchyard at Bamburgh where an ostentatious monument was later raised to her memory. The RNLI awarded William and Grace Darling their silver medal, and a century afterwards it established a Grace Darling Museum at Bamburgh. This commemorates the rescue and contains many family relics, together with manuscripts, books and paintings relating to the event, as well as the sturdy boat used on that stormy September morning in 1838.

which he was associated should be a sanctuary for birds; 17 species nest here, including the eider duck – known as St Cuthbert's chick, or 'cuddy ducks'. A chapel built to his memory during the 14th century was restored in 1845, but parts of the original window and walls are still visible. The islands, owned by the National Trust, can be visited by boat from Seahouses. The best time for birdwatchers to visit is during the nesting season, from the end of May to the beginning of July. For the sake of the birds access is controlled and landing is only permitted on Staple and Inner Farne, but the trip is worth taking, for the birds can be seen at close quarters.

The hard dolerite rocks of the Farnes have always been a danger to mariners, so lighthouses have long been a feature of the islands. It is believed that monks kept beacons burning as far back as the 9th century. The most famous lighthouse is Longstone from where Grace Darling and her father, the keeper, made their dramatic rescue of the survivors of the wrecked *Forfarshire*.

Ford

Map Ref: 88NT9437

Tucked away among trees is the delightful model village of Ford, created by Louisa, Marchioness of Waterford, a bridesmaid of Queen Victoria. She devoted her time to painting after the death of her husband, built the village school and then decorated the walls with water-colour paintings. These depict scenes from the Old Testament and feature local people who were used as models.

Lady Waterford, a notable Victorian beauty, was a pupil of the Pre-Raphaelite artist John Ruskin. He wrote of her work: 'I expected you would have done something better.' However, despite Ruskin's views, Lady Waterford was an accomplished artist and the murals are quite remarkable. The school is no longer used and is now known as Lady Waterford Hall.

Ford Castle, built in 1282, forms part of Lord Joicey's Estate, but is let to the Northumberland Education Authority. It was transformed into a courtyard castle by Sir William Heron, High Sheriff of Northumberland, during the 14th century. The Scots badly damaged the castle on their way to the Battle of Flodden. The castle was altered in 1761 by Sir John Delaval and again by Lady Waterford in the last century. She is buried in the churchyard of the nearby 13th-century church. Although much altered in the 19th century, the huge bell tower may be an original feature.

Like neighbouring Etal, Ford has several craft shops and close by is Heatherslaw Mill, a restored 19th-century water-driven corn mill. Flour is actually ground here and wholemeal flour products are on sale. Next to the mill is a craft shop where demonstrations are sometimes given.

Gainford

Map Ref: 91NZ1716

Darlington people have been retiring to Gainford since the 18th century. Like Croft and Dinsdale, it had its spa, and the font-like mineral water basin can still be seen on the riverbank ¼-mile upstream from the village where the water is available free of charge.

Gainford's village green is without doubt one of the prettiest in the county. On two levels with attractive well-placed trees, always tidy and unblemished by parked cars, it is worthy of the grand and the pretty houses that are built around it. The modern houses on the south side of the green are less attractive; permission to build them was not granted by the local authorities but by a government minister who allowed an appeal.

Gainford Hall, hidden behind high gates and only visible over the wall, is particularly fine. It is a miniature Hardwick Hall, the Derbyshire house reputed to have more glass than wall.

High Row, a group of varied Georgian houses, is the most picturesque part of the village. The beautiful church stands between the river and the green.

Not far to the west and also lying beside the lovely River Tees are Winston and Whorlton. The former has an interesting bridge, built in 1764. The single, semi-circular arch spans 111ft in one exhilarating leap and, unlike most bridges over the Tees, it survived the great deluge of 1771. The 13th-century church has some fascinating carved stones.

Whorlton too has a noteworthy bridge but of the suspension variety. It has lovely riverside footpaths, and a lido on the riverbank.

A round trip of the Farne Islands takes 2½ hours; visitors may only land on Staple (below) and Inner Farne

Numerous delightful paths can be followed through Allen Banks mature deciduous woodland

Haltwhistle

Map Ref: 90NY7064

This small grey market town on the River South Tyne lies just south of Hadrian's Wall and is an ideal base for exploring this great Roman monument. Haltwhistle is in the heart of an important farming area and once claimed to be part of Scotland.

Its odd name was originally spelt 'Hautwessel' and is still pronounced that way by some locals. The town suffered in border raids and is associated with the Ridleys – one of the most powerful border families. In the church of the Holy Cross is a tombstone of John Ridley, brother-in-law of the martyr, Nicholas Ridley. This exceptional Early English church is one of the best in Northumberland.

Carvoran, another fort on the Stanegate – a Roman road built by Agricola – is north-west of Haltwhistle and close to an outstanding section of Hadrian's Wall. The fort itself remains unexcavated, but the adjacent Roman Army Museum is devoted to the Roman soldier and has vivid reconstructions of life at that time. *Carvoran* was once the home of the Wall's only garrison of archers, men from Syria.

AA recommends:
Self Catering: Smithy Cottage, *tel.* (0498) 20565
Guesthouses: Ashcroft, *tel.* (0498) 20213
Broomshaw Hill Farm House, Willia Rd, *tel.* (0498) 20866
Park Burnfoot Farm House, Featherstone Pk, *tel.* (0498) 20378
Ald White Craig Farm House, Shield Hill, *tel.* (0498) 20565
Camp Sites: Burnfoot Campsite, Bellister Estate, Featherstone, 3-pennant, *tel.* (0498) 20106
Yont the Cleugh, Coanwood, 1-pennant, *tel.* (0498) 20274

Haydon Bridge

Map Ref: 90NY8464

The Romantic painter, John Martin, drew pictures in the sand by the banks of the River South Tyne near his native Haydon Bridge. Martin, who became a master of melodrama, is remembered in the straggling grey stone village by a street named after him. He was born in a small cottage at East Lands Farm in 1784, and the scenery of the South Tyne Valley is reflected in many of his paintings.

Haydon Bridge, lying either side of the busy A69 Newcastle to Carlisle road, was once an important place in the movements of Scottish and English armies. The bridge crossing the Tyne was gated, and locked against Scottish invaders. On the right bank of the river is Haydon Spa, a small medicinal spring.

Alone on a hillside stands Haydon Old Church, said to have been one of the many resting places of the body of St Cuthbert after the monks of Lindisfarne fled from the invading Danes. The new church in the village is dedicated to the saint.

South of the village lies Langley Castle, a medieval stronghold that has had a chequered history in recent years, but is now a smart country house hotel. The castle was built in 1360 and was once owned by the ill-fated Earl of Derwentwater who was executed following the 1715 Jacobite Rebellion.

There are some delightful walks in the Haydon Bridge area, but perhaps the loveliest are at Allen Banks – 194 acres of wooded valleys and riverside paths 3 miles west of the village. Several miles of footpaths wind through the woods on either side of the river, between the National Trust car park and Plankey Mill. The Allen is crossed by swaying rope bridges at this secluded beauty spot given to the National Trust by the Honourable Francis Bowes-Lyon, an uncle of the Queen Mother. Nearby is the ruined Staward Pele, once one of the strongest defensive sites in Northumberland, and not far away is the popular Carts Bog Inn.

AA recommends:
Hotel: Anchor, John Martin St, 2-star, *tel.* (043484) 227
Restaurant: General Havelock Inn, Ratcliffe Rd, 1-fork, *tel.* (043484) 376

Heighington

Map Ref: 91NZ2422

Lying just on the northern edge of the River Tees' fertile plain, Heighington has cottages and mansions, and styles galore. Each terrace appears to have its own village green, giving a feeling of space and privacy.

The larger houses, the Old Hall, Heighington Hall and Trafalgar House, have walled gardens and architectural features worthy of note. There are two dovecotes, one in the village and one at Coatsey Moor Farm. Trafalgar House has always been occupied by Cumbys; it was built by Captain William

The Bay Horse Inn faces Heighington's large, attractive green

Bryce Cumby after the great sea battle from which he returned in triumph.

Another claim to fame is the railway station. It was here at Heighington level-crossing, in Aycliffe Lane, that George Stephenson built his *Locomotion No 1*. It was brought in pieces by horses and carts from the Newcastle works and reassembled for its epic journey on 27 September 1825; the first steam passenger train in the world.

The church has just as much variety as the village: Saxon origins with a Norman tower, chancel and tower arches. The vestry is 13th-century, the aisle 14th-century, the tower top 15th-century and the clock opening 19th-century. Back yards and patios abut the graveyard, making the relationship between the church and the people plain to see.

South of Heighington, across the busy A68, are whitewashed villages belonging to the Raby estate. Houghton le Side and Denton, linked by a narrow lane, consist of farms which, with a snow-white dovecote, barns and cart sheds with arched entrances, are timeless. Only the machinery of agriculture has changed; the way of life and the apparent disorder of the layout of the farmsteads is incapable of modernisation.

Hexham

Map Ref: 91NY9364

In 674, Queen Etheldreda of Northumbria gave her spiritual adviser, Wilfrid, land in Hexham on which to build a church. More than 1,000 years later Wilfrid's church, dedicated to St Andrew, dominates this busy market town. Hexham Abbey, at one time, said to be the finest church north of the Alps was built with stones from the Roman fort of *Corstopitum*.

Although much of the present Abbey dates from the 12th century there is a superb Saxon crypt – perhaps the finest in England – and St Wilfrid's Chair or Frith Stool, the Saxon throne of the Bishop. Also of note is a Roman tombstone and the well trodden Monks' Night Stair – still used by the present choir. It is claimed that this ancient staircase is haunted.

Hexham Abbey stands at a corner of the Market Place – lively on Tuesdays when the colourful market stalls are set out in the Shambles, a long shelter with a flagged roof. The town lies at the centre of a large agricultural community and the Hexham livestock market is one of the busiest in the county.

This historic town has some buildings of antiquity. The Moot Hall, built in the 14th century and now a gallery and home for changing exhibitions, is in the Market Place. An archway under the hall leads to the Manor Office and the town's former jail – now a Tourist Information Centre – and the Middle March Centre, a small museum devoted to the history of the Border Reivers.

Like so many border towns Hexham has a turbulent past. It suffered badly at the hands of the Scots, although Robert Bruce could find nothing left to burn when he arrived in Hexham! The last time blood was shed in the town was in 1761 when the Riot Act was read in the Market Place after a group of people, mainly Allendale lead miners, rebelled against new recruiting regulations for the militia. Fifty people were killed and 300 injured. For many years the North Yorkshire Militia were known as the Hexham Butchers.

Now Hexham is a bustling, but peaceful town, popular with tourists visiting nearby Hadrian's Wall. It has a special summer bus service, taking in all the major Roman sites. The town boasts plenty of green open spaces, in particular the Seal (or Sele), next to the Abbey, where monks once meditated, but which is now a lovely public park. Tyne Green Riverside Park is a country park close to the A69 and the Tyne Bridge, from where the best view of Hexham can be seen.

AA recommends:
Hotels: Beaumont, Beaumont St, 2-star, *tel.* (0434) 602331
County, Priestpopple, 2-star, *tel.* (0434) 602030
Royal, Priestpopple, 2-star, *tel.* (0434) 602270
Guesthouse: Westbrooke Hotel, Allendale Rd, *tel.* (0434) 603818
Camp Sites: Causey Hill Caravan Park, Benson's Fell Farm, 3-pennant, *tel.* (0434) 602834
Hexham Racecourse (TRAX) Caravan Club Site, 2-pennant, *tel.* (0434) 606847
Lowgate Caravan Site, 2-pennant, *tel.* (0434) 602827
Garages: Bishops, Alnmouth Rd, *tel.* (0434) 605151
Dale (F Hancock & Sons), Haugh La, *tel.* (0434) 604527

St Wilfrid's throne, or Frith Stool – a place of sanctuary in medieval times

Part of Queen Etheldreda's gift to Wilfrid in 674 was the beautiful tract of land around Hexham known as The Shire

Holy Island

Map Ref: 89NU1241

Holy Island, or Lindisfarne, has played a major role in the history of England. It was from this tiny island, reached by a causeway from the mainland, that the word of God was spread to establish Northumbria as a cradle of Christianity.

Over the centuries Holy Island has attracted many pilgrims following in the footsteps of two saints – Aidan and Cuthbert – who founded this Golden Age, and whose names will always be synonymous with Lindisfarne.

St Aidan and his monks from Iona established a monastery here in 635. He was created Bishop of Lindisfarne and, after his death in Bamburgh, his body was returned to the island and buried beside the high altar. St Cuthbert was a shepherd boy from the Lammermuir Hills who saw a vision of St Aidan and decided to dedicate his life to God. He came to Holy Island in 664, though towards the end of his life he spent more time in solitary retreat on Inner Farne (see page 52).

The monks of Lindisfarne brought Cuthbert's body back to the island where it stayed until the Viking raids of the 7th century. Eventually the monks fled with his body and began a lengthy journey on the mainland that was to end in Durham. They took with them the beautifully illuminated Lindisfarne Gospels – now in the British Museum.

Sir Edwin Lutyens transformed the interior of Lindisfarne Castle to a comfortable Edwardian home in 1903

St Aidan's original monastery was added to over the years to become Lindisfarne Priory. Although now roofless and in ruins, the gaunt remains, dating from the 11th century, are still splendid.

West of the Priory is St Mary's Church of 13th-century origin, where local brides have to go through an unusual wedding ceremony, jumping over a 'petting' stool at the east end of the churchyard to ensure a happy marriage.

Several other strange customs and traditions survive on Holy Island to add to the unique charm that makes it one of Northumbria's most popular tourist spots. Many are connected with the fishing industry, and perhaps the most unusual concerns the word 'pig' – considered to be very unlucky. No fisherman would ever mention the word, instead the animals are called 'yon things', 'grumfits' or 'articles'.

Standing on a high rock at the south-east corner of the island is Lindisfarne Castle, built in 1554 as a fort but renovated by Sir Edwin Lutyens for Edward Hudson, owner of *Country Life* magazine. The fairytale castle became a delightful holiday home with a tiny garden landscaped by Gertrude Jekyll. The property is now in the ownership of the National Trust.

The ancient tradition of brewing mead survives on Lindisfarne and the drink, made from honey and local herbs, is marketed all over the world. Lindisfarne Mead, made to the monks' ancient recipe, is now produced by a commercial company and the modern mead factory is open to the public.

Holy Island is cut off from the mainland at high tide, so visitors are advised to check the tide tables printed in local newspapers, and available at Tourist Information Centres, before attempting to cross.

Holystone

Map Ref: 88NT9502

Seven miles from Rothbury, on the edge of the Northumberland National Park, lies Holystone – one of the loveliest villages in Coquetdale. A tranquil pool of clear water and a sparkling spring form St Ninian's or Lady's Well – now owned by the National Trust.

On Easter Day in 627AD St Paulinus is said to have baptised 3,000 heathen Northumbrians here. However this astonishing claim is disputed because some historians say he was in York that day! The well, set in an enclosure surrounded by trees, is adorned with a cross, and a stone statue of St Paulinus stands at one end of the pool. At the other end is a stone table or altar.

The holy well was once a watering place beside the Roman road from Redesdale to the coast and it is believed that it was walled-in either in Roman or medieval times. It was associated with St Ninian, the fifth-century apostle, but became known as Lady's Well when Holystone was occupied by a group of Augustinian canonesses dedicated to the worship of the Virgin Mary. Nothing remains of the nunnery, but the small village church – largely rebuilt last century – is dedicated to St Mary.

A pretty waterfall lies nearby at Dove Crag, below which is Rob Roy's Cave, reputed to have been a hiding place of the famous outlaw.

Housesteads Fort

Map Ref: 90NY7968

The most dramatically sited of the many forts along Hadrian's Wall occupies a commanding position on the exposed whinstone ridge. It is the most popular tourist attraction on the Wall, perhaps because the views from the fort are quite breathtaking.

Housesteads (*Vercovicium*) is often regarded as the most complete surviving example of a Roman fort. The land was bought by John Clayton of Chesters and the site excavated in the 1890s. In 1930 a descendant of Clayton passed the fort to the National Trust, which protects it and a 3½-mile stretch of the Wall from Housesteads to Steel Rigg – perhaps the classic section of Hadrian's Wall.

The fort is ½ a mile from the excellent visitor centre alongside the Military Road and the walk, up a steepish hill, is not for the elderly or infirm. Special arrangements can be made to obtain vehicular access to the fort for less able people. However, for the able-bodied the walk up to Housesteads is well worth while.

Housesteads Fort covers five acres and its north wall is incorporated into Hadrian's Wall. The fort has the only example of a Roman hospital in Britain and also a 24-seater latrine with flushing tank. At the east gate it is still possible to see the ruts where the Roman chariots entered the fort. Also visible are the remains of the massive granaries with their underground ventilation system.

Hurworth-on-Tees

Map Ref: 87NZ3010

The properties around the green are a glorious mixture of styles. Cottages face virtual castles across the grass, and neither commercialism nor modernity has been allowed to sully the centre of Hurworth. It would make an almost perfect film set for a Victorian melodrama or for Miss Marple to solve a rather superior crime.

Handsome houses built by wealthy Darlington businessmen from the early 18th century to the middle of the 19th century stand

Housesteads, known by the Romans as 'Vercovicium' which means hilly spot

side by side. A datestone on the old Parsonage reads 1480 but, following its restoration in 1938, no building from that period now remains.

In contrast to the elegance of its 'west end', where there are sundials said to date from the time when Emerson – an 18th-century mathematician – lived in the village, Hurworths 'east end' is more modest, with 19th-century linen-weavers' cottages huddled beside the church in a sylvan riverside setting.

A 1½-mile stroll through Rockcliffe Park – now a hospital – which provides one of the loveliest settings for cricket imaginable, brings the walker to Hurworth Place. More work-a-day than its elegant neighbours, the village grew up around a branch of the Stockton and Darlington Railway. Even so, it boasts the rather grand Banks Terrace and Croft House Cottages as examples of mid-19th-century speculative building, the forerunners of modern housing estates. The 15th-century bridge leads to Croft over the Yorkshire border. It has an interesting red sandstone church and Lewis Carroll, author of *Alice in Wonderland*, spent some of his childhood years in the vicarage. The once famous Croft Spa is no more, but the hotel of the same name has retained its glory. The spring which served the Spa still flows but its sulphurous water tastes so awful that it is difficult to imagine why it was once so much in fashion.

Jarrow

Map Ref: 92NZ3265

Best known for the hunger march to London which started here after Palmer's shipyard closed in 1936, the modern town of Jarrow did not exist until 1803. Standing between oil storage tanks and a timber yard, amongst the wasteland of Tyneside's industrial dross, a remarkable amount of St Paul's Monastery,

founded by Benedict Biscop, has survived. Within the church (still in use), a plaque above the chancel arch records the date, 23 April 685, the oldest dedication inscription in any church in the country.

The monastery was part of the split site of the Jarrow/Wearmouth monastery complex. 'One monastery in two places' wrote the Venerable Bede. The roofless walls are preserved and at nearby Jarrow Hall there is an Information Centre where a model of the buildings as they might have looked is on view. The centre also has on display finds from the site which include a superlative Romanesque stone horse head and a reconstruction of a highly-decorated octagonal lectern. An audio-visual display explains the history and the religious importance of St Paul's.

St Paul's Church at Jarrow. It formed part of the monastery where Bede spent his life from the age of seven

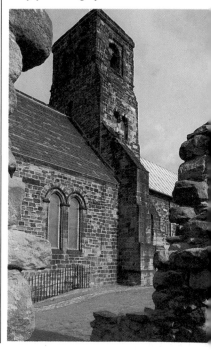

One of the loveliest of the Border towns, Kelso faces the Cheviots across the River Tweed

Jedburgh

Map Ref: 88NT6520

The county town of the old county of Roxburghshire, Jedburgh is a royal burgh on one of the main routes into Scotland, the A68. The town, in the valley of Jed Water, has a colourful past and many attractive historic buildings in its centre.

The beautiful red sandstone Abbey, founded as a priory by David I in 1138, has been sacked and rebuilt many times. However, it is the most entire of the Border monastic houses and has been described as 'the most perfect and beautiful example of the Saxon and early Gothic in Scotland'.

Mary Queen of Scots visited Jedburgh in 1566 and ill health prolonged her stay in the attractive market town. The house she used during her stay, named 'Queen Mary's House', is now a museum to her memory, featuring among the exhibits her death mask. An unusual feature of the 'bastle house' (fortified dwelling) is the left-handed spiral staircase. The house belonged to the left-handed Ker clan, and the special staircase allowed the men to use their sword hands.

The social history of 19th-century

Jedburgh is revealed in a museum at the Castle Gaol, a Georgian prison built on the site of Jedburgh Castle. A town trail links together a number of Jedburgh's historical sites.

Several notable people are associated with Jedburgh. Sir Walter Scott made his first appearance as an advocate at the Court House in 1793 and Robert Burns was made a Freeman of the town. Mary Somerville, founder of the Oxford college, was born here, as was the scientist Sir David Brewster.

A speciality of the town is a dark-brown toffee, flavoured with peppermint and shaped like a snail – known as 'Jethart Snails'. The Jethart Callant's Festival – a series of ride-outs – takes place annually. The Callant is the young man leading the proceedings. An unusual game dating from the Reformation is played in February. Jedburgh Hand Ba' is played by two teams, the 'uppies' and the 'downies' – depending on whether they were born above or below the town's Mercat Cross. The game is played through the streets of the town, using leather balls, although legend says that once the Scots played with the heads of their unfortunate English enemies!

AA recommends:
Hotel: Jedforest Country House (3m S of Jedburgh off A68), 2-star, *tel.* (08354) 274.
Restaurant: Carters Rest, 1-fork, *tel.* (0835) 63414
Self Catering: Stable Cottage, Knowesouth Farm, *tel.* (06053) 2917
Guesthouses: Ferniehirst Mill Lodge, *tel.* (0835) 63279
Kenmore Bank, Oxnam Rd, *tel.* (0835) 62369
Spinney, Langlee (2m S on A68), *tel.* (0835) 63525
Camp Sites: Lilliardsedge Park, Ancrum, 4-pennant, *tel.* (08353) 271
Elliot Park Camping & Caravanning Club Site, Edinburgh Rd, 3-pennant, *tel.* (0835) 63393

Kelso

Map Ref: 88NT7234

Elegant Kelso, situated in the Middle March where the River Teviot joins the Tweed, is not a typical Border town. Facing south towards the Cheviots, Kelso has a 'Flemish' style wide, cobbled market square flanked by gracious Georgian buildings, making it without doubt the most attractive town in the Scottish Borders.

The Tweed is spanned by a beautiful five-arched bridge designed by John Rennie and completed in 1803. The bridge, where a toll was once levied, was used by Rennie as the model for London's Waterloo Bridge – now demolished.

Kelso Abbey, founded by David I in 1128, was probably the greatest of the four Border abbeys; the others are Melrose, Dryburgh and Jedburgh. Benedictine monks from Picardy sited the abbey here and thanks to royal patronage it became extremely wealthy and acquired extensive lands. In 1545, Kelso Abbey was used as a fortress when the town was attacked by the Earl of Hertford, and 12 monks were killed. Over the following centuries the abbey fell into ruins and was given to the nation by the Duke of Roxburgh in 1919. Only fragments of the 12th-century abbey now remain.

Jedburgh Abbey is believed to occupy the site of a 9th-century church

Sir Walter Scott, who was educated in Kelso, referred to Floors Castle as 'altogether a kingdom for Oberon and Titania to dwell in'. Floors is Scotland's largest inhabited house with a window for each day of the year. Situated west of the town on a terraced site overlooking the Tweed, this majestic battlemented house was designed by William Adam in 1721 and extended by Playfair in 1841. It is the home of the 10th Duke of Roxburgh and his wife, the former Lady Jane Grosvenor, but is open to the public in the summer.

The Kelso area is known as horse country, and the town is famed for several related events, including the Horse and Pony Sales, the Border Union Show and horse-racing. A great annual event is Kelso Civic Week that includes traditional 'rides out' to neighbouring villages. During the unsettled days of border raids these were organised to keep control of the burgh boundaries. During Civic Week the Kelso Laddie is chosen, and installed as Kelso Whipman, commemorating the old Whipman's Society of Ploughmen, once active in the town.

AA recommends:

Hotels: Cross Keys, 36-37 The Square, 3-star, *tel.* (0573) 23303

Ednam House, Bridge St, 3-star, *tel.* (0573) 24168

Sunlaws House, Heiton (2m SW A698), 3-star, 1-rosette, *tel.* (05735) 331

Self Catering: Maxmill Park, *tel.* (0573) 24468

Guesthouse: Bellevue, Bowmont St, *tel.* (0573) 24588

Campsite: Springwood Caravan Park, 3-pennant, *tel.* (0573) 24596

Kielder Water and Forests

Map Ref: 88NY6787

Northern Europe's largest man-made lake set in Europe's largest man-made forest is the boast of Kielder Water. The reservoir, with 27 miles of shoreline, is set on the edge of the Northumberland National Park, only 3 miles from the Scottish border.

Kielder Water, opened in 1982, has a surface area of 2,684 acres. The flooding of the upper part of the North Tyne Valley to provide water for industrial Teesside was controversial. However, in creating Kielder, the Northumbrian Water Authority has provided a unique recreational facility for every type of water sport; the lake has already become a stage for many national sporting events, such as water-ski and power-boat championships, as well as angling contests.

Tower Knowe Visitor Centre is a good starting point with its excellent exhibition and video about the massive Kielder project. Close by is the jetty where a ferry service runs regular trips around the lake.

Northumberland National Park

Here is some of the most remote and inspiring scenery in the English uplands. Deep valleys radiate north, east and south from the Cheviot Hills; narrow roads accompany the burns and rivers and provide access to the very heart of these high-domed hills. The central section of the Park includes the heather moors of Harbottle and Simonside and the Rede and North Tyne valleys, infamous for centuries as the resort of moss troopers or border reivers. To the south lies the Whin Sill, along which runs Hadrian's Wall, one of the most important archaeological features in Europe. Altogether, the National Park embraces an area of nearly 400 square miles. A fifth of this is owned by the Forestry Commission, another fifth by the Ministry of Defence, and the rest by private estates and farmers.

The main purpose of the National Park Authority is to conserve the landscape. This is done by discussion and persuasion rather than confrontation, by considering the needs of local people and the character of the land. Some important issues are difficult to resolve. We need wood and paper but spruce forests can alter the landscape and destroy important wildlife habitats. We need an army but rights of way are closed on live training areas and low-flying aircraft can be unbelievably noisy. Compromise has created the countryside we see today; the concept of National Parks requires that the beauty of traditional countryside be recognised and harmful developments prevented.

There are ten National Parks in England and Wales. Of these, Northumberland is the least heavily populated – about 2,500 people live within its boundary – and the least affected by tourism. This adds to its timeless beauty and solitude. Some people walk the hills to escape from civilisation. Others are on a brief family holiday and need help and advice. The National Park Authority produces a range of publications, organises guided walks and maintains information centres.

Conserving such a complex heritage as an entire landscape needs awareness both by residents and visitors of its value, of the fragile balance between the use of the land for farming and forestry, and the protection of wildlife and archaeological sites.

The upper part of the lake, Bakethin Reservoir, is a conservation area. Among the birds to be seen here are herons, and ospreys stop off on their migration for a few days in most years. The track of the old North Tyne Railway and Kielder Viaduct – a unique skew-arch construction – provides a panoramic view over the Bakethin area.

Although Kielder attracts many water sport enthusiasts, most visitors come to see the lake because of its setting – surrounded by the Northumberland hills and great Border Forest. One of the best ways of appreciating the scenery is to take the Forest Drive starting at the Forestry Commission's Visitor Centre based in the 18th-century Kielder Castle – once a hunting lodge for the Dukes of Northumberland. This toll road covers 12 miles of working forest and finishes at Redesdale on the A68 – a short distance from the Scottish border at Carter Bar.

The Kielder Forests is a collective name for four forests – Kielder, Falstone, Wark and Redesdale. Mainly coniferous, the bulk of the afforestation took place between 1940 and 1970 and the area now provides 100,000 tonnes of wood a year for industry. The forests provide habitats for some wildlife and there are plenty of trails for walkers. During the summer the Forestry Commission organises guided walks with a ranger.

AA recommends:

Camp Site: Kielder Campsite, 2-pennant, *tel.* (0660) 20242

Kielder Forest Drive, a 12-mile route between Kielder Castle and Redesdale

Kirknewton

Map Ref: 88NT9130

Huddled at the foot of the Cheviot Hills, Kirknewton can boast of being one of the most beautifully-situated villages in Northumberland. It lies near the junction of the River Glen with the lovely mountain stream, the College Burn.

The remarkable Early English church has a chancel and south transept both with pointed tunnel vaults and little, or no vertical walls. On the wall beside the chancel arch is a strange sculptured relief of the Adoration of the Magi with the Wise Men clad in kilts!

In the churchyard is the grave of Mrs Josephine Butler, the great social reformer, who was born at nearby Milfield in 1828. Several personnel from RAF Milfield are buried in a corner of the churchyard, while at the opposite end are the graves of four German airmen killed in March 1943.

Above the village is Yeavering Bell, one of the most shapely of the Cheviot hills. On its summit is an extensive Iron Age hill-fort, its tumbled ramparts enclosing the shadowy remains of 130 circular huts. The Venerable Bede thought this must have been the palace of Edwin, King of Northumbria, but in fact Edwin's palace, called Ad Gefrin, was sited in the valley. Its location is marked by a stone monument alongside the B3651.

Lanchester

Map Ref: 91NZ1647

Originally the Roman Dere Street fort of *Longovicium*, Lanchester is

All Saints at Lanchester is one of Durham's finest parish churches

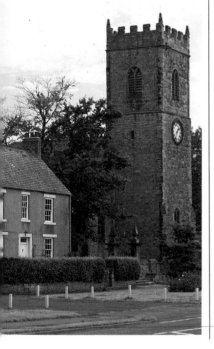

Part of the terraced gardens between the house and the lake at Mellerstain

now a very substantial village. The size and grandeur of its church indicates that this has been an important religious centre since Norman times. By the 13th century, the church was collegiate, having a staff of Prebendaries serving both the parish and the Bishop of Durham.

Both the Norman and the Early English parts of the building are fine examples of these styles, but possibly the most interesting thing about the church is that the massive quoins and the monolithic shafts of the nave, as well as many of the stones in its outer walls, were looted from the Roman fort.

The remains of *Longovicium*, although not open to the public, are visible from the road to Satley, and the stonework most easily seen is laid herringbone fashion, a style associated with Saxon rather than Roman builders.

There are few houses of character in the town as most of the wealthy families lived in grander houses in the surrounding countryside, but fragments of the former village green and the gentle curves of the main street give a feeling of space and prosperity. The railway station has long been closed but the line which runs up the valley is used by walkers and provides a pleasant 7-mile walk to Durham City.

Lanchester Agricultural Show, held in July, is a popular event. It has become known as the Sunshine Show because in recent years it has been blessed by fine weather in even the wettest season. Hall Hill Farm, near Satley, 3 miles south of Lanchester, is open to the public on the first Sunday of the summer months and regularly stages special events enabling visitors to see lambing in progress, sheep shearing and other interesting farming activities.

AA recommends:
Garage: Whitbank (Russell Close Mtrs), tel. (0207) 520336

Mellerstain House

Map Ref: 88NT6439

Scotland's finest Adam mansion is Mellerstain, set in fine grounds 7 miles north-west of Kelso with views across to the Cheviots. The house, built by William and Robert Adam between 1725 and 1765, has ceilings of particular note, with matching fireplaces, woodwork and furniture. The library ceiling is regarded as one of Robert Adam's best works. Among the fine paintings and works of art are Bonnie Prince Charlie's bagpipes.

Opposite Mellerstain is the ruined 13th-century Hume Castle, once a stronghold of the Lords Home.

Middleton One Row

Map Ref: 87NZ3512

No village could be more aptly named or more delightfully situated. The row – and that is all it is – consists of Georgian cottages that have been altered over the years to suit the needs of their occupiers. The arrival of the railway brought commuters and Victorianisation of the row and, in more recent times, the motor car has brought a new breed of commuter and some modern infilling.

Despite the changes, the curving street on its gently sloping green is a happy mixture of styles with each house sharing the same view across the sweep of the River Tees to Yorkshire. The steeply sloping, south-facing grassy river bank is an excellent sun trap with good views in front and a convenient pub behind.

St George's Church, from which the parent village of Middleton St George takes its name, dates from the 13th century but little remains of the original building. There are pleasant walks along the river banks (see Durham County Council

Leaflet Pack – Country Walks in County Durham).

A visit on foot or by car to Low Dinsdale is well worth while as the pink sandstone church surrounded by copper beeches is worthy of a picture postcard. Opposite stands the Manor house, built on the former fortified site of a Norman manor built by the Siward family, who changed their name appropriately to Surtees, and became well known throughout the North.

Beyond the bridge the Victorian wealth of the area is evident. Large houses are dotted amongst the trees and Middleton One Row sparkles in the sun. Stop on the bridge (sur Tees) to enjoy this river at its most idyllic.

Middleton-in-Teesdale

Map Ref: 91NY9425

Set among some of Durham's finest scenery beside the stretch of river that Wainwright, of Lakeland fame, declares to be his favourite in the whole of England, Middleton-in-Teesdale has much to offer in addition to its beauty.

The town has had its ups and downs. Before the 19th century it was a small agricultural settlement much like several others in the dale. However, lead mining and the arrival of the London Lead Company in 1815 to set up its northern headquarters heralded an upsurge in the town's prosperity. For almost 100 years it was like the Klondike – a boom town where lead was as important as gold. The Quaker Company, as it was more commonly known, built virtually

every 19th-century feature of Middleton. The Superintendent's House (Middleton House) is the most impressive example of its work and the Yard nearby, with its clocktower, is beautifully built in the Company's style. Masterman Place, the new town of staff houses, and the Trustee Savings Bank which was built as the Governor and Company's Teesdale Workmans' Corn Association, perhaps the world's first co-operative store, are reminders of the caring attitude the Company had for its employees.

Middleton is a town to wander around. It has lovely, almost secret, back alleys. One behind the church passes what must be one of the first pre-fabs, Greta Lodge. It came from Norway for the 1851 Great Exhibition and thence to its present site. Other paths lead out into the beautiful countryside, even to the Pennine Way, which passes very close by, making the town an ideal centre for a walking holiday. There is easy access to high moorland, pretty villages and waterfalls, which are numerous in the area. The best known of these are High Force and Cauldron Snout, but others, less frequented, such as Low Force and Gibsons Cave, should not be missed. The dale is also famous for its wild flowers and for the fight by conservationists to stop the creation of Cow Green Reservoir. The battle was lost on that occasion and many 'Teesdale rarities' were drowned, but the National Nature Reserve still has unique plant communities as well as interesting upland birds such as ravens and peregrines.

AA recommends:
Hotel: Teesdale, Market Pl, 2-star, *tel.* (0833) 40264

Morpeth

Map Ref: 89NZ1986

The bustling market town of Morpeth, lying in a loop of the River Wansbeck, is the county town of Northumberland.

There are many attractive houses and narrow lanes, and parts of the town have been designated as an 'Outstanding Conservation Area'. Morpeth is well supplied with pleasant wide open spaces, including Carlisle Park which has a riverside walk. To the south of the park is the ruined Morpeth Castle with its 15th-century gatehouse.

The lovely chantry of All Saints, dating from the 13th century, has been restored and houses a Tourist Information Centre and a centre for traditional Northumbrian crafts.

Emily Davison, the suffragette who died after throwing herself under a horse belonging to the King in the 1913 Derby, is buried in the churchyard of St Mary's. Entry to the churchyard is by a fine 1861 lych-gate and on the south side is a watch house built to guard against body snatchers.

Like many Northumbrian market towns, Morpeth retains some old customs. In particular, Riding of the Bounds, when the mayor leads a procession around the town's boundary. Morpeth and Berwick-upon-Tweed are the only two Northumberland towns to keep this ancient custom, although it is popular in Scotland. In recent years the Morpeth Northumbrian Gathering – a week of traditional activities – has grown in popularity.

AA recommends:
Garage: Jennings, 55 Bridge St, *tel.* (0670) 519611

Low Force on the Tees. An island known as Staple Crag divides the falls

Newcastle upon Tyne

Map Ref: 91NZ2464

The vibrant city of Newcastle upon Tyne is the centre of 'Geordieland', and a remarkable blend of ancient and modern. Although a major industrial centre, Newcastle is no cultural desert. It has thousands of years of history and as capital of the north-east it is a major commercial and recreational centre.

This compact regional capital is best seen from one of the six bridges crossing the River Tyne. This is the classic view of Newcastle, with each stage of its development clearly visible.

The story of the city starts with the Romans who built the fort *Pons Aelius* here to guard a bridge over the Tyne. However, the city took its name from the 'new castle' built by William the Conqueror's son in 1080. After a period in Scottish hands, the castle was rebuilt by Henry II in the 12th century. The Norman keep is one of the finest in the country and there are splendid views from its battlemented roof. Next to it is the fortified Blackgate, built by Henry II.

The oldest part of the city is the Quayside – once the heart of Newcastle. Here are some of the most historic buildings in the city including medieval houses. The Quayside is undergoing a massive face-lift to breathe life back into this former commercial centre.

With the decline of river-based trade, the city shifted northwards in the 19th century. The Victorian planners, John Clayton, Richard Grainger and John Dobson, gave the city some fine architecture, including the magnificent curving Grey Street, regarded as one of the most graceful streets in Europe.

Twentieth-century Newcastle includes Eldon Square, one of the largest indoor shopping centres in Europe, and the Metro rapid transport system. This runs partly underground in the town centre, linking the city to its suburbs and the coast.

One way to find out more about the history of the city is to visit Blackfriars, a restored 13th-century monastery. It now houses a Tourist Information Centre, a museum featuring the history of Newcastle and a craft centre and workshops. Blackfriars is close to the West Walls – the remains of the medieval town wall.

Newcastle is well known as a centre for the arts and has many first-class museums and art galleries as well as theatres, including the Theatre Royal – the third home of the Royal Shakespeare Company.

The city has some major annual events. Of particular note is the Hoppings, Europe's biggest travelling fair, based on the Town Moor. This always coincides with Newcastle's biggest race meeting – Northumberland Plate Day, known as the 'Pitman's Derby' – when traditionally miners from Northumberland pour into the city for both events.

AA recommends:

Hotels: For a large selection of hotels see the *AA Hotels and Restaurants in Britain* guide.

Restaurants: Fisherman's Lodge, Jesmond Dene, Jesmond, 3-fork, 1-rosette, *tel.* (091) 2813281

Michelangelo, 25 King St, Quayside, 3-fork, *tel.* (091) 2614415

Mandarin, 14-16 Stowell St, 2-fork, *tel.* (091) 2617960

Jade Garden, 53 Stowell St, 1-fork, *tel.* (091) 2615889

Restorante Roma, 22 Collingwood St, 1-fork, *tel.* (091) 2320612

Guesthouses: Avenue Hotel, 2 Manor House Rd, Jesmond, *tel.* (091) 2811396

Chirton House Hotel, 46 Clifton Rd, *tel.* (091) 2730407

Clifton Cottage, Dunholme Rd, *tel.* (091) 2737347

Western House Hotel, 1 West Av, Gosforth, *tel.* (091) 2856812

Camp Site: Newcastle (TRAX) Caravan Club Site, Gosforth Park, Racecourse, 3-pennant, *tel.* (091) 2363258

Garages: Buist Mtrs, Etherstone Av, *tel.* (091) 2663311

G. Lilley Coachworks, 41/47 The Close, *tel.* (091) 2325481

Minories, Benton Rd, *tel.* (0632) 666361

Skewbridge S/Stn, Shields Rd, Walkergate, *tel.* (091) 2623301

Above: known as the 'Coathanger' Suspension Bridge, this is one of seven structures spanning the River in Newcastle upon Tyne

Tyneside Shipbuilding

The Tyne has a shipbuilding tradition going back to medieval times. Early ships were small – in 1324 the port had only five vessels over 40 tons. As ships became bigger the coal trade – which predominantly used them – needed keels, or lighters, to carry coal from mines and staithes upriver above Newcastle to colliers lying downstream. Tyne keels were oval, flat-bottomed, square-sailed and propelled by two long oars. Tyne colliers were constructed of Baltic timber, with seams caulked with Baltic resins, sails made from Baltic flax, and were built in scores of small shipyards along both sides of the river from Shields to Dunston.

At South Shields the *Tyne*, an early lifeboat, commemorates William Wouldhave, inventor of the self-righting lifeboat. This was launched in 1790 and a replica is on display at the same place at the bottom of Ocean Road, close to the mouth of this great river of shipbuilders.

One of the first iron ships, launched at Walker in the 1840s, was the paddle-steamer, *Prince Albert*, and in 1852 Charles and George Palmer built the *John Bowes*, Tyneside's first screw-propelled collier – capable of carrying 650 tons of coal to London in 48 hours. About the same time the river was improved by straightening, dredging a deeper channel, and building new quays, docks, jetties and piers. Bigger vessels could now be built – paddle-steamers for the Nile, ocean-going steamers for Australia, cable-layers, ice-breakers, dredgers. With the birth of W G Armstrong's armament works at Elswick, the last quarter of the 19th century saw the Tyneside shipyards move into warship construction. By then, most shipbuilding was concentrated along the 5 miles between Bill Point and Albert Dock, with repairers and fitters nearer the river mouth.

In 1876 Charles Parsons, son of the Earl of Rosse, patented his prototype of the steam turbine. By 1889 he had established his own works at Heaton to manufacture marine turbines. The first ship to use them, the *Turbinia*, astonished the Navy at the Spithead Naval Review in 1897 with a speed of 34½ knots. Unusually, individual shipbuilding companies on Tyneside were often short-lived. By the turn of the century mergers and amalgamations linked many famous names: Swan and Hunter, formed as early as 1879, absorbed Wigham, Richardson in 1903, together with a Wallsend company. In 1906 they built, for the Cunard Company, the huge *Mauretania*, powered by steam turbines generating 70,000 horse-power, producing an average cruising speed of 24 knots. However, they needed over 100 firemen to stoke them!

In 1872 Palmer's built a number of oil-carrying ships and until 1913 Tyneside led the world in the building of oil tankers. In 1970, Swan and Hunter constructed the largest vessel to have been built in Britain, the 126,542-ton *Esso Northumbria*.

Between 1914 and 1918 navy contracts kept Tyneside shipyards busy. After the war, once wartime shipping losses had been made good, shipbuilding declined, and many yards closed. From 1936, warship building was resumed, and launchings included HMS *King George V* and HMS *Kelly*. Post-war years again saw great activity followed by decline. Swan and Hunter built even bigger tankers – over ¼ million tons – too large to return to the river.

Order-books now, however, are increasingly dependent on government contracts, and the latest major project saw the commissioning in November 1985 of HMS *Ark Royal*, largest vessel for the Royal Navy in 26 years.

Below: High Level Bridge carrying road and railway, and Swing Bridge – one of the first of its kind

The 'Mauretania' set off for Liverpool on 22 October 1907

Fresh fish is caught and sold daily on the Fish Quay at North Shields

Norham

Map Ref: 88NT9047

The Blessing of the Nets, an ancient fishing ceremony, is performed at Norham every year at midnight on 13 February. The vicar of the village blesses the fishermen and their nets from a coble (a flat-bottomed fishing boat) in the river at the start of the new salmon fishing season. This traditional service is conducted by lantern light, and opens with the well-known passage of the miraculous draught of fishes from St John's Gospel. Norham, a pleasant village of grey cottages, even has a weathervane in the shape of a fish – evidence of the importance of fishing to the village.

Readers of Sir Walter Scott will be familiar with Norham, for its famous castle was featured in *Marmion*. Scott set the scene in the days of the Battle of Flodden:

'Day set on Norham's castle steep
And Tweed's fair river, broad and deep
And Cheviot's mountain lone:
The battled towers, the donjon keep
The loop-holed wall where captives weep
In yellow lustre shone.'

Norham Castle was one of the strongest border fortresses and has one of the finest Norman keeps in the country. It was once the property of the powerful Prince Bishops of Durham. Before the Battle of Flodden the Scots battered the castle with heavy artillery and rebuilding was needed. Norham Castle was the setting of the romantic meeting in 1549 between the firebrand preacher, John Knox, and his wife-to-be, Margaret Bowes, daughter of the governor.

Today the castle is in the care of English Heritage, and although ruined its former glory is apparent.

North Shields

Map Ref: 92NZ3568

This busy fishing port at the mouth of the Tyne lies alongside Tynemouth – yet the two coastal towns are very different. North Shields is no seaside resort, but a working town that has long been famous for its fishing industry. The best time to visit the fish quay is at daybreak when it is buzzing with activity as the catches are unloaded.

The town has a sort of emblem called the 'Wooden Dolly' that represents the traditional Cullercoats fishwife with her creel, or wicker fish basket, over her back. The original Dolly was designed by a Miss May Spence and stood at the end of a passage leading down to the quay, until it became weatherbeaten. Another life-size figure was made and placed in Northumberland Square in the town. Standing on a cliff above the fish quay is the Wooden Doll pub.

North Shields is the terminal for Scandinavian ferries and the famous local ferry service still operates between the town and its 'twin', South Shields.

Otterburn

Map Ref: 88NY8893

On 19 August 1388, the romantic Northumbrian hero, Harry Hotspur (Sir Henry Percy), faced his greatest enemy, James, Earl of Douglas at Otterburn. The battle that followed became one of the most glorified and celebrated in the region's history and inspired poets and minstrels for centuries.

The actual site of the battle is unclear, although it is generally thought that it took place a mile west of the village. A bridlepath starting a few hundred yards along the minor road to Otterburn Hall and the army camp leads to the supposed site of the Battle of Otterburn.

This famous battle, fought by moonlight, was a notable victory for the Scots, who had marched 30 miles from Newcastle after ravaging Northumberland and Durham. Douglas lay in wait for his enemy in the valley of the River Rede where it joins the Otter Burn – later said to have run red with blood. It is claimed that the Earl of Douglas had a premonition that he would die – a dream mentioned by Sir Walter Scott in his epic poem of the battle. Indeed, Douglas was to die – run through by a Percy sword. The place where he fell is marked in Otterburn by a

The site of Norham was well chosen: on one side the Tweed, on the other a ravine

monument called Percy's Cross, situated in woodland to the north of the A696 trunk road, about ¾ mile west of the village.

The Battle of Otterburn is more familiarly known as 'Chevy Chase' and the 'Ballad of Chevy Chase' is the traditional tune of the Northumbrian Pipers. The small-pipes, a sweet-sounding instrument, is undergoing a revival, so visitors to the region may well hear 'Chevy Chase' being played locally.

Until a few years ago, Otterburn Mill, situated by the Otterburn Bridge, produced world-famous tweeds and woollens, using the fleece of the local black-faced sheep. Sadly, production of these woven wools has stopped, but the Mill is still open to the public as a showroom and the quality Otterburn tweeds are still sold. Ironically, for an area so often at war with the Scots, much of the material is now made over the border.

AA recommends:
Hotels: Percy Arms, 3-star, tel. (0830) 20261
Otterburn Tower, 2-star Country House Hotel, tel. (0830) 20620
Guesthouses: Blakehopeburnhaugh Farm House, Byrness, tel. (0830) 20267
Monkridge Farm House, tel. (0830) 20639

Ovingham

Map Ref: 91NZ0863

Thomas Bewick, the illustrious wood-engraver, used to draw pictures in chalk on the gravestones in Ovingham churchyard, where he is now buried. The eldest of eight children, Bewick was born in 1753 at Cherryburn House on the opposite side of the River Tyne at Mickley. Bewick, who was educated in Ovingham, was an artist of great skill who used the birds and wildlife of his native Tyne Valley as his subjects. The illustrations in *The History of British Birds* are among the best examples of his work.

The Thomas Bewick Birthplace Trust has acquired the Bewick family home at Cherryburn, and is turning it into a permanent reminder of this great artist and his work. The project should be completed in 1988.

The riverside village of Ovingham is a charming, old-world place with some interesting houses and a quaint 17th-century packhorse bridge that is a focal point during the annual Ovingham Goose Fair. This popular event goes back centuries, when it was intended as a market place for geese sellers. The geese are gone, but it is still very much a traditional fair, and perhaps one of the last places in Northumbria where the region's oddest delicacies are sold: 'Carlins', a dish of grey peas eaten with salt, brown sugar and rum!

The church where Bewick is buried has an outstanding Saxon tower, and, like several buildings in the area, was built partly with stones from Hadrian's Wall. In a family vault in the churchyard lies Mabel Stephenson, mother of George, the great railway pioneer.

Just across Ovingham Bridge is Tyne Riverside Country Park (see page 72).

AA recommends:
Hotel: Highlander Inn, 2-star, tel. (0661) 32016

Piercebridge

Map Ref: 91NZ2015

The rectangular green is the site of an important Roman fort which guarded the bridge carrying Dere Street across the River Tees. The houses around the green are, almost without exception, unpretentious cottages descended from the dwellings built by the camp following civilians who previously lived outside the fort.

To the east, past the George Hotel where 'the clock stopped, never to go again' – and still fails to tell the right time – there are the remains of a second Roman bridge. Easily reached by a good path, the remains are most impressive, having recently been excavated after discovery during sand and gravel quarrying. One pier, admittedly buried by silt for 1900 years, is as good as new and the well-designed crazy paving, which was laid on the river bed to reduce the water's turbulence, would work as well today were it in the river. The bridge has not been moved but the river has changed its course!

One mile north-west of Piercebridge, Whitecross Farm, whitewashed in the Raby estate style, is visible from the road to Gainford and Barnard Castle. Built in the 18th century, it is totally unspoilt with three bays, tripartite windows and a pantile roof. Greystoke Hall, ½ mile closer to Gainford, and a century earlier in construction, is totally different in style but equally charming.

A memorial in Ovingham churchyard to John Wormald. He was killed in 1874 after a disaster at Prudhoe Colliery

Romaldkirk

Map Ref: 91NY9922

The impressive church is known locally as the 'cathedral of the dale' because of its spaciousness and flamboyant style. The village consists of groups of stone cottages and single detached houses placed haphazardly around a series of village greens which appear to be totally unplanned. Like many of the villages of Teesdale, it is pretty and well cared for.

Prior to 1972 the land on the south side of the river above Barnard Castle was in Yorkshire. Much of it was owned by the Strathmore family and virtually all the buildings are of natural stone, unlike the northern bank where the farms and cottages of Lord Barnard's Raby estate are limewashed. Lartington, Mickleton, Cotherstone and Eggleston, all on the Tees between Barnard Castle and Middleton in Teesdale, have more than enough of interest to occupy the visitor for several hours.

AA recommends:
Hotel: Rose & Crown, 2-star, tel. (0833) 50213

Whitewashed cottages by the bridge at Piercebridge – site of a Roman fort

The sandstone ridges of the Simonside Hills above the Coquet Valley (top) where Brinkburn Abbey (above) was founded beside the river in 1135

Rothbury

Map Ref: 89NU0501

The capital of Coquetdale, Rothbury was once a popular health resort where people came to drink goats' whey and take the air. Goats' whey may not be an attraction today, but Rothbury is still popular with people looking for wide open spaces and fresh air. For Rothbury and its environs are bracing, and the delightful scenery around this ancient market town is a paradise for the walker, fisherman, bird-watcher or pony-trekker.

Rothbury lies on the north bank of the famous salmon and trout river, the Coquet, and is dominated by the heather-clad Simonside Hills. Stone houses typical of the border region line the steep main street with its sloping green planted with shady trees. The winding Coquet passes through Rothbury under a medieval bridge. At the south-east corner of the town centre is All Saints Church, dating from the 13th century, but largely restored in the last century.

The town's market rights (it has a livestock market) date back to a visit from King John in 1205. The road down which he travelled is known as Rotten Row – 'route de Roi'.

If Rothbury seems tranquil now it was not always so. Cockfighting was a popular sport in the area and it had a name for being a lawless place, with its inhabitants described as 'amongst the wildest and most uncivilised in the county'. The locals were certainly dare-devils for they used to play a dangerous jumping game over a spectacular gorge called the Thrum where water forces itself through a narrow chasm. Their leaps over the swirling water often ended in disaster.

At Lordenshaws, towards the Simonside ridge, are the remains of an Iron Age hill-fort, Bronze Age burials, and cup-and-ring marks – mysterious rock carvings etched into sandstone boulders. Brinkburn Priory, founded in 1135 for the canons of the Augustinian Order, lies nearby alongside the River Coquet. It fell into ruins after the Dissolution of the Monasteries, but was completely repaired in 1858.

One of the most breathtaking views in the county can be seen from the B6341 Rothbury to Alnwick road. Looking back towards Rothbury there are spectacular views of the Simonside Hills and the huge Cragside Estate (see page 47).

AA recommends:
Hotel: Coquet Vale, Station Rd, 2-star, *tel.* (0669) 20305
Guesthouse: Orchard, High St, *tel.* (0669) 20684
Camp Site: Coquetdale Caravan Park, Whitton, 2-pennant, *tel.* (0669) 20549

Rowlands Gill

Map Ref: 91NZ1658

This former Victorian suburb within easy reach of Newcastle is now a rural sprawl, famous only for its Tyneside dialect song *Wor Nanny's a Mazer* – the ballad which tells of Nanny missing the train and then over-imbibing in the Towneley Arms.

South of the river lies Gibside. Only the tall column, topped by a statue of British Liberty, and the ruin of the Hall can be seen from Rowlands Gill. The grounds were landscaped by Capability Brown (see page 35) and once contained a gothic banqueting house, an orangery, a lake and fine avenues of trees.

The beautiful, Palladian style round chapel (now in the care of the National Trust) was built by James Paine for Sir George Bowes. He died in 1760 leaving a million pounds, but his mausoleum, erected by masons paid twopence an hour, has survived two centuries of devaluation more successfully than his vast fortune.

The simple central altar, surrounded by cherry-wood pews, stands beneath the dome. From below it resembles an inverted Wedgwood bowl, and the triple-decked pulpit with a parasol-shaped sounding board is perfect. Beneath the chapel is the mausoleum. Not open to the public, it is occupied by the remains of the Bowes family – the ancestors of Elizabeth Bowes-Lyon, Queen Elizabeth the Queen Mother.

AA recommends:
Camp Site: Derwent Park Caravan Site, 2-pennant, *tel.* (0207) 543383

St Cuthbert's Cave

Map Ref: 89NU0031

Legend has it that Northumbria's beloved St Cuthbert was tending his sheep in a cave in the heart of Northumberland's countryside when he saw a vision of St Aidan. After seeing the saint ascend to heaven in the arms of angels, the young shepherd decided to dedicate his life to God.

Whether this story is true is

debatable, but St Cuthbert's Cave does exist to the south of the quiet village of Doddington in romantic Glendale. It may be that the cave – known locally as Cuddy's Crag or Cove – was used by the future Bishop of Lindisfarne, as his early boyhood was spent tending sheep at Wrangham, a large farm on the hill at Doddington North Moor. The cave is now owned by the National Trust.

This part of Glendale to the north of Wooler is steeped in mystery and legend. St Cuthbert's Cave stands next to a 20ft-high stone bearing vertical grooves which were supposedly made by the chains the Devil used when he hanged his grandmother! The cave and stone are on the south side of Dod Law, a hill capped with the remains of an early British fort where there are some mysterious rocks carved with cup-and-ring marks.

The site of the battle called Milfield Plain is part of the bed of a prehistoric lake. In the month before the Battle of Flodden, this Arthurian battlefield was the site of one of the many skirmishes between English and Scots. Led by Lord Home, the Scots – who had been burning English villages – were defeated heavily by the English under Sir William Bulmer of Brancepeth, Durham. For many years after the Scots named the route through Milfield 'The Ill Road'.

The lead-crushing mill wheel at Killhope, where the story of mining is brought to life

St John's Chapel

Map Ref: 90NY8838

This is the only village in Durham with a town hall but otherwise it is typical of upper Weardale settlements. Above Stanhope, the capital of the dale, the villages all nestle by the river and without exception line the road. They are working villages, built by miners and quarrymen.

In recent years weekenders have made their mark but Weardale has changed little. Quarrying is still the main industry and the valley sides are scarred, but its rugged beauty is softened by meadows full of wild flowers. Stone walls enclose the fields and run up the valley sides to meet the heather on the fells.

Killhope, beyond Weardale, is the site of a 19th-century lead-crushing mill and mine. It is being restored by Durham County Council and is open to the public. There are many ruined lead mines in the dale but at Killhope the ruins and the process of restoration is explained.

Durham's Coast and the Denes

It is unfortunately true that colliery waste is dumped on Durham's beaches, but it is equally true that 80 per cent of the coastline between the Tyne and the Tees is unspoilt. There is considerable wildlife and geological interest, the sand is clean and soft and the cliffs are beautiful. Large stretches of the coast are nature reserves protected by Acts of Parliament and one area is likely to be acquired in the near future by the National Trust.

Even man's rubbish can be exciting. Down a little track at Ryhope there is a beach of man-made shingle. Worn and polished by the movement of the tides, broken glass and concrete have been transformed. Bricks are rounded but have retained their regular patterns, while concrete has been converted to pebbles, marbled by the colours of the aggregate they contain and glass has changed to jewels of many colours, dull when dry but brilliant when wet.

The cliffs from Whitburn to Crimdon Dene are of magnesian limestone. They support a rich limestone flora and provide nesting sites for colonies of sea birds. The hinter-

Bloody cranesbill, a bushy member of the geranium family

land also shelters northern European migrant birds such as snow and Lapland buntings. Oystercatchers and turnstones congregate on Whitburn beach, from where, at very low tides, a submerged forest can be seen.

The Denes are the greatest delight. At Hawthorn, where the Dene is managed by Durham County Conservation Trust, bloody cranesbill, dyer's greenwood, orchids, and a host of other flowers can be seen. Castle Eden Dene is a National Nature Reserve with many miles of footpaths. Both the Dene and the cliffs southwards to Blackhall Rocks are fascinating. There is magnesian reef limestone with breccias and fossil cephalopods. Where boulder clay covers the limestone of the Dene the flora is particularly rich.

To the south, towards Teesmouth, there are both mobile and stable sand dunes, mud flats and salt marsh – ideal bird-watching country.

Seaham Harbour was built in the 1830s by Lord Byron's family, the Londonderrys

Seaham

Map Ref: 92NZ4149

Apart from the Saxon church of St Mary, the vicarage and Seaham Hall – now an hotel – the original village of Seaham has disappeared completely. Like Escomb, Seaham's ancient church is also built of Roman stone. Discovering St Mary's, tucked away, and reached by a very rough track from the cliff top road, is a wonderful surprise.

The Seaham Hall Hotel was the home of Ann Milbanke who was wooed and wed by Lord Byron in 1815. The marriage ceremony took place in the upstairs drawing room which is still intact with its original pretty frieze and fireplace. Six years after the wedding, Lord Byron's family, the Londonderrys, bought the whole of Seaham in order to build a harbour from which coal from the Londonderry collieries could be shipped. The dock and the town that grew around it lie to the south of the Hall. The police station, originally the company offices, and the Londonderry

Institute in Tempest Road are the best remaining grand buildings erected by the 3rd Marquis of Londonderry as part of his massive scheme of town development. Bath Terrace, no doubt inspired by the city of that name, is in the style intended for Seaham but the finances could not keep up with the imagination. Only the Londonderry Arms, now the Harbour View in North Terrace, has retained some elegance with its pillared portico.

Still mining coal under the North Sea, Seaham is very much a working town. It does however have potential for leisure activities. Part of the harbour provides berths for a flotilla of cobles crewed by miner/fishermen who with lines, nets and lobster pots make part of their living from the sea. Angling trips can be arranged and the catches can be extremely good. North of the harbour rocky outcrops give way to miles of empty beach. No candyfloss or fairgounds, but there is a promenade.

Seahouses see Beadnell.

Seaton Sluice

Map Ref: 92NZ3376

The curious harbour at the mouth of the Seaton Burn was built in 1670 to cope with the increasing trade in coal. Sir Ralph Delaval built a sluice near the present road bridge and the gates opened and shut automatically with the tide. When the harbour became too small to cope with the number of ships, the 1st Lord Delaval cut a new entrance in the rocky cliff enabling the water from the harbour to take a short cut into the sea. The Cut, 52ft deep, 30ft wide and 900ft long, is still spectacular. Although Seaton Sluice is on the edge of an industrial belt, it has beautiful golden beaches backed by dunes.

The former busy coal port fell into disrepair and the harbour remained derelict for about 100 years before local authority workers and volunteers set about repair work for the benefit of small sailing vessels that now occupy it. This is a good place to watch seabirds, as in strong easterly gales they fly close to

Sailing boats now occupy the harbour at Seaton which at one time was busy with coal ships

the shore.

As well as coal, Seaton Sluice had a salt trade from the 13th to the 19th century. Sea water was evaporated in big tanks heated by coal. The site of the salt pans is below the present bridge, but all the workings have been swept away.

A few miles inland is Seaton Delaval Hall, ancestral home of the Delaval family and a magnificent Vanbrugh mansion, regarded as one of the finest houses in the north. The Hall, built in the early 18th century, is based on the Palladian style introduced into this country by Inigo Jones. It has had an unlucky history – fire badly damaged one wing and a later blaze almost gutted the main block of the house. Until recently, Seaton Delaval Hall was used for Elizabethan banquets, but the present owners are now carrying out extensive restoration and the Hall may re-open to the public in the future.

Sedgefield

Map Ref: 92NZ3528

Fertile farmland surrounds this smart little town. It has a large green, a grand church and leafy back lanes. Its wide roads have been quieter since the building of bypasses in recent years and Sedgefield has become a very pleasant place in which to live. Situated close to industrial Teesside and adjacent to excellent road links, residential expansion has been inevitable. The changes have not harmed the centre. It now has good shops and a remarkable selection of comfortable pubs and restaurants. The gardens are pretty and the places of refreshment seem to vie with each other in providing the best display of hanging baskets and window boxes.

Views to the south encompass the Cleveland Hills which dwarf the cooling towers and chimneys of Teesside's chemical works. On its outskirts Sedgefield has a superb country park, an 18th-century landscape garden rescued from complete decay by Durham County Council in the 1970s. The town also has a National Hunt racecourse which is small and friendly. The area is famous for foxhunting and the South Durham Hunt have kennels close to the town. There is an agricultural show in August and on Shrove Tuesday the traders and the farmers compete in a traditional free-for-all football match which uses the whole town as its pitch.

Some attractive houses, especially at the west end, overlook the green. Bishop Cosins was responsible for the church's woodwork which is of superb quality. Much of the work is thought to have been done in the 1630s by Robert Barker who also worked on Brancepeth church and Durham Cathedral.

Hardwick Hall Country Park, to the west of Sedgefield

AA recommends:
Hotels: Hardwick Hall, 3-star, *tel.* (0740) 20253
Crosshill, 1 The Square, 1-star, *tel.* (0740) 20153
Guesthouse: Dun Cow (Inn), High St, *tel.* (0740) 20894
Campsite: Sedgefield (TRAX) Caravan Club Site, Sedgefield Racecourse, 2-pennant, *tel.* (0740) 21925
Garage: Turners, Sedgefield Ind Est, *tel.* (0740) 20338

Shildon

Map Ref: 91NZ2325

Now a place of pilgrimage for railway enthusiasts, the town sprang up to serve the Stockton and Darlington Railway and went on serving railways until 1985, when its last major connection, the Wagon Works, was finally closed by British Rail.

Timothy Hackworth, an apprentice engineer to George Stephenson, became the Locomotive Superintendent of the Stockton and Darlington Railway and set up his business, the Soho Engine Works here. He built the *Sans Pareil* for the Rainhill Trials, which, although it was beaten by Stephenson's *Rocket*, later proved itself in service on the Bolton and Leigh Railway. This workshop led to the development of Shildon as a railway town.

For true railway 'buffs' there is plenty of memorabilia. Hackworth's house is now a museum and fragments of the world's early railway systems can be seen scattered around the town.

Shincliffe

Map Ref: 92NZ2940

Close to Durham City on the A177, Shincliffe consists of two parts. The older village lies on the valley floor close to the river and the 19th-century colliery village, High Shincliffe, now extended by modern residential development, is on the glacial plain above. The collieries are long gone.

The Village, as the lower part is called, has a pretty tree-lined main street flanked by high verges where daffodils and crocuses have become naturalised. The 18th- and 19th-century cottages which line both sides of the street have, without exception, been improved without detracting from the overall charm. It is a village much loved by its inhabitants, always clean, tidy and beautified by flowers. Only the ever-present parked cars intrude on the serenity of this lovely place.

Modern housing in both parts of the village has been added with care. St Mary's Close, near the church, won a Civic Trust Award. Footpaths along the riverbank or through Houghall Woods lead to Durham.

Shotley Bridge

Map Ref: 91NZ0852

This is the fashionable suburb of Consett, which, until 1983, was a steelmaking town. Strange as it may seem, it was at Shotley Bridge that local steel making began, long before Consett existed. German craftsmen settled here in the 17th century and began making swords. A furnace of the type they used can still be seen at Derwentcote, 4 miles to the east, beside the River Derwent.

In the 19th century, with the coming of the railway to serve the Consett Iron Works and the developing collieries, Shotley Bridge found fame as a spa. Some wealthy visitors chose to stay and build grand houses in the vicinity of the healing waters. The railway line, notwithstanding its real purpose, became a popular scenic route and even today, many years after the last train passed through Queens Road Station, locals and visitors use the line – now developed as a walkway – as a pretty alternative to the road.

The 10-mile track follows the valley downhill to Swalwell on the outskirts of Newcastle; it offers easy walking or cycling, with attractive views all the way.

Raby – an impressive medieval castle – is surrounded by a deer park

South Shields

Map Ref: 92NZ3666

Resort, port, shipbuilding centre and prosperous cosmopolitan town, South Shields has a lively shopping centre with modern shops and some traffic-free streets. Only the continuous screech of seagulls above the malls reminds shoppers of their close proximity to the sea. The Old Town Hall in the riverside market place is a reminder of a long history of trade, while later municipal buildings express the Edwardian prosperity the town enjoyed. Corporation Street has retained its 19th-century shop fronts featuring carved and painted figureheads.

The oldest and most unexpected part of the town is where *Arbeia*, a 2nd-century Roman fort, was established. It became the supply base for the Roman army's 3rd-century Scottish campaign and was occupied intermittently for 200 years. The remains are extensive and well displayed. On the site of the West Gate a replica of what archaeologists believe the original was like is being built. This is a massive undertaking with two three-storey towers, and two gates with lengths of wall on either side. Planned to open to the public in 1987, it will be the biggest Roman reconstruction of its kind in Britain.

The seaside facilities of South Shields are also being refurbished and include a glass-fronted promenade. There is a Yacht Club, wide sandy beaches and a leisure pool, as well as the usual amusements. A coastal railway track, which has now been removed, preserved the seafront from development. The cliff-top with its rolling lawns provides ideal sunbathing spots and the Marine Parks, created from levelled ballast heaps, separate the beaches from the town. Riverside Drive, a town-centre bypass, offers splendid views across the Tyne to North Shields, the Fish Quay and a galaxy of bobbing boats. Further east, the silhouette of ruined Tynemouth Priory can be seen against the northern sky.

AA recommends:
Hotel: Sea, Sea Front, 3-star, *tel.* (091) 4566227
New Crown, Mowbray Rd, 2-star, *tel.* (0632) 4553472
Guesthouse: Sir William Fox Private Hotel, 5 Westoe Village, *tel.* (091) 4564554
Campsite: Lizard Lane Caravan & Camping Site, 1-pennant, *tel.* (0632) 544982 or 557411
Garage: Lynch Mtrs, No 5 Unit, Evans Yard, Commercial Rd, Temple Town, *tel.* (0632) 564665

Staindrop

Map Ref: 91NZ1220

This ancient village, said to have been visited by King Canute, has had its periods of glory. The Nevilles and the Vanes, the owners of Raby Castle before and after the Rising of the North, made Staindrop a prosperous market town.

The church of St Mary is one of the most fascinating churches in Britain. It has a Saxon nave and considerable Norman remains. The altar screen is plain but of considerable interest, as it is the only pre-Reformation screen in the county of Durham. Monuments are the church's speciality. As one would expect, they are all effigies of long dead lords and ladies of Raby. In life they influenced England's history and after death they contribute to English monumental art. They are of oak, alabaster and marble, so numerous that an overflow mausoleum was built in 1850 by the 2nd Duke of Cleveland to house the surplus. The organ, once pumped by a water engine (still beneath the floor), has remarkable tones created by the automatic combination of different pipes.

The houses of the village are mostly set around an extensive green. They range from the 17th-century manor house to 1970 council houses of local stone. Mullioned windows, dignified bows, classical doorcases, coach house arches and delightful fanlights adorn both sides of the green.

Raby Castle is inseparable from Staindrop. The castle and its Masters have lorded over the village and its residents since the 14th century. Like Brancepeth and Barnard Castle, it was a Neville stronghold until 1569. Forfeited to James I, it was acquired in 1616 by his Secretary of State, Sir Henry Vane of Kent and has remained in the ownership of the Vane family ever since. The castle is set in spacious walled parkland with herds of deer, lakes, follies, beautiful gardens, grand stables and coach houses, the result of combining military strength with spacious accommodation. Added to in virtually every century since it was built, the castle is most impressive and ably illustrates different ages of the castle builder's craft.

The Raby estate, which occupies a large tract of land on the north side of the River Tees, surrounds the castle. Hundreds of farm houses and cottages which make up the estate are whitewashed every year by the tenants, in accordance with their tenancy agreements. This practice, together with 380 years of experience in managing this naturally beautiful area, gives the Raby land a well-cared for look.

Sunderland

Map Ref: 92NZ3957

By 1830 the port of Sunderland, which received its charter in 1183, had given its name to an area on both sides of the River Wear which included Bishop Wearmouth on the south side and Monkwearmouth to the north. Sunderland is now the biggest town between the rivers Tyne and Wear and as an administrative, cultural and shopping centre serves a large population. The port is still busy and ships are still being built on the river. In recent years, the banks of the river, which for centuries suffered from industrial despoilation, have been much improved and there are now very pleasant walks along the water's edge.

Monkwearmouth Church, the Wearside part of Benedict Biscop's split-site monastery is the oldest building in the town and Phoenix Lodge, in Queen Street East, is the oldest masonic hall (1785) in the country. Monkwearmouth Station, now a Transport Museum, is considered by many to be one of the most handsome stations in existence. It was built in 1848 when that great Baron of the railways, George Hudson, was the local MP. Could it have been a practical expression of his political awareness?

Roker and Seaburn to the north face the sea, and offer golden beaches of soft clean sand, but holiday facilities are limited and the crowds of old are gone.

Even further north lies Whitburn.

Recently popular with the football stars of Roker Park, it was Sunderland's 'stockbroker belt' a century ago. Consequently the houses of the village, particularly on Front Street, reflect the characters or fortunes of the men who had them built. Cleadon is a similar Georgian enclave.

Charles Dickens was a friend of the Abbs family who lived at Cleadon House.

AA recommends:
Hotels: Seaburn, Queens Rd, Seaburn, 3-star, *tel.* (0783) 292041
Mowbray Park, Toward Rd, 2-star, *tel.* (0783) 78221

Gelt House, 23 St Bedes Ter, 1-star, *tel.* (0783) 672990
Restaurant: Maltings, Bonner's Field Complex, Monkwearmouth, 2-fork, *tel.* (0783) 654862
Garages: Minories, Newcastle Rd, *tel.* (0783) 491277
Warwick, Warwick Ter, Silksworth, *tel.* (0783) 210838

Coal Mining

Coal may well have been worked in the north-east in Roman times. Open-cast mining certainly occurred on properties of the Bishops of Durham in the 12th century, while the monks of Tynemouth and Newminster (near Morpeth) were creating early wealth from coalpits on their estates in the following century. In 1239 Henry III gave the freemen of Newcastle the right to dig coal from good seams outcropping on what is now the famous Town Moor. Thirty years later, local roads were considered dangerous because of unfenced workings.

Throughout the next three centuries coal was extracted from hundreds of small surface 'bell-pits', or from levels driven into the steep banks of the Tyne as far as Wylam, the Wear to about Chester-le-Street, and the Derwent below Chopwell. Most of the coal produced was shipped away from Newcastle, initially as ballast but then as cargo exported down the coast or across the North Sea.

By Tudor times, diminishing supplies of timber for fuel stimulated the coal trade to the extent that, in 1600, Queen Elizabeth granted a monopoly of this to merchant adventurers of Newcastle called the Society of Hostmen, who controlled the shipping of 200,000 tons of coal a year from the city. Most of this came from pits within a few miles of the river. By 1670 a network of waggonways had arisen – wooden-railed tracks along which horse-drawn waggons, replacing pack-horses of earlier centuries, transported coal from pit to riverside staithes. These were soon to be known as 'Newcastle roads'.

An engraving of South Hetton Colliery, Durham, in the days of pit ponies

Throughout the 17th century trade expanded. Older seams because exhausted and were replaced by new ones more distant from the rivers Tyne and Wear, resulting in turn in the need for longer waggon-ways. By the middle of the 18th century, mining methods had started to improve, and it became possible to sink shafts on to deeper seams. Over the coal-rich areas, land-owners lucky enough to have seams below their estates were working their own pits. The Dukes of Northumberland, the Delavals and Blacketts, the Lambtons, Lumleys, Milbankes, the Dean and Chapter at Durham; between them the 'Grand Allies' – Russells of Brancepeth, Liddells of Ravensworth, Strathmores of Gibside – owned the best pits between Tyne and Wear.

Flooding was a constant problem in the new deep pits. In 1718 Thomas Newcomen's steam engine was used to pump water from a mine on Washington Moor. In 1735 coke was used for the first time to smelt iron, heralding the 'industrial revolution'. By the end of the century seams 800ft below the surface were being exploited at Byker,

Felling and Jarrow, but mining remained hazardous, particularly because of 'firedamp' explosions. By 1816 George Stephenson and Sir Humphrey Davy had invented similar safety-lamps for miners.

Although the 18th century had seen much industrial progress, it was the advent of the railways after 1825 which saw the massive spread of coal-mining, particularly in the triangle roughly between Sunderland, Bishop Auckland and Hartlepool. Simple figures illustrate the growth. In 1787 two million tons of coal were shipped from Tyne and Wear ports, and in 1913 (the peak year) 41 million tons were produced in County Durham alone.

Now the industry has contracted, and is concentrated on a few huge, deep pits near the coast from Ashington to Horden. Pithead gear, spoil-heaps, even colliery villages, have vanished from the landscape. Yet the remains of waggonways, of small remote collieries in the hills – Elsdon, Bellingham, Lambley, Coanwood and others – of old lines and substantial bridges, are haunting reminders of past endeavour and a life of hardship.

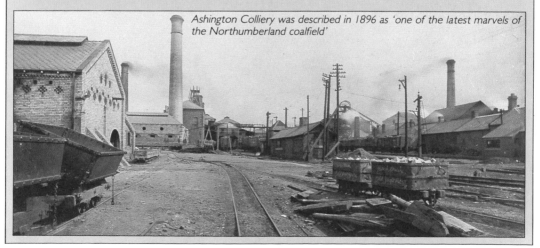
Ashington Colliery was described in 1896 as 'one of the latest marvels of the Northumberland coalfield'

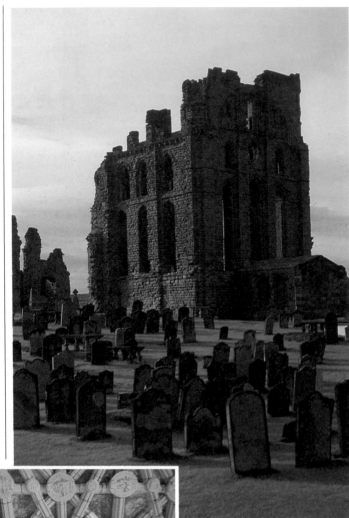

After the dissolution, Tynemouth Priory (top) remained as a fortress because of its almost impregnable position. The Lady Chapel at the east end was a later addition.
Above: detail of the chapel roof

Tow Law

Map Ref: 91NZ1139

The Tow rhymes with how, not mow. This rather bleak and windswept village was once the headquarters of the Weardale Iron Company whose foundry can still be seen here. Once a company town, it has become a country village where a thriving cattle and sheep market is held each autumn. 'Mule gimmers', the young females of a particular cross-breed of sheep, are auctioned and despatched to all corners of the land.

The screen in the parish church, decorated with fir cones and nuts glued to a wooden frame, is the work of a former vicar and two local men.

Tynemouth

Map Ref: 92NZ3669

The ancient kings of Northumbria lie buried by the ruins of Tynemouth Castle and Priory which guard the headland at the mouth of the River Tyne. Since earliest recorded time this headland has been fortified, and for well over 1,300 years monastic buildings have stood here – destroyed many times by invading Danes.

These historic ruins are the most outstanding feature of this elegant seaside resort. The priory, which at one time was founded as a Benedictine Priory by Robert de Mowbray, was dissolved in 1539, but due to its commanding position, continued to be used for coastal defence.

The castle and priory ruins look out over the resort's other main attraction – impressive golden beaches at the Long Sands and King Edward's Bay. The coast here is popular with windsurfers and yachtsmen and there is an open-air swimming pool at the south end of the Long Sands.

As befits a seaside resort Tynemouth has a rich maritime history. Standing not far from the priory on a 50ft-high pillar, is the statue of Lord Collingwood, looking out to sea. Admiral Cuthbert Collingwood was the hero of the Battle of Trafalgar and four cannons from his ship *Royal Sovereign* are sited below the statue. He was born in Newcastle, and is buried beside Nelson in St Paul's Cathedral.

Below the monument are the Black Middens – dangerous rocks that have seen some terrible tragedies. In a bid to prevent further deaths at sea the Tynemouth Volunteer Life Brigade was formed in 1864 – the first institution of its kind in the world. Based in a weather-boarded building on the cliff-top, the Brigade headquarters can be visited and contains many artefacts and figureheads from wrecks, together with a breeches-buoy and rocket lifelines.

Tynemouth has some fine old houses that give the town an air of refinement. Old Tynemouth is best illustrated by Front Street, now the main shopping street. One of the most attractive 18th-century houses has been turned into a craft shop and gallery specialising in the cream of British crafts.

AA recommends:
Hotels: Grand, Grand Pde, 3-star, *tel.* (091) 2572106
Park, Grand Pde, 3-star, *tel.* (091) 2571406

Tyne Riverside Country Park

Map Ref: 91NZ1665

Two parks, one on either side of the county boundary, make up a continuous stretch of riverside, beginning in industrial Tyne and Wear and running into scenic Northumberland. The parks allow people from the towns to explore beautiful countryside within a walk, train or bus journey, from their homes.

To the east is Newburn Country Park where engineer William Hedley was born. To the west is Low Prudhoe. A walk between the two takes in the picturesque village of Wylam (see page 77).

Sections of the park are of particular interest to naturalists and there are two visitor centres as well as several picnic sites. To the south of the Park is Prudhoe Castle; recently re-opened by English Heritage, its imposing ruins stand high above the River Tyne. The castle's massive walls and position on top of a steep slope gave it greater protection against attack. William the Lion of Scotland swore to destroy it in 1173, but gave up after three days! The 12th-century keep – one of the oldest in Northumberland – was built by Odinel de Umfraville. Later the castle passed into the hands of the powerful Percy family and the barbican and gatehouse were added.

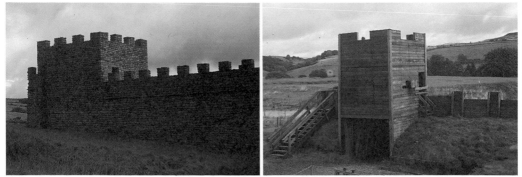

Full-scale reconstructions of a stone turret (left) and a wooden gate-tower (right) on Hadrian's Wall at Vindolanda

Vindolanda

Map Ref: 90NY7766

The first fort at Vindolanda was built more than 40 years before work began on Hadrian's Wall, a mile to the north. Vindolanda was part of a frontier system devised by Agricola, and became the base for up to 500 Roman auxiliary soldiers. The headquarters building is very well preserved. Just west of the fort a civilian settlement has been excavated. Special features of Vindolanda include reconstructions of the Wall and a tower. Close to the fort are ornamental gardens and an excellent museum housed in a country house called Chesterholm. In the museum, displays and reconstructions aid the visitor's understanding of both civilian and military life at the time. Among interesting finds are sandals, shoes and a child's money box.

Wallington Hall

Map Ref: 89NZ0284

Elegant Wallington Hall, 12 miles west of Morpeth, reflects a more peaceful era in the history of Northumberland. The hall is set in 100 acres of lakes and woodlands, which, together with cottages and farms dotted in and around the village of Cambo, make up one of the National Trust's largest estates in Northumbria.

The early history of Wallington is obscure, although during the 14th century it belonged to Alan Strother, whose name Chaucer gave to one of the rascals in the *Reeve's Tale*. The present house dates from 1688, but was altered in the mid 18th century by William Paine.

Sir William Blackett, a Newcastle shipping and mining magnate, bought Wallington from Sir John Fenwick, who was later beheaded for conspiring to kill William III. In 1777 Sir Walter Blackett died childless and Wallington Hall passed to his nephew, Sir John Trevelyan. The Trevelyan family, whose members include the famous historian G M Trevelyan, lived at Wallington until 1936 when Sir Charles gave it to the National Trust.

The Hall is famed for its delicate plasterwork and china, as well as a series of murals in the central hall. Painted by Newcastle artist William Bell Scott, a follower of the Pre-Raphaelite movement, they depict famous scenes in Northumbria's history, including the Death of Bede and the Building of the Roman Wall. Among the trappings of this fine stately home is a magnificent collection of dolls' houses.

Wallington is famed for its beautiful gardens – set some way from the house. They were partly planned by Capability Brown, who was born at nearby Kirkharle and educated in Cambo. The landscape gardener who went on to revolutionise the design of many of the finest parks and gardens, including Blenheim, was born Lancelot Brown in 1715. It is often said that the natural beauty of his home county acted as inspiration for the gardens he planned in the south of England (see page 35).

The grounds at Wallington are used for several summer events, including open-air productions of Shakespeare's plays.

Above: a scene from the life of St Cuthbert in the central hall of Wallington Hall
Below: fine plasterwork on the ceiling in the library

Given to Lord Percy of Alnwick in 1332, Warkworth Castle has belonged to the family ever since

Wark

Map Ref: 90NY8677

The quiet village of Wark, beside one of the loveliest reaches of the River North Tyne, was once the capital of Tynedale. When the area was part of Scotland the Scottish kings held court on the Mote Hill where the Normans had raised a motte-and-bailey castle.

Wark was probably the scene in 788 of the murder of Alfwald of Northumbria – a Christian king whose death led to the lowering of moral standards in the north!

In the churchyard at Wark is the grave of the sportsman/naturalist, Abel Chapman, whose home was Houxty, on a hill overlooking the Tyne. Chapman made a list of 134 bird species spotted within 2 miles of his home. Although he travelled all over the world, Abel Chapman was always eager to return home; he bought the former sheep farm because it was the haunt of the black grouse.

Chapman's writing brought him world-wide acclaim. His first book published in 1889 was *Bird Life of the Borders* and he carried on writing until his death – he actually finished dictating his memoirs on his deathbed. Part of his collection of big game trophies has been used in an imaginative display called 'Abel's Ark', at the Hancock Museum in Newcastle.

Pleasant walking can be enjoyed in the Wark Forest area west of the village in the Northumberland National Park. Here, on the banks of the Warks Burn, is Stonehaugh Picnic Site – well known for its decorative totem poles.

AA recommends:
Hotel: Battlesteads, I-star, *tel.* (0660) 30209

Warkworth

Map Ref: 89NU2406

Nikolaus Pevsner in *The Buildings of England* insists that Warkworth must be approached from the north for it allows 'one of the most exciting sequences of views one can have in England'. He should have added that it should be seen in spring when hundreds of daffodils bloom on the steep-sided slopes of Warkworth Castle. For this is when many people consider the picturesque town looks its best.

Dominated by the dramatic ruins of the Percy stronghold, Warkworth is situated on a winding loop of the River Coquet, a short distance from where it spills into the North Sea. Spanning the river is a narrow medieval stone bridge, one of a handful of fortified bridges in the country. The main street and market place are lined with Georgian and early Victorian houses.

Three scenes from Shakespeare's *Henry IV* are set at Warkworth Castle, which dates from the 12th century. It was here that the 3rd Earl Percy and his son Harry Hotspur plotted to set Henry IV on the throne. Until the 16th century the castle was the home of the Percy family while Alnwick Castle, although larger, was used as a fortress. It is still owned by the Duke of Northumberland, but cared for by English Heritage. Although now in ruins, Warkworth Castle has some fine medieval masonry and the keep was restored and made habitable last century.

The lovely church of St Laurence, an almost complete Norman building, was the scene of a terrible massacre in 1174. The Scots, under Earl Duncan, murdered men, women and children who had taken refuge there.

About ½ mile up the river from the castle is Warkworth Hermitage. Reached by rowing boat, this tiny 14th-century chapel and a sacristy are hewn from the cliff, while the hermit's house was built outside. The last hermit was George Lancaster, chaplain to the 6th Earl of Northumberland, who lived there in the early 16th century.

Cottages on the green at Wark – one-time capital of Tynedale

The Lambton Worm

Events described in the most famous of Northumbrian legends occurred on the River Wear in County Durham, near Washington, presumably in medieval times. Like most such tales it has different versions, embellished round the same foundation. The youthful heir to the Lambton estates was fishing on the River Wear and caught a strange 'worm', probably an eel-like fish. On his way home he threw it into a well at Lambton Castle and forgot about it.

When he was older he joined a Crusade to the Holy Land, but during his absence the 'worm' grew to be enormous, and was able to wriggle out of the well. It soon began to terrify the neighbourhood, feeding on lambs, calves, sheep, and even human babies, and apparently at night slept coiled 'ten times round Penshaw Hill'. This prominent, grass-covered conical hill above Penshaw village is now crowned with the monument erected in 1844 to the Earl of Durham, whose family name is Lambton. The family version of the legend, going back at least 10 generations, asserts that the worm wrapped itself nine times round Worm Hill, a smaller green knoll on the Wear's opposite bank. All attempts to kill the monster failed – when cut in two, the halves merely joined themselves together.

Seven years later young Lambton returned home, full of remorse at his earlier folly of throwing the mysterious worm into the well. Seeking the advice of a local witch he was told to cover his armour with razors, to carry his sword, and to fight the monster in the middle of the river. Naming her price for this advice, the witch demanded that Lambton slew the first living creature to greet him from the castle after his victory.

The ploy succeeded. As the worm coiled itself round Lambton, the razors cut it into pieces which were carried away in the river before they could rejoin themselves. He signalled success to the watchers

According to old local tales, the Lambton Worm was just one of many dragons that terrorised the north-east

in the castle expecting his father to release a dog, as planned, as he returned home from victory. But in his excitement the old man forgot and came out himself to greet his son, who naturally refused to kill him. Accordingly, the witch put a curse on the family that no male Lambton would die in his bed. Since they were rather a wild bunch, and this was medieval England, it was scarcely unexpected that many Lambtons afterwards did die, in battles or through accidents.

A final thought – why does Durham claim so many 'worm' legends – the Stockburn Worm, the Lindley Worm, and the Pollard Brawn, as well as other monsters?

Washington

Map Ref: 92NZ3056

Present-day Washington is a second generation new town. Modern, self-sufficient 'districts' are scattered over a wide area surrounding the town centre. Each district, often with its own industrial estate, is insulated from its neighbours by landscaped parkland. All districts are linked by a network of highways, cycle tracks and footpaths.

Strangers are advised to study the roadside maps before entering the area. The districts have numbers which appear on the directional signs.

District 4 is the original Washington. In past years, together with several other small villages, it served four collieries which, for 100 years provided work for the male population. Long before that time, between the 12th and 14th centuries, the de Wessington family lived here. After many generations, they provided the United States of America with their first President, George Washington.

Washington Old Hall, the family home, was rebuilt in 1613 from the ruins of an earlier house. In 1937, it was restored to its present immaculate condition. Funds for the restoration came from both sides of the Atlantic and the house is now owned and opened to the public by the National Trust. Furnished in 17th-century style, it feels as though it is still lived in by a family of the period.

Washington also has a Wildfowl Park, run by the Wildfowl Trust, 110 acres on the north bank of the River Wear. There are 1,200 birds of 100 different kinds, including a number of Hawaiian geese – a rare species saved from extinction by the efforts of the Trust. Visiting or migratory birds are encouraged. To find the Park follow signs to District 15.

The 'F' Pit Industrial Museum in Albany, District 2, is one of the four defunct collieries of Washington. Now a museum, it still has the steam engine, winding gear and headstock which were installed in 1888.

Less than 3 miles north-west of Washington Town Centre at Springwell it is possible to see one of the last rope-hauled railways to operate in Britain, the Bowes Railway designed by George Stephenson.

AA recommends:
Hotels: George Washington, Stone Cellar Rd, 3-star, *tel.* (092) 4172626 Post House, Emerson, 3-star, *tel.* (091) 4162264

Washington Old Hall, family home of US President George Washington

Whalton's Baal Fire ceremony is said to date back to Saxon times

Whalton

Map Ref: 91NZ1381

Many years ago Whalton villagers used to leap through the flames of a bonfire on Old Midsummer's Eve. This pagan fire festival has survived, but the villagers are now more restrained! At sundown on 4 July the people of Whalton gather round an enormous bonfire on the village green. The Baal Fire is an ancient tradition and its origins are not known.

Whalton is an exceptionally pretty village with a broad main street flanked by grass. At the east end is the Manor House created from a group of four cottages by Sir Edwin Lutyens in 1908 – his well-known colleague Gertrude Jekyll helped with the garden design.

The church has a tower dating from the 12th century, and the rest of the building dates from the 13th and 14th centuries.

Two miles south of Whalton is Ogle – a hamlet with a castle consisting of a 14th-century tower house and 15th- to 16th-century manor house. Ogle was once the seat of the famous Northumbrian family of the same name.

Whitley Bay

Map Ref: 92NZ3572

Smugglers used to land their contraband on St Mary's Island, lying off the coast at Whitley Bay, a busy seaside resort close to Tyneside. The island, reached by a causeway at low tide, is dominated by a 126ft-high white lighthouse. The stone house on the island was once an inn – but lost its licence at the end of the last century.

Whitley Bay is a popular family resort with all the trappings – including a large amusement park called Spanish City and a first-class leisure pool with aqua slide and wave machine. The resort has long stretches of fine sandy beach, an imposing promenade, and a smart shopping centre with several specialist shops.

Along the coast from Tynemouth is Cullercoats; once a busy fishing village, its identity has merged now with its neighbour's. Not so many years ago the Cullercoats fishwife, in a traditional costume, was a common sight, selling her fish by a cottage door. A few local fishermen still launch their boats from Cullercoats and the village has a beautiful sandy bay.

AA recommends:
Hotels: Ambassador, South Pde, 2-star, *tel.* (091) 2531218
Holmedale, 106 Park Av, 2-star, *tel.* (091) 2513903
Windsor, South Pde, 2-star, *tel.* (091) 2523317
Cavendish, (formerly Manuels), 51-52 Esplanade, 1-star, *tel.* (091) 2533010
Downton, South Pde, 1-star, *tel.* (091) 2525941
Newquay, 50-54 South Pde, 1-star, *tel.* (091) 2532211
Guesthouses: Lindisfarne Hotel, 11 Holly Av, *tel.* (091) 2513954
York House Hotel, 30 Park Pde, *tel.* (091) 2528313
Camp Site: Whitley Bay Caravan Park, The Promenade, 3-pennant, *tel.* (091) 2531214
Garages: Colebrooke & Burgess, Hillheads Rd, *tel.* (091) 2528225
Whitley Lodge Motor Co, Claremont Rd, *tel.* (091) 2523347

Whittingham

Map Ref: 89NU0611

Clustered on the banks of the River Aln are the stone houses of one of the most picturesque of Northumberland's villages. Meaning 'the dwelling in the white meadow', Whittingham was an important place many centuries ago because of its central position in the Vale of Whittingham and its command of the fords at the point where the Alnwick road joined the Newcastle to Edinburgh route.

Crowds of people used to flock to the village for an annual fair held on 29 August. It became celebrated in

Once famous for its inshore catches, Cullercoats is home to some of the oldest fishing families in Northumberland

Wooler continues its tradition of agricultural fairs and markets with the Glendale Show, held every August

Northumberland's folklore by the song 'Whittingham Fair' – also sung as 'Scarborough Fair'.

Whittingham, like Alnmouth, claims to be the place where St Cuthbert was elected Bishop of Hexham. The saint and the village appear together in another Northumbrian story. Edred, Bishop of Lindisfarne, had a vision in about the year 800 of Cuthbert ordering the Danes to take as their leader a Danish boy called Guthred, a slave to a widow in Whittingham.

The Danes followed Edred's advice and took Guthred to a hill called Oswigedune where Edred had the coffin of St Cuthbert. Guthred and the Danes swore peace and gave to the saint's followers all the land between Tyne and Wear to the east of Hadrian's Wall. The story may have some truth because a man called Guthred was actually proclaimed King of Northumbria at Whittingham in 883.

Two miles south-west of Whittingham lies Callaly Castle, where a 13th-century pele tower is incorporated into a fine 17th-century mansion.

Wooler

Map Ref: 89NT9928

Towards the end of her young life Grace Darling came to the health resort of Wooler, hoping that the change of air would cure her of consumption. Sadly, it did not and Grace died. However, this quiet market town in the shadow of the Cheviot Hills is bracing and a good centre for those who enjoy outdoor pursuits.

The town is set on a slope above the Wooler Water within easy reach of the Northumberland National Park. It is the centre of a large farming community and has an important livestock market: in the past it was renowned for its cattle fairs.

Wooler has a distinguished place in the history of wood engraving, for it was the birthplace of the Brothers Dalziel. George, Edward, John and Thomas were responsible for a large number of illustrations in Victorian books and many early blocks for *Punch* magazine were engraved by them.

To the south-west of Wooler is the Harthope Valley. There are excellent walking routes from Harthope Burn.

AA recommends:
Hotels: Tankerville Arms, Cottage Rd, 2-star, *tel.* (0668) 81581
Ryecroft, Ryecroft Way, 1-star, *tel.* (0668) 81459

Wylam

Map Ref: 91NZ1164

Prosperous Wylam, straddling the River Tyne, was once a pit village. Now it is one of the few rural villages on the edge of industrial Tyneside.

It is a charming place, lying either side of the leafy-banked river with neat rows of terraced houses now popular with commuters. Its most famous son is George Stephenson, inventor of the *Rocket* and nicknamed 'Father of the Railways' (see page 48).

Stephenson was born here in 1781 in a small red-roofed cottage that is now owned by the National Trust. It stands beside the river on what was once a main thoroughfare through Wylam. Only one room is open, and access is by foot or bicycle only, as the path in front of the cottage is now a walkway linking the riverside parks at Newburn and Low Prudhoe. Originally it was a wooden tramway running from Wylam to Lemington that was later equipped with rack-rail for William Hedley's *Puffing Billy*.

Wylam's importance as a centre for the development of the railway is shown at a small museum at the Falcon Centre. Wylam Railway Museum also commemorates the region's railway pioneers, including Stephenson, Timothy Hackworth and William Hedley.

The cottage in Wylam where railway pioneer George Stephenson was born

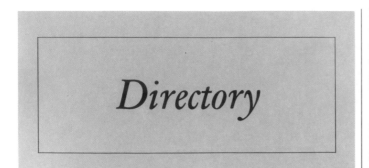

Directory

ACTIVITIES

Angling
Northumbrian rivers provide excellent fishing, as does the coast for sea anglers. Write for permits, etc to the Northumbrian Water Authority, Northumbria House, Regent Centre, Newcastle upon Tyne NE3 3PX.

Bird watching
The open moors of the Northumbrian uplands are famous as a refuge for uncommon breeding birds such as merlin and golden plover, whilst the coast is notable for its seabirds and rare migrants.

Golf
Links golf courses abound; some hotels are situated in or on the edge of golf courses. A full list of clubs that welcome visitors may be obtained from the Northumbria Tourist Board, address on page 82.

Walking
Northumbria is ideal walking country with many miles of public footpaths and bridleways, including part of the Pennine Way long-distance footpath. The Northumbria Tourist Board (see page 82) produces a booklet detailing numerous walks and trails throughout the region which are graded according to their suitability for families, and the fit and the experienced walker. The Northumberland National Park Department has published a series of Walks books on areas of the National Park and coast. A large number of guided walks are organised; and these vary from one to six hours' duration with the emphasis on 'discovery'. Contact the National Park Department (see page 82) for walks in Northumberland, and the County Planning Officer, County Hall, Durham DH5 1UF, *tel.* (0385) 64411 ext 2354, for walks in Durham.

Water sports
You can swim, sail, windsurf, water-ski and canoe in many places, both on the coast and inland at centres like Kielder Water, where there are facilities and accommodation for disabled people. The Northumbrian Water Authority will supply information (address above, under Angling).

Other participator sports
There are specialist activity centres in Northumbria where the visitor can learn to climb, parachute, hang-glide, fly microlights, cross-country ski or pursue indoor sports such as skating or squash. There are also several riding centres in the area. Details from information centres and the Sports Council (see page 82).

CRAFT WORKSHOPS

Craftsmen, and workshops selling handmade goods abound in Northumbria. Here is a selection, by county, of the most interesting – with details of demonstrations and tuition.

Durham
Ireshopeburn, Weardale: Michael & Mary Crompton, Forge Cottage. Spinning and weaving workshops in old blacksmith's forge; handmade articles for sale; one-day courses. Open daily except Thu.
Tel (0388) 537346

Mickleton, nr Barnard Castle: *Mickleton Pottery.* Makes ceramic figures of local people past and present; and domestic earthenware and stoneware. Demonstrations and one-day courses. Open Easter to Oct, daily except Tue; winter by appointment. *Tel* (0833) 40225

Pickering Nook, Burnopfield: Steve & Jean Strathearn, *Craft Centre.* Stonebuilt Victorian school, now a working craft centre; spinning, weaving, screen printing; picture framing, guitar making and brass rubbing. Craft Shop; refreshments, fairs, exhibitions and demonstrations. Open Tue to Sun; evening parties by appointment. *Tel* (0207) 71682

Winston: Brian Russell, *Little Newsham Forge.* Hand-forged wrought ironwork; fire grates, fire-irons, weather vanes; gates, etc. Open Mon to Sat. *Tel* (0833) 60547

Witton Gilbert: David Reynolds, Woodcarver, 17/18 Front Street. Woodcarver at work in workshop; sculptures range from abstract, religious, natural history to dressed walking sticks. Also registered firearms dealer. Open daily. *Tel* (0385) 710512.

Northumberland
Alnham, nr Whittingham: *Alnham Woodcraft,* The Old Schoolhouse Workshop, making wide varieties of wooden toys: puzzles, Noah's Arks, rocking horses, etc. Callers welcome by prior arrangement. *Tel* (0669) 30204

Alnwick: *Freestone Ceramics,* Corn Exchange Court, Bondgate. This pottery produces a range of domestic oven-to-tableware and complementary tableware; hand decorated. Demonstrations by appointment. Open Mon to Sat. *Tel* (0665) 602352.
The Narrowgate Pottery, Narrowgate, makes a wide range of ornamental and domestic stoneware. Workshop and gallery open to view; painting; sculptures and other crafts on display. Open Mon to Sat. *Tel* (0665) 604744.
John Smith of Alnwick Ltd, West Cawledge Park, 1m S of Alnwick, by A1. Galleries in traditional Northumbrian farm buildings, with large display of hand-made antique furniture; also craftwork, coffee and local information. Visitors can watch cabinet-making and furniture restoration in the workshops. Regular classes on furniture restoration. Open daily. *Tel* (0665) 604363

Bedlington: *Craftwise:* Hilary Town, 22a Front Street East. Pottery and Craftshop; visitors may watch potter at work. A speciality is fine relief decorated giftware. Open most days, except Sun. *Tel* (0670) 822238

Belford: *Hazon Mill Knitwear,* 6 High Street. Handframed knitwear and tweed skirts are produced and sold by this workshop and shop. Open daily except Thu. *Tel* (06683) 808.

Berwick-upon-Tweed: *Lindisfarne Pottery,* Palace Green. Pottery producing bottles and containers for Lindisfarne Liqueur Company's mead; badged china for tourists and a range of hand-made stoneware. Large viewing window. Open Easter to end Sep, daily except Sun. *Tel* (0289) 305153.
Meadow Cottage Craft Workshops, 12 Knowehead, Tweedmouth. Pottery producing hand-thrown pots; kitchenware, etc. Open most days; visitors welcome. *Tel* (0289) 307314

Chathill: *The Textile Workshop,* Margaret Blackett Hunter. Teaching workshop near coast; spinning and weaving tuition in summer; course programme available. Equipment for sale and demonstrations given. Open Easter to Sep, Fri & Sat; other times by arrangement. *Tel* (066 589) 218

Etal: Old Power House, Etal Village. Hand-made furniture, wood turning. Open daily. *Tel* (089 082) 376.

Erroll Hut Smithy and Workshop,
Letham Hill. Working smithy
producing ornamental ironwork.
Wood-turning workshop producing
hardwood furniture; spinning and
plant-dyeing demonstrations and
courses. Parking area; small garden
with picnic facilities. Open daily.
Tel (089 082) 317

Ford: *Fountain Craft*, The Estate
House, Ford Village. Local crafts:
wood-carving, prints, paintings.
Open daily. *Tel* (089 082) 297

Harbottle: *Spindles of Harbottle
Craft Studio*, Lightpipe Hall. Small
cottage and workshop in foothills of
Cheviots, ¾ mile from Harbottle
village; magnificent scenery.
Spinning wheels; small hardwood
furniture. Studio offers crafts and
accessories for hand spinners;
demonstrations, tuition by
arrangement. Open Apr to Sep,
daily; other times by appointment.
Tel (0669) 50243

Heatherslaw Mill: *High Kiln Craft
Shop.* A wide variety of British craft
in granary next to drying kiln.
Demonstrations of glass engraving
and pyrography; pets' corner;
natural history exhibits. Open
Easter to Sep, daily; Oct, Sun only.
Tel (089 082) 291

Holy Island: *Lindisfarne Liqueur Co,*
St Aidan's Winery. Showroom
with full range of products; free
sample of Lindisfarne mead, open
Easter to Sep, daily; winter
weekdays when tide permits.
Tel (0289) 89230

Longframlington, D G & E M
Burleigh, Rothbury Road.
Northumbrian smallpipes are made
here. Display on the history of the
smallpipes, music, books and
records of piping on sale.
Proprietors will play visitors local
tunes. Coffee. Open Mon to Sat,
but please ring. *Tel* (066 570) 635

Morpeth: *Chantry Silver & Art
Gallery*, Chantry Place. Hand-made
jewellery; pictures by local artists;
silversmith. Open Mon to Sat.
Tel (0670) 58584

Otterburn: *Redesdale Dairy*, The
Soppitt, Elsdon. Sheep and cow
cheeses made here by only cheese-
maker in county; farmed on organic
principles. Open all year. *Tel* (0830)
20276. *Otterburn Mill Ltd.* Pure
wool tweeds and sweaters;
Icelandics and hand-knits; travel and
pram rugs; sheepskin products, etc.
Open Mon to Fri; and Sat from
May to Christmas.
Tel (0830) 20225

Shilbottle: *Shilbottle Glass Studio,*
West End. Hand-made free-blown
glass goblets, vases and other
glassware; glass blowing
demonstrations. Coffee shop. Open
all year Tue to Sun.
Tel (066 575) 521

*Mr and Mrs Burleigh of
Longframlington playing their
Northumbrian pipes*

Stamford, nr Rennington: *The
Workshops*, Craig Dhu. Custom
designed furniture; skilled craftsmen
at work. Open daily.

Warenford: *Norselands Gallery*, Old
School. Drawings, paintings, prints
and other skilled craftwork.
Craftsmen at work. Open Tue to
Sun & BH. *Tel* (06683) 465

Tyne & Wear
Newcastle upon Tyne: *Blackfriars
Craft Centre.* Workshops, usually
open to public. Shop open Mon to
Sat & BH.

INFORMATION CENTRES

Durham
Tourist Information
Barnard Castle: 43 Galgate.
Tel (0833) 38481
Darlington: Darlington District
Library, Crown Street.
Tel (0325) 469858/462034
Durham City: 13 Claypath.
Tel (0385) 43720/47641
Peterlee: The Upper Chare.
Tel (0783) 864450

Forestry Commission
Hamsterley: Hamsterley Forest
Visitor Centre, Hamsterley Forest, nr
Bishop Auckland. *Tel* (038888) 312

National Trust
Durham: 61 Saddler St.
Tel (0385) 45285

Northumberland
Tourist Information
Alnwick: The Shambles.
Tel (0665) 603120/603129.
Open summer only.
Berwick-upon-Tweed: Castlegate
Car Park. *Tel* (0289) 307187.
Open summer only.
Corbridge: The Vicar's Pele.
Tel (043 471) 2815.
Open summer only.
Haltwhistle: Council Offices,
Sycamore Street. *Tel* (0498) 20351
Open summer only.

Hexham: Manor Office, Hallgates.
Tel (0434) 605225
Kielder: Tower Knowe Visitor
Centre (NWR), Falstone, Hexham.
Tel (0660) 40398
Seahouses: 16 Main Street.
Tel (0665) 720424.
Open summer only.
Wooler: High Street Car Park.
Tel (0668) 81602.
Open summer only.

Forestry Commission
Kielder: Kielder Castle Visitor
Centre, West View, Bellingham,
Hexham. *Tel* (0660) 20242

National Trust
Craster: Craster Car Park, Craster,
Alnwick. *Tel* (067 074) 691
Holy Island: Lindisfarne
Information Centre, Elm House,
Marygate, Holy Island.
Tel (0289) 89253
Housesteads: Housesteads Car
Park, Military Road, Bardon Mill,
Hexham. *Tel* (04984) 525
Rothbury: Cragside.
Tel (0669) 20333
Cowhaugh Car Park, Rothbury.
Tel (0669) 20333
Wallington: East Coach House,
Wallington Courtyard, Cambo,
Morpeth. *Tel* (067 074) 673

National Park
Cawfields: (Hadrian's Wall)
Harbottle: Harbottle, Morpeth
Ingram: Ingram, Powburn,
Alnwick. *Tel* (0665) 78248
Once Brewed: Once Brewed,
Military Road, Bardon Mill,
Hexham. *Tel* (04984) 396
Rothbury: Church House, Church
Street, Rothbury. *Tel* (0669) 20887

Tyne & Wear
Tourist Information
Gateshead: Central Library, Prince
Consort Road. *Tel* (091) 4773478
Jarrow: Jarrow Hall, Church Bank.
Tel (091) 4892106
Newcastle upon Tyne: Central
Library, Princess Square.
Tel (091) 2610691
Blackfriars: Blackfriars, Monk
Street. *Tel* (091) 2615367
North Shields: Tyne Commission
Quay, North Shields Ferry
Terminal. *Tel* (091) 2579800.
Open summer only.
South Shields: South Foreshore.
Tel (091) 4557411.
Open summer only.
Sunderland: Crowtree Leisure
Centre, Crowtree Road SR1 3EL.
Tel (0783) 650960/650980
Whitley Bay: The Promenade.
Tel (091) 2524494.
Open summer only.

National Trust
Washington: Washington Old
Hall, The Avenue, Washington Old
Village. *Tel* (091) 4175037

PLACES TO VISIT

Besides offering a wide and varied
choice of landscapes to explore

The original dedication inscription of St Paul's, Jarrow, founded in 684

Northumbria is rich in other places that amply repay the interest of visitors. Brief details of the best-known and most impressive follow.

Dates, times and similar details relating to such places have a tendency to change, so it is always a good idea to check with a local information centre before making a special trip.

Abbeys, Cathedrals & Priories

Durham
Barnard Castle, Egglestone Abbey. Premonstratensian Abbey ruins; most of nave and chancel have survived with remains of cloisters. Open EH standard hours.

Durham Cathedral. One of the finest examples of Norman architecture in Europe; the burial place of St Cuthbert and the Venerable Bede.
Open all year at varying times.

Finchale Priory. Benedictine Priory built on site of chapel of St Godric on banks of River Wear. Substantial ruins.
Open EH standard hours.

Northumberland
Hexham Abbey. Most of the present building dates from the 12th century, but the abbey was founded by St Wilfred between 674 and 678AD. The 7th-century crypt is virtually intact.
Open daily.

Lindisfarne Priory on Holy Island. This ruined priory, the north's cradle of Christianity, was founded in 635AD by St Aidan. The present ruin dates from 1090.
Open EH standard hours.

Brinkburn Priory, Rothbury. Founded in 1135 for the canons of the Augustinian Order. The church was allowed to decline after the Dissolution of the Monasteries, but was repaired in 1858.
Open EH standard hours.

Tyne & Wear
Jarrow. St Paul's Church and Monastic site. 7th-century church, now chancel of present church. The Venerable Bede worshipped here.
Open daily.

Newcastle upon Tyne. St Nicholas Cathedral. This mostly 14th/15th-century building has a 12th-century Norman arch. Open daily.

Sunderland. St Peter's Church and Chapter House, Monkwearmouth. Saxon church, sculptured stones and finds from monastic site. Open daily in summer. Other times and winter by appointment.

Tynemouth Priory/Castle. The remains of several Northumbrian kings are buried in this now ruined priory, dating from the 7th century with 14th-century fortifications. Open EH standard hours.

Castles, Houses, Parks & Gardens
Durham
Auckland Castle and Deer Shelter, Bishop Auckland. Home of the Bishop of Durham, parts date from 12th century. Castle open May to Sep, Wed only. Deer shelter open daily during daylight hours.

Barnard Castle, Barnard Castle. 14th-century ruins; great hall and keep overlooking River Tees. Open EH standard hours.

Bowes Keep, Bowes. Three-storey 12th-century stone keep. Open EH standard hours.

Durham Castle, Durham City. The Norman castle of the Prince-Bishops. Open (except during University functions) weekdays in the first weeks of Apr, Jul, Aug & Sep; at other times Mon, Wed & Sat.

St Aidan's College and Gardens, Durham City. Sir Basil Spence designed this college which has a splendid landscaped garden. Open daily all year.

Raby Castle and Deer Park, Staindrop. Medieval castle, great kitchen; period furniture, fine paintings, carriage collection, walled gardens, stable tea-rooms. Open Easter to end Sep. BH Sat to Tue; Apr to Jun, Wed & Sun; Jul to Sep, daily except Sat.

Northumberland
Alnwick Castle, Alnwick. Home of Duke and Duchess of Northumberland. Rugged border fortress dating back to 11th century; a treasure house of furniture, painting and china. Open May to early Oct, daily except Sat (but open BH weekends).

Aydon Castle, nr Corbridge. An outstanding example of a late 13th-century fortified house. Open Easter to Sep, EH standard hours.

Bamburgh Castle, Bamburgh. The home of Lord and Lady Armstrong. The outcrop on which the medieval castle stands has been occupied since prehistoric times and has a grand outlook over the coast. Open Easter to last Sun in Oct, daily. Also the Armstrong Museum.

Belsay Hall, Castle & Gardens, near Morpeth. 19th-century hall built in the Doric style by Sir Charles Monck; 14th-century castle with adjoining 17th-century house; picturesque gardens. Open Apr to Sep, EH standard hours.

Berwick-upon-Tweed Castle and Town Walls. The walls are an outstanding example of 16th-century fortifications built in Tudor times to resist artillery.

Chillingham Wild Cattle. Open Apr to Oct, Mon, Wed, Sat & BH, & Sun pm.

Cragside House and Country Park, Rothbury. NT. The house was designed by Richard Norman Shaw for the first Lord Armstrong who created around it the magnificent wooded country park with lakes and rhododendrons. Cragside was the first house in the world to be lit by water-generated electricity. Open: Country Park Apr to Sep, daily; Nov to Mar, weekends only; House Apr and Oct, Wed, Sat, Sun & BH Mon; May to Sep, daily.

Dunstanburgh Castle, Craster. NT/EH. Built by Thomas, Earl of Lancaster in the 14th century; now a ruin. Open EH standard hours.

Howick Gardens, Craster. Noted for spring and early summer flowers. Open Apr to Sep, daily.

Elsdon Tower, Elsdon. 14th-century pele tower, grounds and gardens, grounds open May to Sep, daily; house by appointment.

Lindisfarne Castle, Holy Island. NT. 16th-century castle restored by Sir Edwin Lutyens in 1903. Open Apr, Wed, Sat & Sun, May to Sep, daily except Fri.

Norham Castle, Berwick-upon-Tweed. Border fortress with Norman keep.
Open EH standard hours.

Preston Tower, Chathill. 14th-century pele tower.
Open Apr to Sep, daily.

Prudhoe Castle, Prudhoe. Ruined 12th-century castle.
Open EH standard hours.

Wallington House, Walled Garden and Grounds, Cambo, Morpeth. NT. Late 17th-century house with mid 18th-century interior. Dolls house collection; coach display, woodland, lakes, walled flower garden. Open: House Apr and Oct, Wed, Sat & Sun; May to Sep, daily except Tue. Walled garden all year, daily.

Warkworth Castle, Warkworth. Ruins of castle dating from 12th century with 15th-century keep. Hermitage 1½ miles downstream reached by boat in summer. Open EH standard hours.

Tyne and Wear
Newcastle Keep, Newcastle upon Tyne. Built 1168-1178. One of the finest surviving examples of a Norman keep in the country. Panoramic views of the city from the roof. Open Apr to Sep (except Mon).

Hylton Castle, Sunderland. Keep built by William de Hylton – plus a 15th/16th-century chapel. Now a ruin. Open EH standard hours.

Washington Wildfowl Trust, 1m off the A19 on the A1231. Over 1,250 wildfowl, viewing gallery, hides and picnic areas. Open daily except 24 & 25 Dec.

Washington Old Hall, Washington, NT. Ancestral home of George Washington. Open Apr, Wed, Sat & Sun; May to Sep, daily except Fri; Nov to Mar by appointment.

Museums
Durham
Barnard Castle: *The Bowes Museum.* Internationally important art collection; painting; period rooms; English and French furniture, porcelain, textiles, costumes, music galleries. Children's gallery. Open daily.

Beamish: *North of England Open-Air Museum,* nr Chester-le-Street. Open-air museum of North Country life; a town street, shops, pubs, stables, farm, houses, Victorian park, colliery and related buildings and cottages; NER railway station, locomotives, etc. Open daily (closed Mon in winter).

Darlington Museum, Tubwell Row. Museum of local natural and social history; fossils, rocks; angling tackle display; observation beehive (best in summer). Open daily, except Sun. *Railway Museum,* North Road station. Dedicated to the history of the Stockton & Darlington & North Eastern Railways. Open daily, Sun pm only.

Durham City:, *Cathedral Treasury Museum.* Including 7th-century coffin of St Cuthbert. Open daily. *Monks Dormitory,* also in cathedral. Anglo-Saxon carved stones and local history items. Open daily. *Durham Heritage Centre,* St Mary-le-Bow, North Bailey. Medieval church with heritage exhibition. Open daily, from Jun to end Sep. *Durham Light Infantry Museum and Arts Centre,* nr County Hall. History of county regiment since 1758, changing exhibitions and events. Open daily, except Mon but open Bank Holidays. Closes 25 & 26 Dec &

1 Jan. *Town Hall & Guildhall,* modelled on London's Westminster Hall, and a 14th-century guildhall rebuilt in 1752 which houses the City regalia and silver. Admission on application to Mayor's office. *Old Fulling Mill,* River Bank. A museum of local archaeology. Open daily. *University of Durham Museum of Oriental Art,* Elvet Hill, open weekdays; also weekends from May to Oct.

Ireshopeburn: *Weardale Folk Museum.* Small museum in Minister's House at High House Chapel next to Methodist Chapel where Wesley preached. Visits by arrangement.

Shildon: *Museum.* Home and workplace of Timothy Hackwood, railway pioneer. Open Apr to Sep, daily.

Shotley Bridge: *Heritage Centre.* Features all aspects of local and natural history, geology, and the surrounding countryside. Displays of local crafts. Open daily.

Upper Weardale: *Killhope Wheel.* Lead-mining centre. Open Apr, May, Jun & Sep daily, except Mon. Jul & Aug, daily.

Northumberland
Ashington: *Woodhorn Church Museum.* 11th-century church with relics of the region's Christian evolution. Open Apr to Sep, Tue to Sat.

Bamburgh: *Grace Darling Museum.* Memorabilia of Grace Darling, her family and the famous rescue – including the rescue boat. Open Apr to mid Oct daily.

Berwick-upon-Tweed: *Museum and Art Gallery,* Ravensdowne Barracks. Local history, natural history, archaeology and fine and decorative art. Open daily, except Christmas and New Year. *Guildhall.* Has buttermarket, guildhall, council chambers, and a newly-restored cell block museum. Open two-day week in summer, or by arrangement. *King's Own Scottish Borderers Regimental Museum.* Displays of uniform, silver, medals, weapons. Open daily, except Sun and public holidays in winter. *Wine and Spirit Museum and Pottery.* Artefacts of wine and spirit trade, potter at work and craft workshop village. Open Mar to Oct daily.

Heatherslaw Mill. Restored water-driven corn-mill. Demonstrations given and produce on sale. Open Easter to Sep, daily. Oct weekends only.

Hexham: *Middlemarch Centre for Border History.* In Hexham gaol; Border Reivers exhibits and reconstructed interior of 16th-century pele tower. Open Apr to Oct weekdays.

Newton: *Hunday National Tractor and Farm Museum.* Agricultural museum; farm machinery; water-powered cornmill; farm animals; narrow-gauge railway. Open daily.

Wylam: *George Stephenson's Birthplace.* NT. Built about 1750. Open Apr to Oct, Wed, Thu, Sat & Sun. *Railway Museum,* Falcon Centre. Open Tue & Thu pm & Sat am.

Tyne & Wear
Jarrow: *Bede Monastery Museum,* Jarrow Hall. Archaeological finds from Saxon and Norman monastery sites; Saxon glass; scale model of the 7th-century site, audio-visual programme on monastic life. Open daily except Mon, but open Bank Holidays.

Newburn: *Newburn Hall Motor Museum.* Collection of veteran and vintage and post-vintage cars. Restoration work can be seen. Open daily except Mon.

Newcastle upon Tyne: *Museum of Antiquities.* From pre-history to medieval times with models of Hadrian's Wall and Roman soldiers, Temple of Mithras, etc. Open daily except Sun and 24 – 26 Dec. *Blackfriars.* 'The Story of a City'. Exhibition illustrating the development of Newcastle. Open Apr to Sep, daily; Oct to Mar, Tue to Sat. *Hancock Museum.* New displays of Abel's Ark and Bewick Shrine, also collection of birds and geological exhibits. Open daily. *John George Joicey Museum.* In Holy Jesus Hospital and the 17th-century Austin Tower; furnished rooms from early Stuart to late Victorian times; displays of local history and European arms and armour including one of sporting guns; also houses *Regimental Museum of 15th/19th The King's Royal Hussars* and the disbanded *Northumberland Hussars.* Open daily except Sun. *Military Vehicle Museum,* Exhibition Park. Set up in 1983 to display

19th-century water-driven corn mill at Heatherslaw. Products are on sale

armoured and fighting vehicles, including the jeep. Opening details from Tyneside 281 7222. *Museum of Science and Engineering*, West Blandford Street. Full-size examples of windmills, watermills, steam, internal combustion and hot-air engines; also Engineering Gallery in process of development. Open daily except Sun. *National Bagpipe Museum*, Black Gate. Comprehensive collection of bagpipes, particularly the Northumbrian smallpipes. Open daily.

South Shields: *Central Museum and Art Gallery*. Displays covering the history of South Shields. Open daily.

Sunderland: *Grindon Museum*, Grindon Lane. Edwardian period rooms and shop interiors. Open daily except Thu & Sun but open Sun from Jun to Sep. *North East Aircraft Museum*, Sunderland Airport. Post World War II British and foreign aircraft, and collection of aero engine and aircraft parts dating back to 1908. Also a Vulcan V bomber. Open Sun and Bank Holiday Mon or by prior arrangement. *Museum and Art Gallery*, Borough Road. Regional natural history and geology. Wearside archaeology and history. Open daily. *Ryhope Engines Museum*. Two large beam water pumping engines in 1868 pumping station. Also museum. Open Easter to Dec. In steam at certain times.

RAILWAYS & BOAT TRIPS

Bowes Railway Co Ltd, Railway Manager, Springwell Village, Springwell, Gateshead NE9 7QJ. Mon to Fri and special open days; steam train rides and rope haulage demonstrations.

Browns Boathouse, The Boathouse, Elvet Bridge, Durham DH1 3AF. Rowing boats for hire and launch trips on 2½ miles of water with fine views of city and cathedral.

River Tyne Cruises Ltd, 2nd Floor, Exchange Buildings, Quayside, Newcastle upon Tyne NE1 3BJ

Kielder Water Boat Trips. Operate May to Sep. For details contact Tower Knowe Visitor Centre. *Tel* (0660) 40398

Billy Shiel's Farne Islands Boat Trips, 4 Southfield Avenue, Seahouses NE68 7YT. Daily sailings all year round to the Farne Islands; charter trips to Lindisfarne.

St Cuthbert's Boat Trips, H J Harvey & Sons, 16 Union Street, Seahouses, Northumberland NE68 7RT. Boat trips daily to Farne Islands from Easter to end Sep.

SEASONAL EVENTS

A list of dates can be obtained from the Northumbria Tourist Board (address under Useful Addresses).

Spring
Morpeth Northumbrian Gathering. A week in early spring for traditional pastimes: morris and sword dancing
Teesdale Country Fair, Lartington Park, Barnard Castle. Includes gun dog displays, riding and shooting
North-East Camping, Caravan & Boat Show, North-East Exhibition Centre, Newcastle Racecourse, Gosforth, Newcastle upon Tyne
Riding the Bounds Ceremony, Berwick-upon-Tweed. A May Day custom for horseriders
May Fair, Berwick-upon-Tweed. First held in 1302. The fair starts at noon on the last Friday in May
May Week, Seahouses. A traditional carnival week

Summer
Ovingham Goose Fair. No longer for marketing geese, this is a traditional midsummer fair where the inhabitants of this riverside village dress in Northumbrian costumes and craftsmen exhibit their wares
Durham Regatta. The oldest rowing event in Britain, in mid-June
Miners' Picnic at Bedlington, Northumberland, and *Durham Miners' Gala* where the gathering is addressed by trades union and Labour Party leaders
Ponteland Round Table Highland Games. Ponteland, a Newcastle suburb, holds this annual event at its Castle Ward Sports Centre
Allendale Sheep Dog Trials. A traditional fair
Alnwick Fair. This popular Northumbrian event lasts for a week in June/July with many local customs and traditional events
Newcastle Hoppings. This opens on Race Saturday for the last full week in June, and is the world's largest mobile fair
Whalton Baal Fire Ceremony. A pagan celebration of old Midsummer's Eve
North of England (International) Motor Show, The Links, Whitley Bay, Tyne and Wear
Hexham Abbey: Festival of Music and the Arts. This week-long event is held in early July
Tweedmouth Feast. A 13th-century religious festival on the first Sunday after 18 July; local schools nominate a 'Salmon Queen' and her coronation is followed by the traditional Salmon Supper after which a church service is held
South Tyneside Festival & Flower Show, South Shields. Displays of flowers, vegetables and crafts
Tyneside Summer Exhibition. A county show with special events
Billingham International Folklore Festival. Eight days of international songs, music and dancing in mid August
Bellingham Show. A traditional agricultural show

Durham Beer Festival. At the end of August; the largest festival for real ale in the North of England with traditional jazz and folk groups

Autumn
Hexham Town Fair. A festival week in September
Eggleston Show. A September agricultural show
Alwinton Border Shepherds' Show. An agricultural show on the second Saturday in October. Fell racing, sheepdog trials and wrestling are additional attractions
Durham Music Festival. Musical events take place throughout the city

Winter
Allendale Baal Fire Festival. A pagan custom to bid farewell to the previous year and welcome in the New Year
Morpeth to Newcastle Road Race. Held on New Year's Day
Blessing of Nets, Norham-on-Tweed. This ancient ceremony is held annually on 14 February
Shrove Tuesday Football Matches. These take place at Alnwick and Sedgefield

USEFUL ADDRESSES

National Park Officer: Eastburn, South Park, Hexham NE46 1BS. *Tel* (0434) 605555
Forestry Commission: Walby House, Rothbury NE65 7NT. *Tel* (0669) 20569 and Eals Burn, Bellingham NE48 2AH. *Tel* (0660) 202042
National Trust (Regional Office): Scots Gap, Morpeth, Northumberland NE61 4EG. *Tel* (06704) 691
Northumberland Wildlife Trust: The Hancock Museum, Newcastle upon Tyne NE2 4PT. *Tel* (091) 2320038
Northumbria Tourist Board: Aykley Heads, Durham. *Tel* (0385) 46905
Ramblers' Association (NE Secretary): Mr M Ruddick, 14 Moor Place, Gosforth, Newcastle upon Tyne NE8 4AL *Tel* (091) 2857279
Youth Hostels Association: Regional Office: Bowey House, William St, Newcastle upon Tyne NE31 1SA. *Tel* (091) 2847471
Northumbrian Mountaineering Club: Mr N Jamieson, 52 Angerton Avenue, Shiremoor, Newcastle upon Tyne NE27 0TU. *Tel* (091) 2532703
Sports Council (Northern Region): Aykley Heads, Durham. *Tel* (0385) 49595
The Countryside Commission: Northern Regional Office, Warwick House, Grantham Road, Newcastle upon Tyne. *Tel* (091) 2328252
Royal Society for the Protection of Birds: Milburn House, Dean St, Newcastle upon Tyne. *Tel* (091) 2324148

NORTHUMBRIA

Atlas

The following pages contain a legend, key map and
an atlas of Northumbria.

*Above: the Penshaw Monument, County Durham.
This 'Grecian temple' was erected in 1842 to commemorate
John George Lambton, 1st Earl of Durham*

Northumbria Legend

TOURIST INFORMATION

入	Camp Site	⚲	Nature reserve
⚘	Caravan Site	☆	Other tourist feature
ℹ	Information Centre	⬛	Preserved railway
P	Parking Facilities	⚔	Racecourse
☀	Viewpoint	⚘	Wildlife park
✕	Picnic site	⬛	Museum
⚑	Golf course or links	⚘	Nature or forest trail
⛫	Castle	m	Ancient monument
⚑	Cave	⌒⌒	Telephones : public or · motoring organisations
♈	Country park		
✿	Garden	PC	Public Convenience
⛪	Historic house	▲	Youth Hostel

GRID REFERENCE SYSTEM

The map references used in this book are based on the Ordnance Survey National Grid, correct to within 1000 Metres They comprise two letters and four figures, and are preceded by the atlas page number.

Thus the reference for Hexham appears 91 NY 9364

91 is the atlas page number

NY identifies the major (100km) grid square concerned (see diag)

9364 locates the lower left-hand corner of the kilometre grid square in which Hexham appears

Take the first figure of the reference 9, this refers to the numbered grid running along the bottom of the page. Having found this line, the second figure 3, tells you the distance to move in tenths to the right of this line. A vertical line through this point is the first half of the reference.

The third figure 6, refers to the numbered grid lines on the right hand side of the page, finally the fourth figure 4, indicates the distance to move in tenths above this line. A horizontal line drawn through this point to intersect with the first line gives the precise location of the places in question.

ORIENTATION

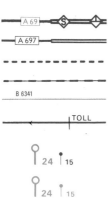

True North

At the centre of the area is 10′ E of Grid North

Magnetic North

At the centre of the area is about 6½° W of Grid North in 1987 decreasing by about ½° in three years

KEY-MAP 1:625,000 or 10 MILES to 1"

ROAD INFORMATION

Motorway with service area, service area (limited access) and junction with junction number

Motorway junction with limited interchange

Motorway, service area and junction under construction with proposed opening date — Mid 1987

Primary routes ⎫
Main Road ⎬ { Single and dual carriageway with service area

Main Road under construction

Narrow Road with passing places

Other roads { B roads (majority numbered) — B 6341
Unclassified (selected)

Gradient (1 in 7 and steeper) and toll — TOLL

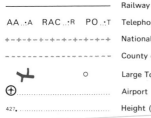

Primary routes and main roads

Motorways

Primary Routes

These form a national network of recommended through routes which complement the motorway system. Selected places of major traffic importance are known as Primary Route Destinations and are shown on these maps thus DURHAM. This relates to the directions on road signs which on Primary Routes have a green background. To travel on a Primary Route, follow the direction to the next Primary Destination shown on the green backed road signs. On these maps Primary Route road numbers and mileages are shown in green.

Motorways

A similar situation occurs with motorway routes where numbers and mileages, shown in blue on these maps correspond to the blue background of motorway road signs.

Mileages are shown on the map between large markers and between small markers in large and small type

1 mile = 1·61 kilometres

GENERAL FEATURES

———————	Railway
AA..:A RAC..:R PO..:T	Telephone call box
+-+-+-+-+-+-+-+-+	National Boundary
- - - - - - - - - - -	County or Region Boundary
✈ ○	Large Town Town / Village
⊕	Airport
427.	Height (metres)

WATER FEATURES

By Sea { Internal ferry route
External ferry route

Ferry............................. Short ferry routes for vehicles are annotated Ferry

——————— Canal

⌒⌒⌒ Coastline, river and lake

TOURS AND ATLAS PAGES
1:250,000 or ¼" to 1 MILE

ROADS   Not necessarily rights of way

M 6   Motorway with service area and junction with junction number

A I(T)   Dual Carriageway   Trunk road

A 697   Dual Carriageway   Main road

A 697   Dual Carriageway   Roundabout or multiple level junction

B 6276   Dual Carriageway   Secondary road

Other tarred road

Other minor road

Gradient 1 in 7 and steeper

RAILWAYS

Road crossing under or over standard gauge track

Level crossing

Station

Narrow gauge track

WATER FEATURES

Cliff

Slopes

Short ferry routes for vehicles

Flat rock

Lake

Transport for vehicles

Bridge   Ferry

Low water mark

Canal   Dunes   High water mark

ANTIQUITIES

Native fortress

Roman road (course of)

Castle · Other antiquities

CANOVIVM · Roman antiquity

GENERAL FEATURES

Buildings

Civil aerodrome (with custom facilities)

Wood

Radio or TV mast

Lighthouse

Telephones : public or motoring organisations

RELIEF

Feet	Metres	
		.274
		Heights in feet above mean sea level
3000	914	
2000	610	
1400	427	
1000	305	Contours at 200 ft intervals
600	183	
200	61	
0	0	To convert feet to metres multiply by 0.3048

WALKS 1:25,000 or 2½" to 1 MILE
ROADS AND PATHS Not necessarily rights of way

M 6   Motorway

A 6   Trunk road

A 697   Main road   Narrow roads with passing places are annotated

B 6272   Secondary road

A I(T)   Dual carriageway

Road generally over 4m wide

Road generally under 4m wide

Other road, drive or track   Path

RAILWAYS

Multiple track   Level crossing

Single track   Cutting

Narrow Gauge

Road over & under   Embankment

Siding   Tunnel

GENERAL FEATURES

Church or Chapel   with tower   Electricity transmission line

with spire   pylon pole

without tower or spire

Gravel pit   NT   National Trust always open

Sand pit   NT   National Trust opening restricted

Chalk pit, clay pit or quarry   FC   Forestry Commission pedestrians only (observe local signs)

Refuse or slag heap   National Park

HEIGHTS AND ROCK FEATURES

Contours are at various metres / feet vertical intervals

50 ·   Determined   ground survey
285 ·   by   air survey

Surface heights are to the nearest metre / foot above mean sea level. Heights shown close to a triangulation pillar refer to the station height at ground level and not necessarily to the summit .

Vertical Face

75
60
50

Loose rock   Boulders   Outcrop   Scree

PUBLIC RIGHTS OF WAY

Public rights of way shown in this guide may not be evident on the ground

Public Paths   Footpath
Bridleway

By-way open to all traffic

Road used as a public path

Public rights of way indicated by these symbols have been derived from Definitive Maps as amended by later enactments or instruments held by Ordnance Survey between 1959 and 1st May 1986 and are shown subject to the limitations imposed by the scale of mapping.

Later information may be obtained from the appropriate County Council.

The representation on this map of any other road, track or path is no evidence of the existence of a right of way.

WALKS AND TOURS (All Scales)

7   Start point of walk

Route of walk

Line of walk

Alternative route

3   Start point of tour

Route of tour

Featured tour

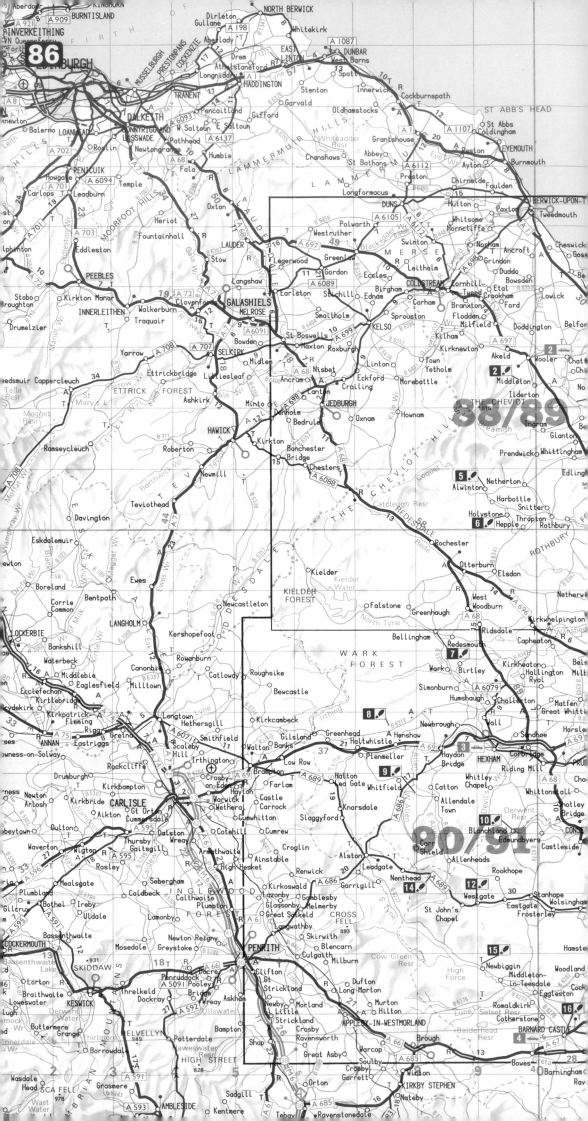

Key to Atlas pages

Distances in miles to HEXHAM
Map Ref: 91 NY 9364

Carlisle	38	Leeds	101
Durham	31	London	287
Edinburgh	96	Newcastle	22
Glasgow	130	Penrith	43
Lancaster	98	York	96

NORTHUMBRIA

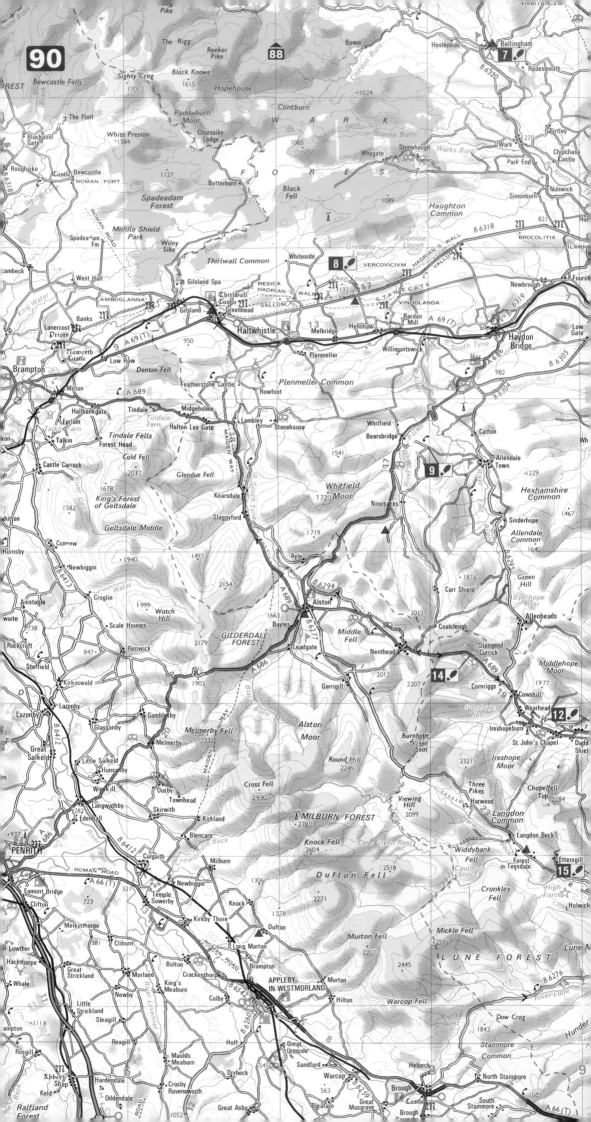

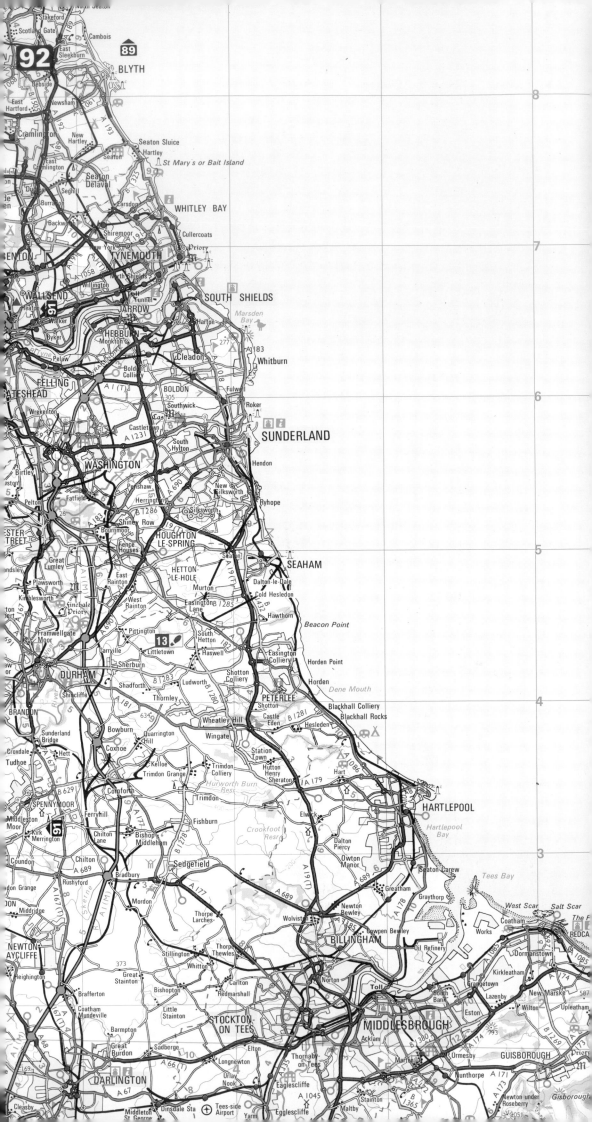

NORTHUMBRIA

Tours & Walks

This section contains four circular motor tours
and 16 planned walks covering the
Northumbrian countryside.

*Above: open all the year round, Jesmond Dene is a haven for wildlife
as well as a delightful recreational area for Newcastle*

TOUR 1 86 MILES
Dale and Coast

This route takes in part of the county's beautiful coastline, before turning west from Bamburgh Castle to sample the foothills of the Cheviots and the delights of Coquetdale. It allows for detours to ancient castles such as Chillingham and Callaly, the mansion and vast estate of Cragside, and Brinkburn Priory, before returning to Alnwick via Warkworth.

The drive starts at Alnwick (see page 34), a delightful grey stone market town on the River Aln; its medieval castle is the home of the Percy family, the Dukes of Northumberland. There is a Tourist Information office in The Shambles. The annual medieval fair starts on the last Sunday in June and lasts for seven days.

From Alnwick town centre follow the signs for Morpeth, and then Bamburgh to leave the town by the B1340. Cross the River Aln by Denwick Bridge for Denwick. At Denwick Church keep left, then branch right onto an unclassified road signed Longhoughton; in 2½ miles turn left onto the B1339. After 1 mile turn right. In another ¼ mile keep forward onto an unclassified road, past the entrance to Howick Hall on the left. The Hall has long associations with the Northumberland Grey family; the garden is often opened to the public.

Turn sharp right, signed Craster, after ½ mile turn left at a T road; in 1½ miles turn right at a crossroads, and in ⅓ mile turn right at a T road. A further ¼ mile leads into Craster village. This is a fishing community, famous for its oak-smoked kippers. The coastal scenery from here to Dunstanburgh is wild and beautiful, with many pleasant walks (see page 47).

From Craster return for ¼ mile, then keep forward, signed Embleton, and in ⅓ mile turn right; keep on for ¾ mile and turn right again at a T road. About 1½ miles on at Embleton Church turn right onto the B1339, signed Beadnell. Minor roads lead from Embleton to its golf course, and to Dunstan Steads on Embleton Bay, and the coastal footpath.

At a mini-roundabout in Seahouses turn right, then left at the War Memorial, signed Bamburgh. In 3 miles pass Bamburgh Castle; the town is ¼ mile further on. The massive castle on a 150ft-high basalt rock is visible for miles across the Northumberland countryside (see page 36).

In 1¼ miles keep forward on the B1340, and in nearly 3 miles at a crossroads, turn right. In 1½ miles on the edge of Beadnell, the road, signed Seahouses, leads forwards for nearly 2 miles to Seahouses. This is the embarking point for the Farne Islands, and is a yachting and holiday centre (see page 37). Fine views of the islands may be had from the harbour, and landing tickets are obtainable from the Information Centre.

In Bamburgh town, branch right onto the B1342, signed Belford, and in 2½ miles at Budle Bay (T road) turn left. In 1¾ miles the road traverses a level crossing; ½ mile onwards turn right, then left to join the B6349 for Belford. Belford was once a famous coaching stop on the Great North Road; just outside the town is the 18th-century Belford Hall.

Leave by the Wooler road B6349, then in ¾ mile turn left onto an unclassified road, and after 3 miles, turn right at a T road onto the B6348, signed Chatton. In two miles the Percy Arms public house at Chatton is reached. This is named after the Percy family, one of the great Northumbrian dynasties – and there are many more such reminders in the area.

At the end of Chatton turn left onto an unclassified road, signed Chillingham. In 1½ miles at Chillingham pass a road to the ruined Chillingham Castle – a short detour to the left. Chillingham is most renowned nowadays for its herd of wild white cattle (see page 44).

From Chillingham village continue for just over 4 miles to join the B6346, then proceed ahead for nearly 2 miles to the edge of Eglingham. Turn right onto an unclassified road, signed Powburn. At this turning is a glimpse of Eglingham Hall – early 18th-century, with some parts dating back to the 16th century.

In just over a mile, branch left, signed Glanton, and in 2½ miles cross the main A697. More than ½ mile further on enter Glanton. From this village, 500ft up in the Cheviot foothills, there are good views over the valleys of the Rivers Breamish and Aln.

Turn right in Glanton, and then left, signed Whittingham. After 1½ miles enter Whittingham; cross the river bridge and take a right turn, signed Rothbury, and pass the entrance to Callaly Castle 2 miles further on, on the right. This fascinating building is on the site of a 13th-century pele tower which became a Border fortress in the 15th century.

In ¼ mile bear left, and 1¾ miles later, turn left at a T road. In more than ½ mile take a left turn, signed Thropton, Rothbury, and just over 3 miles further on, enter the edge of Thropton. This village is divided in two by the Wreigh Burn, and has a footbridge over the River Coquet; it also has a early 15th-century fortified house, Thropton Tower.

Turn left at a T road onto the B6341, signed Rothbury, and in 1¾ miles enter Rothbury. The capital of Coquetdale, the busy market town of Rothbury is a perfect centre for exploring the Cheviots and the Northumberland National Park.

From Rothbury drive for nearly ½ mile and bear right on the B6344, signed

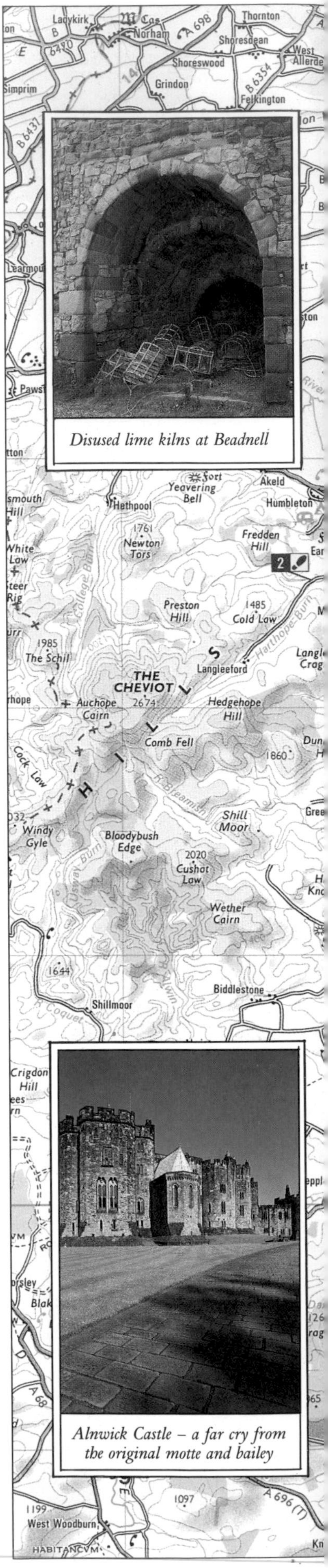

Disused lime kilns at Beadnell

Alnwick Castle – a far cry from the original motte and bailey

Morpeth. In another mile pass the National Trust's Cragside estate on the left (see page 46), and in a further 1¼ miles pass Brinkburn Priory on the right. In 1¼ miles turn left, signed Coldstream, and join the A697. Less than 1¼ miles further on turn right onto the B6345, signed Felton; in 2½ miles bear right, and in just under 2 miles enter Felton. In the 13th century the English barons met here to transfer loyalty from King John to King Alexander of Scotland. This insult was avenged the following year when King John burned Felton to the ground.

Turn right, signed Morpeth, Newcastle, and in ¼ mile the B6345 turns very sharply left, signed Amble, Warkworth. In 2 miles keep left, still on the B6345, signed Acklington, and in 1½ miles enter Acklington. Continue through the village, and in 1½ miles continue ahead, joining the A1068, signed Alnwick. After 2¼ miles turn left and enter Amble; turn left and in ⅓ mile pass Amble Braid Picnic Site on the right. In a further mile at a T road turn right into Warkworth. Here is another Percy stronghold, Warkworth Castle, still a home of the Percy family (see page 74).

In 3½ miles at the Hipsburn Roundabout (Alnmouth is to the right), take the 2nd exit, and in nearly ½ mile on the edge of Lesbury keep left and in 3¾ miles re-enter Alnwick.

TOUR 2
Around the Cheviots

This circular tour starts at the edge of the Northumberland National Park, skirts the Bowmont Water Valley, takes in Carter Bar where there are fine views northwards, and then descends to Otterburn, passing Catcleugh Reservoir and Redesdale Forest before turning north again to Wooler.

The drive starts from Wooler (see page 72), a good place from which to explore the Cheviots. There is a Tourist Information Centre in the High Street Car Park, from which visitors can obtain information about Northumberland in general and the Cheviots in particular.

Take the A697 from Wooler, signed Coldstream. After 2¾ miles, branch left on the B6351, signed Yetholm, and follow the road for 1¾ miles to a plaque on the right. This indicates the Saxon village of Ad Gefrin, first discovered in 1955, its timber hall structures and stockades long since decayed.

Follow the B6351 for a further mile to Kirknewton. This lovely village was once a vulnerable Border town, and the scene of many skirmishes.

Leave Kirknewton and after 2¾ miles, on the edge of Kilham, go forward on an unclassified road signed Kirk Yetholm, Town Yetholm, and drive for 3 miles, to a small stream which marks the Scottish Border; 1½ miles further on is Kirk Yetholm, and the road leads on to the main village under ½ mile away at Yetholm – or Town Yetholm as it is locally known. Kirk Yetholm marks the end of the Pennine Way, and is a walking and climbing centre with camp sites and fishing and riding facilities.

Take the B6401 from Town Yetholm church, signed Morebattle, Jedburgh. In 3⅓ miles, cross a bridge over the Kale Water, and continue towards Morebattle. After ⅓ mile keep left and in another ½ mile the road reaches Morebattle. This small village is on the Kale Water and is surrounded by hills which have many prehistoric forts and other settlements.

1¾ miles from Morebattle turn left along an unclassified road, signed Cessford; 1½ miles further on keep left into Cessford. A short detour along a road to the left leads to ruined Cessford Castle.

Leave the village and bear to the right; after 3½ miles turn left at a crossroads, signed Oxnam. Just over a mile further on cross a narrow bridge, and in another ½ mile at a T road turn left and follow the road for ¾ mile into Oxnam, from whose Post Office it is just over 4 miles to the A68. Turn left, signed Newcastle, and ascend from here 5¼ miles to Carter Bar. This viewpoint (1,371ft) is on the Border, and from the lay-by on a clear day the view reaches 50 miles to Edinburgh and the Firth of Forth, with the Eildon Hills a mere 18 miles away at Melrose.

The long 5½-mile descent leads past the Catcleugh Reservoir on the right to Byrness. There is a memorial in the tiny 18th-century church here, to the construction workers who died while building the reservoir. Byrness has a small village built for Forestry Commission employees, a picnic site and fishing facilities.

In a further 1¾ miles, on the right, is the Redesdale Forest Park. The A68 passes the peaceful and attractive picnic site of Blakehopeburnhaugh on the right, beside the River Rede. There are waymarked walks through Redesdale Forest, and a 12-mile forest drive – with a toll – to Kielder Castle.

Follow the A68 for 3¾ miles to Rochester, the 'camp on the high rock', and a little more than 2½ miles beyond Rochester, go forward on the A696, signed Otterburn, which is a further 2¼ miles. Otterburn is another holiday centre, with an early 19th-century mill, and noted for the Battle of Otterburn in 1388 (see page 64).

In just under a mile from Otterburn, branch left onto the B6341, signed Rothbury, and in 2½ miles enter Elsdon. One of the finest pele towers in the county, and the remains of a Norman motte-and-bailey, illustrate Elsdon's one-time strategic importance, set as it is at the junction of two major routes from the border into Redesdale.

From Elsdon continue northwards on B6341 for nearly 5 miles to the Harehaugh Picnic Site on the left. About ¼ mile further on turn left onto an unclassified road, signed Holystone, Harbottle. Follow this road for 2¾ miles into Holystone. Here, the famous Lady's Well will be found behind the Salmon Inn (see page 56).

Bear right out of Holystone and ¾-mile north at a T road turn left, signed Harbottle, Alwinton, to Harbottle. This lovely Coquetdale village nestles beside the river at the foot of the ruined 12th-century castle on its mound, or knowe.

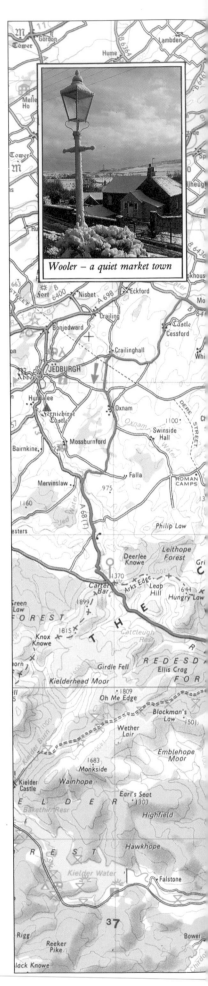

Wooler – a quiet market town

A mile after leaving Harbottle, cross the River Coquet, and turn right after ¼ mile, signed Netherton; follow the road for 4¾ miles to Netherton and turn left at the post office, signed Whittingham, which is 6 miles further on. This village has a former pele tower, now almshouses, and the Whittingham Games and Fair are held here in late summer (see page 76).

Leaving Whittingham, turn left at a T road in ¼ mile, signed Glanton, Wooler, and follow this road for practically 2 miles to Glanton. Here are lovely views over the Breamish and Aln valleys.

Turn left at the crossroads, and then bear to the right, signed Powburn, Wooler. In 1⅓ miles the road reaches Powburn and joins the A697. In a further 3½ miles pass the Cat's Paw Picnic Area and the last lap into Wooler is 5 miles.

Catcleugh Reservoir, completed in 1906

Elsdon pele tower

TOUR *3* 80 MILES

Hadrian's Wall and the Derwent Valley

This route explores the North Tyne Valley; travels over moorland to run parallel with Hadrian's Wall before descending again to Haltwhistle and across further moorland to Allendale town and the upper Allendale Valley. The road climbs to 1,829ft before it descends to Upper Weardale and crosses the Stanhope and Muggleswick Common uplands to reach Edmundbyers, with views of the Derwent Reservoir. It then passes through Slaley Forest and Dipton Wood to return to Hexham.

The drive starts from Hexham (see page 55), one of the best places from which to explore Hadrian's Wall. The administrative centre for Tynedale, this historic market town is built on a terrace overlooking the Tyne. There is a Tourist Information Centre at Manor Office, Hallgates, NE46 1XD (tel (0434) 605225).

From Hexham town centre follow the signs to Carlisle and the A6079; cross the River Tyne and in ¾ mile at a roundabout take the 1st exit, A69, and in another ¾ mile turn right onto A6079, signed Rothbury. In just under ½ mile pass the edge of Acomb (on the right), and in 2 miles pass Wall and reach a crossroads at Brunton House. There is a stretch of Hadrian's Wall here, in the care of English Heritage.

Turn left onto the B6318, signed Chollerford, and in ¼ mile cross the River North Tyne into Chollerford. The single-track, five-arch bridge was built after the river flooded in 1771 and washed away the previous structure; there are Roman bridge abutments about ½ mile south of the present bridge.

At the roundabout in Chollerford take the 1st exit, signed Carlisle, and in ½ mile pass the entrance to Chesters Park on the left. Here the Wall can be seen again, with the Roman fort of Cilurnum, excavated by a Victorian amateur archaeologist, John Clayton, who lived in the 18th-century Chesters House in the Park.

After a long 3½-mile ascent pass Brocolita Roman fort on the left and drive for a further 4¾ miles to the car park for Housesteads Roman fort on the right. Housesteads is probably the finest fort on the Wall, in the joint care of the National Trust and English Heritage (see page 57).

Continue along B6318 for 2¾ miles to the Twice Brewed Inn, passing a National Park Information Centre on the left. In a further 2½ miles turn left at a crossroads onto an unclassified road, signed Haltwhistle, and after a ½-mile descent, and a further ½ mile, turn right at a T road, signed Town Centre, and in ½ mile enter Haltwhistle. The town lies between the Haltwhistle Burn and the South Tyne River, and has a notable Early English church and the remains of a Roman fort and marching camp (see page 54).

In ¼ mile at a T road, turn right onto the A69, signed Carlisle, and ½ mile further on turn left onto an unclassified road, signed Plenmeller, and cross the River Tyne; shortly at a T road turn left, signed Plenmeller, Whitfield. In 1 mile enter Plenmeller. A left-hand turn in this hamlet leads to Unthank Hall, partly 15th-century, and built on the site of an earlier house, claimed to be the birthplace of Nicholas Ridley, who as the Protestant Bishop of London, died at the stake with Latimer in 1555.

From Plenmeller there is a 3¼-mile-long ascent over Plenmeller Common; then turn left and in a further 2¼ miles turn right and descend for ¾ mile to Whitfield. This village, scattered about the rivers West and East Allen, about 1½ miles short of their meeting point, is sited in one of the most beautiful parts of Northumberland.

From Whitfield travel forward for ¾ mile, and at a T road turn right onto the A686, signed Alston. In ¼ mile turn left across the River West Allen, on an unclassified road, signed Allendale. (Almost immediately there is a hairpin bend in the road.) In 3¾ miles join the B6295 and after ¼ mile enter Allendale. Allendale is a popular holiday town with many amenities: good walking, trout fishing, golf (see page 34).

Follow the B6295 as it turns right at the Hotspur Hotel, signed Allenheads, Cowshill, and in 7¾ miles reach Allenheads and begin a 3¼-mile ascent and descent to a T road; turn left onto the A689 (unsigned) and in ⅓ mile enter Cowshill. In ½ mile reach Wearhead, and follow the signs for St John's Chapel, passing through Ireshopeburn after another ¾ mile. The Weardale Museum is a further ½ mile along on the right. In ¾ mile, enter St John's Chapel, and in just over ½ mile pass through Daddry Shield. A mile further on is the village of Westgate, and in another 3 miles is its twin, Eastgate. Westgate was the site of the Bishop of Durham's castle, the foundations of which can be seen at

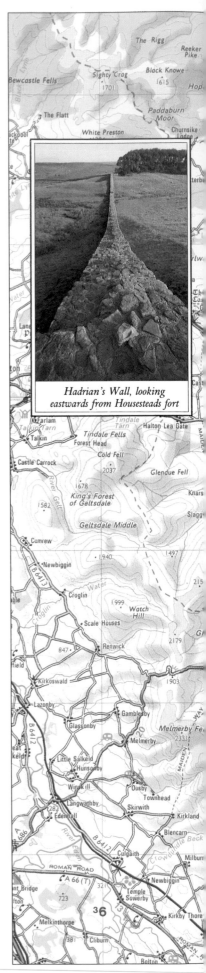

Hadrian's Wall, looking eastwards from Housesteads fort

High Westgate, with the remains of an old mill and waterwheel. Eastgate and Westgate border Weardale Park, a deer park before the 16th century, and a camp for Edward III's army in the 14th-century border wars.

2½ miles further on, enter Stanhope and at the Grey Bull public house turn left onto the B6278, signed Edmundbyers, and climb to Stanhope Common. In 3 miles bear right, and in practically a mile descend a 1-in-7 then 1-in-10 incline for 3½ miles to Edmundbyers. Turn left onto the B6306, signed Blanchland, and skirt the southern edge of the Derwent Reservoir, passing Pow Hill Country Park after a mile, on the right. In another ⅓ mile pass a picnic area on the right, and 2 miles further on pass a road to Carricks Picnic Area. Cross the River Derwent in another 1¾ miles, and enter Blanchland. This is the most famous 'model' village in Northumbria, with a 12th-century abbey (see page 40).

Turn right, signed Hexham, and in 2¾ miles keep left; in another 2½ miles reach the edge of Slaley, and in just over 3 miles cross Linnels Bridge and continue for 2 miles into Hexham.

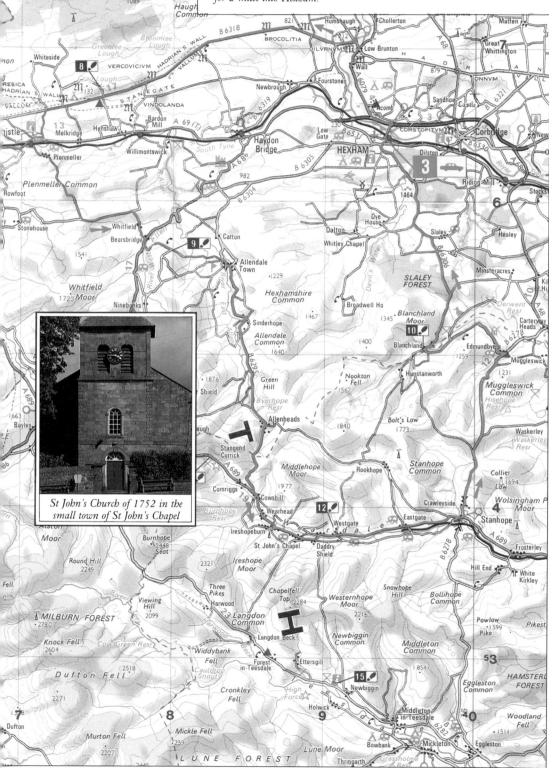

St John's Church of 1752 in the small town of St John's Chapel

TOUR 4 60 MILES
Weardale and Teesdale

Taking a main road through undulating country to Staindrop and Raby Castle, this route continues along minor roads, skirting Hamsterley Forest before rejoining another main road through Weardale, ascending to 2,056ft before descending to Langdon Beck and returning through Teesdale to Barnard Castle.

The drive starts at Barnard Castle (see page 36). The 12th-century castle that gives the town its name is a ruin now, but it still dominates the town from its hill above the River Tees. It is in the care of English Heritage. The town has many interesting buildings; the Tudor Blagrave house was once an inn, reputed to have been patronised by Oliver Cromwell in 1648. Dickens researched Nicholas Nickleby here, and the town's famous Bowes Museum houses important art collections. Market day is on Wednesday. There is a Tourist Information Centre at 43 Galgate, DL12 8EL (tel (0883) 38481; Sat & Sun 37913).

From Barnard Castle follow signs for Darlington and the A67. In ¾ mile turn left onto the A688, signed Bishop Auckland. In 5¾ miles reach Staindrop Post Office, and in ¼ mile keep left at the church. In just under a mile is the entrance to Raby Castle on the left. The Castle in its deerpark is one of the finest fortresses in England, dating back to the 12th century, with a medieval great kitchen, collections of furniture, paintings and other works of art; also carriages and other horse-drawn vehicles.

In just over ½ mile from Raby Castle entrance turn left onto an unclassified road, signed Woodland, Cockfield, and after ½ mile keep forward, signed Butterknowle, Woodland. A mile further on enter Burnthouses, then after another 1¼ miles turn left onto the B6282, signed Copley, Woodland. Pass through Copley and after a further mile reach Woodland. Turn left here, keeping on B6282, and in about ¼ mile turn right onto an unclassified road (unsigned). In 5½ miles reach Hamsterley; turn left, signed Wolsingham, and cross Redburn Beck. In 1¼ miles reach Hamsterley Forest Drive. A toll here gives access to Hamsterley Forest, a Forestry Commission recreation area with several picnic sites, nature trails and walks.

Continue for 4½ miles to Wolsingham, turn left onto the A689, signed Alston, and in ½ mile pass the Windy Nook Picnic Area on the left, and Frosterley Post Office after a further 2½ miles. Another 2½ miles further on enter Stanhope. This market town is the gateway to Upper Weardale; it has a 15th-century market cross, and an 18th-century castle.

After 3 miles enter Eastgate, and in another 3 miles enter Westgate. A further mile leads to Daddry Shield, and another ½ mile leads to St John's Chapel; turn left onto an unclassified road, signed Langdon Beck. The road ascends and descends over moorland to meet a T road after 4¾ miles. Turn left onto the B6277, signed High Force, Middleton. This is Teesdale; farmland and moorland on the Pennines. These beautiful remote hills have changed little since prehistoric times.

Half a mile further on by the Langdon Beck Hotel, pass a road on the right to Cow Green Reservoir, and in 2¾ miles pass the High Force Hotel on the left. Here is a parking area for the tourist to visit the famous High Force Waterfall, 70ft high and part of the huge Raby estate.

In 1¼ miles reach Bow Lees, and after ¼ mile pass the Bow Lees Picnic Area on the left. Another ½ mile leads into Newbiggin. After 2¾ miles pass Middleton-in-Teesdale Post Office on the right. Middleton is the capital of Upper Teesdale, and last century was the centre of Northumbria's lead mining industry.

Turn right onto the B6277, signed Barnard Castle, and in ¼ mile cross the River Tees. In ½ mile keep left, and in ¾ mile reach Mickleton Post Office. Remains of prehistoric man have been discovered in this single street hamlet.

In 2 miles reach Romaldkirk, and 2 miles further on reach Cotherstone. This pretty village produces its own cheese. There are attractive walks, especially at the meeting point of the two rivers, Balder and Tees.

In 1⅓ mile enter Lartington and in 2¼ miles at traffic signals turn left to enter Barnard Castle.

Spectacular High Force between Durham and Yorkshire

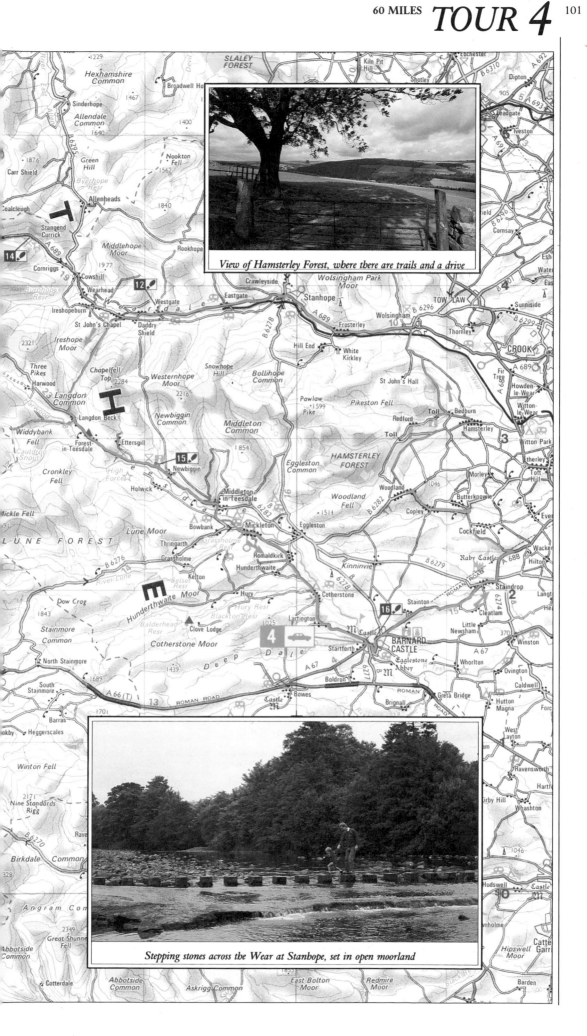

View of Hamsterley Forest, where there are trails and a drive

Stepping stones across the Wear at Stanhope, set in open moorland

Holy Island

Allow 1½ hours

Experience the charm of Holy Island on this walk which takes in Lindisfarne Priory, harbour and castle on a short but fascinating excursion. Note: the causeway floods at high tide and in order to avoid a delay of up to two hours check the times in advance.

Park in Holy Island car park (NU127422). Turn right out of the car park and left at the next junction. Then turn right and sharp left for the church and priory. If you wish to look around the priory there is an entrance charge payable at the wicket gate; if not, go through the gate, keep to the path which loops around the church and exit via a small gate on the west side of the church. Turn left down the track. At the bottom of the hill, bear left up the steep path onto the top of the rocky outcrop which is a dolerite dike. Go up to the coastguard's lookout for a superb view south across Fenham Flats to Bamburgh Castle. There is also a bird's-eye-view of the priory looking north from here. In 634, Oswald invited the monks from Iona to Lindisfarne (another name for Holy Island; Lindis is the name of the river which flows across the causeway and farne means island) and Aidan founded a wooden monastery here. This was wasted by Vikings in 875 and the brothers fled for their lives. The present ruin is all that remains of a priory built in 1093.

Bear left at the dip in the hill and then right along a gravel path to the harbour. Lobster and crab pots are very much in evidence here although the main catch is now salmon. Go around the harbour, noticing the boathouses which are listed buildings!

At the end of the track, turn right towards the castle and follow the road to a gate. Go through the kissing gate and walk around the base of the castle. It was

The old lime kilns below Lindisfarne Castle

built in 1539, a year after Henry VIII dissolved the monasteries and the island became a military rather than spiritual base. Seymour, the Queen's brother, used the castle to land men before going on to Scotland. It has had a peaceful history with no battles and bloodshed, and was bought as a private house at the turn of the century by Edward Hudson, founder of *Country Life* magazine. It is now in the care of the National Trust. The old lime kilns a little further on were fed by limestone from the north of the island and the reduced quicklime was shipped to Dundee in return for coal.

Turn along the old wagonway through a kissing gate and keep to this track which leads away from the sea via a freshwater pool on the left. Cross one stile and a second kissing gate leading into the National Nature Reserve which extends across the north of Holy Island. Turn left at the next track crossing the path (before the dunes) and follow this path along the foot of the dunes. In spring and summer the flowers and insects here are a delight.

This path will eventually lead onto a well-defined track which turns left and leads directly back to the car park. A brief sortie into the dunes for a closer look at dune flora is always a treat in the summer months.

Happy Valley

Allow 3 hours

The smooth grassy slopes of the Cheviot Hills make excellent walking country. This route follows Happy Valley downstream before ascending a small hill above the Harthope Burn for really magnificent views.

Park in Harthope Valley on the gravel verge at the bottom of the steep hill which leads into the valley, just before Carey Burn Bridge (NT976249). From here, turn left along the road and in about 20 paces, cross a stile on the right beside a gate. A short way upstream from here, the Harthope Burn which rises on the Cheviot joins forces with the Carey Burn to form Coldgate Water. Both tributaries have large water catchment areas and the channel ahead signifies Coldgate Water's capacity to flood. In June the bank of gorse on the left is aflame with yellow flowers and its rich scent is strongly reminiscent of coconut.

Keep to the track through the gorse to an alder grove and fork left along a path which leaves the main track and starts climbing. Once over this rise, watch for herons which frequently lift from the river beside Grimping Haugh. 'Haugh' means flat pasture in the valley bottom.

Keep straight on, more or less following the river and eventually bear to the left beside a plantation and go through a gate. Continue on the haugh, avoiding the steep sheep paths which lead up the bank on the left. Eventually the path reaches a stile, cross this into a wood. Now the path is right beside Coldgate Water as it rushes through a series of lovely pools.

Near the end of this woodland track, turn right through a kissing gate and cross the footbridge. Pause halfway across to look for dippers and wagtails. The dipper is a characteristic bird of clear, rocky streams; it looks like a chubby blackbird with a white breast, and has a habit of dipping and curtseying when standing on stones. It feeds on aquatic insects and is able to swim or walk on the bottom of stream beds, using its wings as paddles.

Bear right up the road for about ¼ mile past Old Middleton Farm, and just past the farm turn right along the track waymarked 'Old Middleton, Harthope Valley and Langlee'. Follow the drystone wall uphill, and take a breather at the first gate. Turn round for a fine view of the sandstone edge of Bewick Moor.

Continue to the brow of the hill where the red pantiled roofs of Old Middleton come into view. Behind the deserted cottages the tip of the Cheviot appears.

At the next gate, notice the splendid drystone wall on the left. This has been beautifully restored with help from the Northumberland National Park Authority in an effort to preserve the character of the old village. The houses left standing are not of any great age, but further on, there are hummocks in the fields which are remnants of a much older settlement. The site is scheduled as an ancient monument.

There is a public footpath through the village if you wish to explore, otherwise, bear right immediately after the gate, over a bank of wild flowers. Go down the bank and cross a footbridge at the head of a very unexpected and precipitous gorge. Now go up the bank, cross the stile and keep to the fence on the right which encloses a plantation of Scots pine trees. Cross another two stiles and follow the side of the hill around as the path begins to climb a little. At the next gate, turn left to follow the yellow waymarker straight up along the edge of a field to another waymarker. This points the way across a thistle field which has a lovely view of the Harthope Valley.

Keep straight on as the track leads through an isolated gateway (the fence was removed long ago) and, to avoid a small marsh, keep right and another waymarker again signals the way. There is a duck pond nestling in the bracken on the right which can be seen as the path loses height.

Just beyond the next gate, turn left on a path through the bracken. At the bottom of this section of path, bear left again over a broken wall and go over a stile. Now keep to this path as it hugs the valley side and passes beneath a group of lovely old oaks. Finally, the path leads down some steps, across the footbridge, almost straight across a field and then over a stile on the left to come out onto the road. *Turn right over Carey Burn Bridge.* Look back for a fine view up Harthope Valley with Housey Crags high up on the left. Beyond is the great dome of Hedgehope Hill.

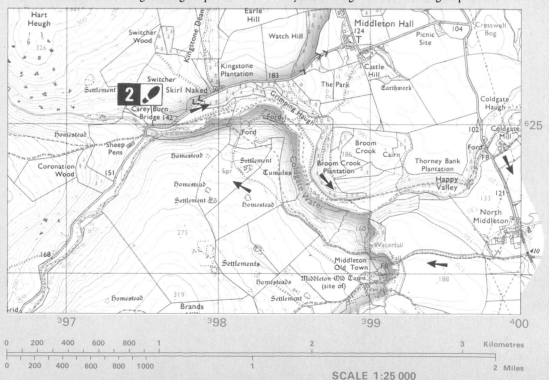

SCALE 1:25 000

WALK 3
Hill-fort and Heather

Allow 2½ hours

This moorland walk offers a great feeling of space and isolation with some of the finest views in Northumberland overlooking the valley of the Till with the Cheviots behind.

Park in the hamlet of Old Bewick (NU067215) taking care not to block farm entrances. Go up the track which runs beside a small row of cottages and through a gate. Up the hill on the right is an old reservoir surrounded by sycamore, larch and Scots pine trees. The steep hill ahead, faced with Scots pine, leads to a flat-topped summit which was the site of an ancient hill-fort and settlement. It is well-preserved and has four ridges on the north side. This hill is part of an escarpment which extends away to the left where it is cloaked mainly in sitka spruce trees. This is Hepburn Wood and behind it on a hilltop is Ross Castle, the site of another Iron Age fort.

Go through two gates keeping to the roughly cobbled track with a drystone wall on the left. Take a look back at the panoramic view of the Cheviots. Hedgehope is the dome-shaped hill and to its right is The Cheviot itself.

The land changes at the third gate from rough pasture and bracken to rush and heather moorland. Fork right where the track divides and head for the sycamore trees which can just be seen above the rise. On the left a little further on, a strange pile of stones comes into view. This is a Bronze Age burial mound dating back to 1600BC. The mound contains three cists or stone graves where various treasures have been found, including a jet necklace, shell beads

and a broken flint knife. As well as these remains, there are also strange rock carvings which decorate some of the moors above Rothbury. These 'cup-and-ring' carvings, as they are known, have fascinated and puzzled archaeologists for decades.

Continue up to the ruin of Blawearie and have a look at this lonely settlement, which has been derelict for more than 40 years. The outcrop of sandstone behind the house was incorporated into a garden once with stone steps linking the levels.

Retrace your steps for 40yds back down the track and follow the direction of a yellow waymarker in the bracken on the left, just before a small stream. Follow this path through the bracken and make plenty of noise in warm weather to warn any snoozing adders of your approach. Cross a boggy area and follow the direction of the yellow waymarker opposite which leads to a good path, marked through the heather with cairns. At the white-topped marker post, head directly away from Blawearie between two small valleys. In the bracken on the left is another ancient camp, while further down the path a pillbox looks out from the right-hand valley, a more recent relic of defensive measures.

Go past the rocky gulley on the left which is known as Corbie Crags; corbie is the local name for crow. Eventually, the path leads into a mossy area which is the meeting point of two streams. Head straight across this, toward a gate and just before this, turn right keeping the wire fence on the left, and go up the side of the small valley ahead. As the path gets steeper, various small paths lead off into the bracken. Keep roughly to the valley on the left and eventually come to a fence. Follow it to a gate.

Now, either turn left through the gate, down the track which eventually leads to the minor road and turn right to walk the mile back to Old Bewick; or, at the gate, turn right along a deeply rutted bridleway. Keep in sight of the fence on the left and as it bends left, follow it to a wicket gate in a drystone wall. Bear left down a steep hill and right beneath an area of rhododendrons. Keep to the contour and eventually cross a stile in the fence ahead.

Turn left back to Old Bewick.

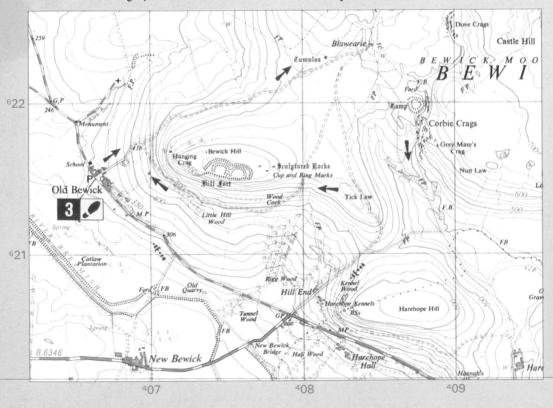

Kippers, Kittiwakes and the Kern

Allow 2 hours

The celebrated coast of Northumberland features in this walk, together with the tiny fishing village of Craster, home of the famous kippers.

Park in Craster car park (NU257198). This was the site of whinstone quarrying until before World War II. Here the Whin Sill, a narrow arc of volcanic rock sweeping from Teesdale to the Farne Islands, outcrops in a series of heughs (heugh means 'heels of land') which are accessible and easy to quarry. Wander up to the coach park area; the

Kittiwakes rarely venture inland except to breed

sheer quarried faces attract fulmars in search of a nest site.

Leave the car park and turn right down to the harbour. The concrete block on the south pier is part of a hopper into which the quarried whinstone was emptied from an overhead cableway.

Turn right alongside the harbour to pass the kipper sheds of Robsons and Sons, curers of the famous Craster kippers. The process of smoking herrings over oak chippings has not changed since the business was founded, and kippers from Craster find their way into the most exclusive food hampers.

Bear slightly right at the end of this road and go along Heugh Road before turning left onto the coast path. The Northumberland coast is well known for its sea birds, and cormorants, kittiwakes and eider ducks can be seen throughout the year.

The path goes around Cullernose Point which is part of the Great Whin Sill mentioned earlier. Man has utilised the defensive properties of the Sill for diverse fortifications over the centuries. One of these lies to the north in the shape of a graceful ruin – Dunstanburgh Castle. Building work on the castle was started in 1313 by Thomas of Lancaster. Throughout the Wars of the Roses, it was a Lancastrian stronghold, but fell into disrepair in the 1500s. The cliffs to the south of Cullernose are a nesting site for house martins, small blue and white birds, similar to swallows but with short forked tails. They build small, inverted mud huts under rock ledges in which to nest but the top corner of a window or gutter seems to suit them just as well, hence their name.

Eventually, the coast path leads to a beautifully chimneyed house, right on the edge of the cliff. This was built as a bathing house for the Grey family who owned Howick Hall (less than a mile up the road). The salt spray has weathered the rock into fantastic shapes, carving deep grooves into the softer bands of sandstone. On the seaward side of the promontory ahead is Rumbling Kern, a deep cleft in the cliff which earns its name from the sound effects created by an incoming tide. On the landward side of the Kern is the quarry which provided stone for the Greys' first house.

Turn right along the track waymarked Howick Burn Mouth and keep straight on at the road. In about ½ mile is the entrance to Howick Hall. The gardens in spring and early summer are breathtaking with an outstanding array of azaleas and rhododendrons; well worth a visit.

Turn right through the car park (just before the Hall entrance) and go through a gate to follow a farm track along the edge of a wood on the left. At the end of this wood, go through a gate (ignore the stile on the left) and cross the field ahead, which has a very narrow footpath leading straight through it towards a heugh. Cross a stile at the end of the field and now keep to the stone wall on the left. In the corner of the field is a ladder stile on the left, cross this, and now follow the right hand field boundary round to Craster South Farm. Here, turn right and go down to the road. Cross to the gate opposite and follow the well-surfaced footpath through the field to the wooded heugh. This is a small nature reserve owned by the Northumberland Wildlife Trust and dedicated to Dr Arnold Lawrence.

Follow this path back to Craster car park.

WALK 5

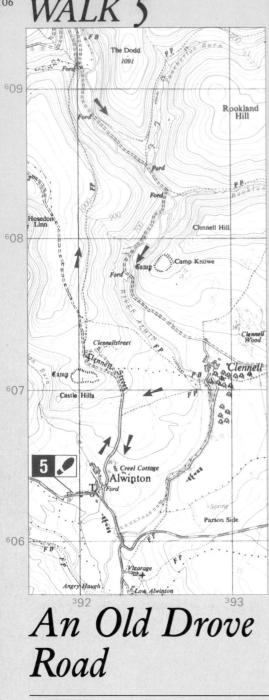

Long Crag south-west of Alwinton above Linshiels Lake

An Old Drove Road

Allow 2 hours

The small village of Alwinton nestles in the beautiful valley of the Upper Coquet which runs its course here between the ancient laval flows of the Cheviot Hills and the sediments of the fell sandstones. The landscape is wild and dramatic and empty but for sheep and the odd isolated farm.

Park in Alwinton car park (NT919063) and turn left out of the car park. Go straight across the village green over a small footbridge and turn left along the track. This is Clennell Street, one of many ancient roads which cross Northumberland and which remain because of the isolated nature of much of the county. The Roman marching camps here in the north were garrisoned by the ninth legion and were of great strategic importance. Chew Green was one; it lies 8 miles west of here, high in the hills on the Scottish border.

Begin the slow steady climb up the track and at the

first gate across Clennell Street cross the ladder stile and take a breather. The small knoll on the left was once the site of a well fortified or palisaded settlement. It is about 2,700 years old and was defended by wooden barricades. Why the ancients should choose such an exposed site is a mystery but it is thought that pressure of population forced people into less favourable areas and because of their isolation these sites have survived into the present century. The large hill on the right is Silverton Hill. In the valley bottom on the right is Clennell Hall which once belonged to the ancient family of that name. The name means 'hill that was clean' or 'free from undergrowth'.

Continue as the track sweeps around the tiny settlement of Clennellstreet. Cross the step stile over a wire fence just beyond the settlement, and follow the waymarker to another stile. The view back from here is excellent, with the Simonside Hills to the south-east and Long Crag due east.

Keep on this contour along the small, well-defined footpath well above a circular stone pen, known as a stell. This is the traditional gathering point for hill shepherds to herd their sheep into, for counting and checking.

Eventually the path goes past a stone cairn, complete with waymarker, and this points to another cairn and to the track to Kidlandlee Dean. Kidlandlee Forest stretches away in the distance, almost to the border. This is a good vantage point from which to view the steep valley sides of the River Alwin. The scree slopes are a relic of the last Ice Age when freeze-thaw action was intense enough to break up the exposed rock of the valley sides, creating a series of loose rock sheets. After the ice melted, vegetation crept back and most of this area became wooded. The trees have in turn been grazed out of existence by sheep.

Go through the gate at the bottom of the track and turn right to follow the river to Clennell. Keep to the main track as it skirts the hamlet and cross the cattle grid. Either keep straight on for about ¼ mile and turn right along the minor road past Alwinton church (this is of Norman origin and has the unusual feature of being separated from its chancel by about ten steps) or take the footbridge across the river. The footpath sign points the way up a bank, over a stile and along a raised bank across a field eventually meeting Clennell Street again. Turn left and retrace the beginning of the outward route back to the car park.

Lady's Well

Allow 1 to 1½ hours

Situated in the Coquet Valley, Holystone is one of Northumberland's prettiest villages with its well-built stone houses and delightful cottage gardens. This route passes the famous 'Lady's Well' before going on to Sharperton.

Park in the village of Holystone (NT954027) and take the waymarked path for Lady's Well in front of the Salmon Inn. After about 30yds, fork right over another stile and keep to this track to Lady's Well. The Well is now owned by the National Trust and the explanatory plaque here mentions St Ninian, the 5th-century apostle. In fact, Holystone is named after a stone which commemorated the fact that St Paulinus baptised 3,000 people at the spring here. If one considers that the total population for Northumberland was probably less than 10,000 at the time, this was either an extraordinary event or has been slightly exaggerated in the telling. However, the well was afterwards called St Ninian's and this was changed to Lady's Well when Holystone became the site for an Augustinian Priory in the first half of the 12th century.

After looking at the Well, continue along the track to cross another stile. Now follow the edge of the field and at the top of the rise, turn round for a superb view of the Simonside Hills. Go on to a gate where it can be extremely muddy if it has rained recently, but is easily passable if it has been dry. Head straight to a squeeze stile and cross another stile immediately ahead. Now follow the line of the fence. The village of Sharperton lies to the north-east and the River Coquet is to the east (on the right). Red squirrels frequent the Scots pine plantation on the right. Most of their diet is derived from conifer seeds, and the expansion of Northumberland's forests have been to their distinct advantage, although this expansion has not benefited all animals and plants mutually.

Go through the gate in the corner of the field and walk along the edge of this field, keeping the hawthorn trees on your right. At the end of the hawthorns, go through the metal gate which leads to the road. Turn right and go down the hill. In spring, the hedgebanks burgeon with wild flowers.

Ignore the road to Holystone at the bottom of the hill and cross the bridge over the River Coquet. Enjoy the view from the bridge with the river sweeping in wide bends along the wide flat bottom of the valley. The river is fed by many tributaries, most of which rise in the Cheviots close to the border 10 miles upstream. Oystercatchers, grey wagtails, pied wagtails and common sandpipers may be seen below the bridge.

Continue up the road, beyond the left-hand turn to Sharperton village and where the road bends left, go through a small gate on your right. Go down the path but beware the strip of dock leaves; these mark the course of a tiny but deep stream; the water is obscured by the vegetation. Take a big step across to the bank opposite and climb up through the trees keeping the fence on your left. The marsh on the right has a rich flora of lady's smock, lady's mantle, great willowherb, crosswort and horsetails. On the way up towards the woods, enjoy an excellent view of the River Coquet as it meanders seawards leaving great banks of boulders and pebbles in its wake. Downstream are workings belonging to the Ryton Sand and Gravel Company. The company has converted most of the old workings into a nature reserve, and this has proved hugely successful. Visitors are welcome, and should contact the site manager.

Go through the gate at the top of the wood and turn right along the edge of the field down to the footbridge. Cross the bridge and take the track straight ahead across the haugh to the minor road. The last section of the walk into the village passes a lovely water meadow on the left after a little bridge. Such flower-rich meadows have become rare as farming methods have advanced.

Just beyond the meadow, turn right into Holystone village.

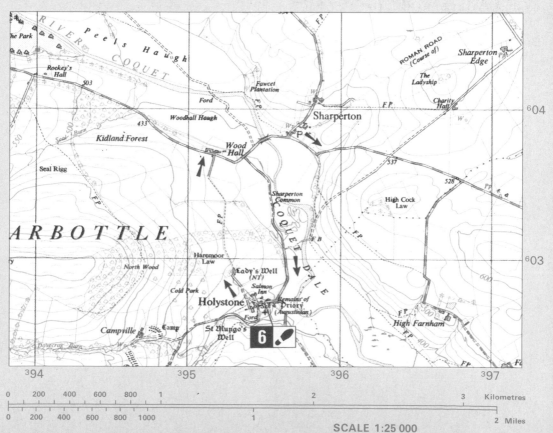

WALK 7

During the last century lovely Hareshaw Linn was a fashionable place for picnics

Hareshaw Linn

Allow 1½ hours

This is a delightful walk through a wooded gorge which leads to an unexpected waterfall in a rock amphitheatre.

Park in Hareshaw Linn car park (NY834840). The new factory units opposite are sited on an old iron

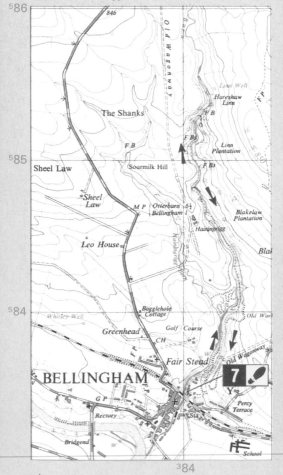

foundry yard. In the 1850s, for a few years only, this was the scene of a full-scale heavy industrial operation; coal and iron were brought down the Dene along a small railway, and water was carried to a water wheel to work bellows which fanned the furnace. The iron was of good quality and was used in the High Level Bridge in Newcastle, but although the product was good, competiton from foundries in Teesdale and Tyneside bankrupted the company.

Follow the finger-post signposted 'Hareshaw Linn' past Foundry Yard Farm on the right and through a kissing gate. Hareshaw means Grey Wood; linn is a northern word for waterfall.

The track now leads uphill and passes on the left old spoil heaps from the mining days. The spoil is alkaline and an unexpected result of the mining disturbance is that lime-loving plants such as quaking grass, salad burnet and thyme do well here.

Go through another kissing gate. The buttresses in the stream on the left are remnants of a dam which held back a head of water sufficient to turn the water wheel.

Keep to the line of the small railway which carried the iron ore from mines just around the corner. The small falls on the left were the result of a flood in 1975.

Wander up through the spoil heaps to a kissing gate which leads into the woods. The path through these woods was laid by people from Bellingham at the turn of the century. Its surface and six footbridges are now periodically restored with the help of volunteers. So great is the woods' botanical and wildlife interest that they are now in the care of the Northumberland National Park Authority. The plastic tubes which look like strange triffids are part of the woodland management programme; they encourage the growth of small trees by protecting them from rabbits and deer as well as wind and frost. On the way up the gorge, if you are here in the warmer months, have a go at identifying some of the plants; as well as the more obvious flowering plants there are many interesting mosses and ferns.

Eventually turn left over the sixth footbridge to see the Linn shooting over a ledge into a deep, dark plunge pool below. Enjoy the atmosphere and accoustics of the spot before retracing your steps back to the car park.

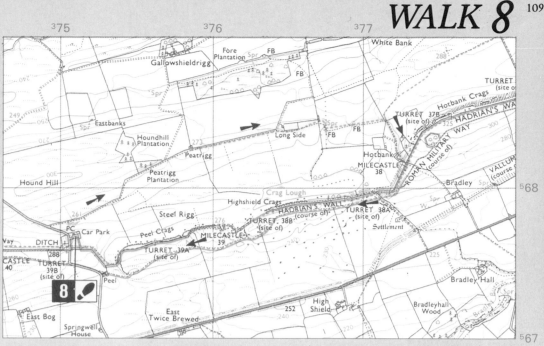

Hadrian's Wall

Allow 2 to 2½ hours

The impressive crags of the Great Whin Sill topped by the best remaining Roman monument in Europe make this an exciting and dramatic route, with fine views from both sides of the Wall. The track is prone to flooding and unless the ground is very dry, good boots or wellingtons are advisable.

Park in the National Park car park at Steel Rigg (NY751677) and turn right out of the main entrance onto a minor road. At the bottom of the hill turn right and go over the ladder stile, waymarked 'Hotbank'. Notice the crags rising above Crag Lough.

Follow the track. In the evening, when there are long shadows, the columnar structure of the Great Whin Sill is revealed. The sill is a wedge of volcanic rock which was forced in molten form through existing layers of sedimentary rock. It is at its most impressive here, forming continuous crags for several miles overall. The sill stretches in an arc from Teesdale through the south of Northumberland right to the Farne Islands. The castles of Bamburgh and Dunstanburgh are built on outcrops of it; as it is more resistant to weathering than the surrounding rock it stands proud, providing a natural defence. The Emperor Hadrian must have seen the crags here before commissioning the Wall and sensibly had them incorporated into the plans.

The track passes a plantation and a barn on the left and continues straight ahead. Cross two ladder stiles, now bear right and follow the path over a small stream and up through a meadow taking care to keep to the footpath. The low nutrient value of the soil means that grass growth is meagre here and farmers have to buy in expensive feed in the winter for their animals. Therefore the hay crop is very important and should not be damaged by trampling.

Cross a step stile. In the spring the ditch ahead is full of large yellow marsh marigolds. *Now make for the gate and stile almost straight ahead. Cross the stile, turn right through a gate and head towards Hotbank Farm.* On the approach to the farm look to the right for a good view of Crag Lough. This shallow lake is owned by the National Trust and is a good habitat for summer flowers and winter birds. The flat, marshy area extending to the right indicates the lake's former area. It is gradually silting up and will eventually disappear as the reeds are succeeded by mosses, birch and alder trees.

Keep straight ahead through a gate with the farm on the right; ignore the gate on the right to the farmyard and cross a stone step stile built into the wall. Now turn right and walk along the line of Hadrian's Wall. In a short distance is the site of Milecastle 38 which is now an overgrown ruin. This was built in AD122–6 to shelter the troops who patrolled the Wall. There was a milecastle every Roman mile (1,620yds) along the Wall and two turrets between each milecastle. As well as these minor fortifications, there were the forts, the most well preserved of which is Housesteads.

Continue along the Wall to a ladder stile, cross this, turn right over another ladder stile, turn left and climb up the path as it rises above Crag Lough. At the top, the path levels out and the views are exhilarating with sheer crags falling away to the Lough below.

From the top of the next ladder stile there is an excellent view of a newly excavated section of Hadrian's Wall. Notice the structure; there are properly faced outer sandstone blocks with awkwardly shaped chunks of whinstone (which are extremely difficult to cut and dress) used as the in-fill. Current archaeological evidence suggests the Wall once had a white mortared finish. On completion, it was about 15ft high and may have had a parapet, so with a rendering of creamy white mortar it would have stood out for miles!

Once over the stile, follow the footpath diversion down to a further stile in the wall (not the gate). Cross this and keep to the path past the work huts and bear right via an excavation-in-progress (c.1986) back onto the Wall. The path now undulates but the climbs and descents are short. At the next step stile, beware, the path descends via slippery steps which have been well polished by the feet of thousands of visitors. After the descent, the path has been diverted once again to allow fresh archaeological work to be carried out. *Follow the small valley on the right back towards Steel Rigg car park.* If excavations permit, go on to the Wall itself up the small ladder with its handrail, and turn around for a memorable view.

After about 50yds, step down through the wicket gate and take the path back into Steel Rigg car park.

WALK 9

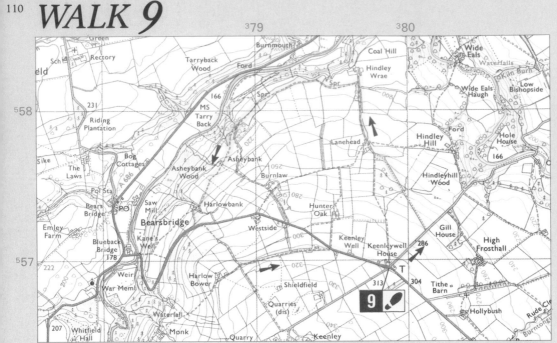

The Meeting of the Allens

Allow 1½ to 2 hours

This is an exhilarating walk high on the valley side, overlooking the meeting point of two rivers – the East and West Allen.

Park at the crossroads near Keenleywell House (NY798569) and take the minor road signposted Oakpool. Then turn down the first road on the left. Enjoy good views of the River East Allen which carves a valley on the right. Keep on this road as it passes a house on the left and a coniferous plantation a little further on. At the bottom end of the plantation turn left through a gate. The house which lies at the end of the track is Hindley Wrae and derives its name from 'the hill where the hinds graze' indicating that red deer may once have featured in the landscape here.

Follow the line of the drystone wall on the right and at the end of the wall follow the track to the small hawthorn tree in the corner of the field, over to the right, and go through the gate beside it. Look through the trees on the right for a view of the meeting point of the Allen rivers. *Now follow the line of the track onto a cobbled path which is an old drovers' road.* From this track, the views over the West Allen Valley are excellent with the wooded valley sides falling away steeply to the fast flowing river below. The variety of trees make a splendid show of colour in the autumn.

As the path leaves the wall, pass beneath an avenue of trees and then go through the gate ahead (beware of the wet patch). The path now crosses a small burn and turns slightly right to head up through the field, in front of a small cottage. Turn left through the gate and then bear right in about 15yds along the fence line to continue parallel with the river valley. Cross an old field boundary and head for the large ash tree ahead; just to the right of the tree, the roof of a house called Harlowbank comes into view. Keeping the row of mature trees and hawthorns on the right, walk along to

The fast-flowing East Allen seen from Cupola Bridge. It joins the West Allen nearby

the end of the field, through a gate and turn right in front of Harlowbank. This name relates to a gathering of people; Harlow Bower, less than ½ mile away, means the cottage where people assembled.

Bear left up the track (by kind permission of the owner) being sure to fasten the gate onto the road. Pause at the road for a look at the view; the cluster of houses in the valley to the south is Whitfield. Lead mining was a principal industry in the Allen valleys in the last century and ore was brought from Alston to be smelted at Whitfield. Two miles downstream was one of the principal mills, and Cupola Bridge, carrying the A686, takes its name from a type of furnace used in the smelting process.

Turn left up the road and in about 30 paces cross a stone stile built into the drystone wall on the right. Now walk straight up this field (it is quite steep) keeping in a line parallel with the conifer plantation to the far right. At the end of the field is a gate beside a wych elm; go through this and keep the drystone wall on the right.

At the top of this field cross the ladder stile. The farm on the right is Harlow Bower, mentioned earlier. *Turn left along the track and in about ½ mile it joins the road, turn right for a short distance to return to the crossroads.*

Moor and Mine

Allow 2 hours

From the historic village of Blanchland, this walk leads up to open moorland which offers spectacular views, on a clear day, of the northern Pennines, before returning to the Derwent Valley.

Park in the public car park in Blanchland (NY964505). Turn left onto a minor road which follows a stream. In the spring and early summer the hedgebanks lining this road are thick with cow parsley, germander speedwell, greater stitchwort, meadow cranesbill and creeping buttercup. As the path passes by the plantation on the right, listen for the song of wrens, chaffinches, blackbirds and the thin 'zis' of the goldcrest.

The road climbs up a small, steep hill to the little settlement of Shildon. This is surrounded by relics of the leadmining days of the last century. Spoil heaps behind the cottages remain bare of vegetation and on the left of the track is an old smelt mill chimney. Do not attempt to explore the workings as there are hidden shafts which are dangerous. Lead mining is probably Northumberland's oldest industry; it began in Roman times, and apart from a lull in the Dark Ages, lead has been consistently sought after and was mined up to the 1920s.

Keep left at the road fork and continue as the track climbs steadily past a sitka spruce and Scots pine plantation on the left and a barn on the right. The country changes from the intimate reaches of the burn to open pastures leading to the moorland of Bulbeck Common. The flora changes too and in summer there are northern marsh orchids in the ditch on your right, among the fairy flax, birdsfoot trefoil and lady's mantle. Orchids rely on a particular micro-organism in the soil to sustain their growth and this is why they cannot withstand being transplanted. On the approach to the heather moorland, listen for the bubbling call of the curlew which nests here before returning to its winter feeding grounds around the coast.

The track is gated just before Pennypie House; go through the first gate, ignore the track up to the house and go through another gate straight ahead. Turn left and cross a small plank bridge. Now follow this moorland track which is a public road. Lapwings also nest on the moors. In the spring they tumble earthwards at alarming speeds in spectacular aerobatic display flights. As the track begins to lose height, the views across the northern Pennines are superb. Bolts Law on the right is the highest point on the skyline and Edmundbyers Common rises on the left. Between them an old lead-mining chimney punctuates the horizon and on a clear day you can make out other relics of lead-mining workings below it.

Go through the gate at the end of the moor and follow the track down the steep hill. Be careful going down as the loose gravel on this steep track can be slippery. Baybridge nestles at the foot of the hill.

At the road junction turn right, pass Baybridge picnic site on the right and take the waymarked footpath for Blanchland on the left, just before the river bridge. Cross the boardwalk, turn right and follow the River Derwent back to Blanchland.

The abbey here was founded in 1175 by Premonstratensian monks (after Prémontres in Normandy). It takes its name from an abbey near Cherbourg called Blancheland, which means White Glade, or Lawn. Like many places in Northumberland the abbey was subject to raids from the Scots and on one occasion, when mist foiled an attempted raid by the Scots, the monks rang the abbey bells in thanksgiving at being saved, only to guide the Scots back with disastrous consequences.

Go up through the village past the old school to return to the car park.

Lapwings, or peewits, feed over farmland

SCALE 1:25 000

WALK *11*
Derwent Valley Woodlands

Allow 2½ to 3 hours

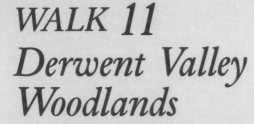

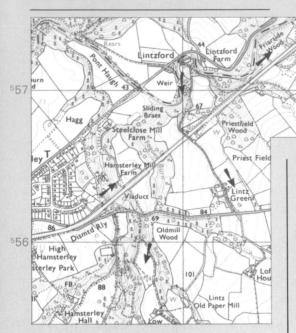

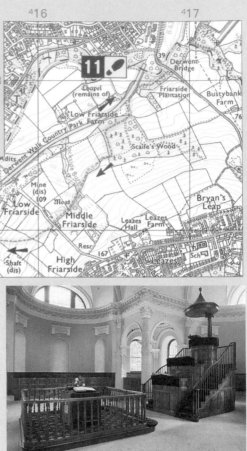

Built in 1760, Gibside Chapel was repaired and redecorated in 1966

This walk is varied with woodland, stream, and riverside stretches, ending with a final easy return along a reclaimed railway track – part of the Derwent Walk which follows the old railway line from Swalwell to Consett.

Park in the car park on the northern side of the River Derwent at Rowlands Gill (NZ161581). Cross the river by the former railway viaduct which now carries the Derwent Walk. Take the footpath to the left immediately beyond the concrete decking. This leads to Scaifes Wood, a commercial plantation of Norway spruce (better known as the Christmas tree).

Further on, follow a lovely grassy path through an avenue of mature larch trees. After a sharp climb, the path emerges on the valley side at a point where there is a stile with a grand view of the valley, Rowlands Gill and Chopwell Woods. Turn left and follow the path up the side of the field. At Middle Friarside, cabbages and cauliflowers alternate with Christmas trees, a strange mixture but an indication of the variety of soils and farming systems present in the valley.

After crossing the road the path descends and meets a perfectly straight downhill track. This once provided the collieries up the hill with an outlet for their coal. Trainloads of coal were lowered down the incline to join the railway. Before the invention of the steam engine, wagons with wooden wheels were hauled by horses along wooden rails from these collieries to the river.

Continue in a straight line and at the Derwent Walk turn left. After 50yds turn right towards Lintzford. Oak and birch woodland, unaffected by man and as natural as any wood can be, reaches down to an idyllic riverside. Only 50yds upstream stands Lintzford Mill, once a water-driven paper mill and little changed since Georgian times. The bridge, house and granite-paved roads reflect the pride and perhaps the affluence of its builder.

Take the cart-track uphill behind the mill towards Lintz Green. At the tarmac road turn right (be careful, this ia busy road) and then left after the 'road narrows' sign to enter Old Mill Wood by the public footpath. This beautiful mixed mature woodland is owned by the Woodland Trust, a charity formed to protect English woods. Footpaths lead in all directions; some are public, others 'permissive' (usable by the permission of the owners).

Cross the footbridge and follow the path into the next valley. Step over the stream and aim for the waterfall – audible from some distance. *Cross the Pont Burn either above or below the falls and at the Hamsterley Hall drive, turn right towards the road again.* Hamsterley Hall stands at the end of the drive. It has recently been divided into three separate residences but was once the home of R S Surtees of Jorrocks fame and later, Lord Gort, the Commander of the British Expeditionary Force in France before Dunkirk. The bridge along the drive is known as Handley Cross Bridge, and is thought to have been built with the proceeds of Surtees' novel of that name. The gates beside the lodge are a fine example of real wrought ironwork.

Turn left at the road, then right opposite the car park to join the Derwent Walk and return to Rowlands Gill. From the viaducts the views of tree tops and the countryside beyond are superb. Even in Victorian times, when one-shilling excursions from Newcastle were popular, this railway was renowned for its scenery. Gibside Chapel, now in the care of the National Trust, is close to Rowlands Gill and should not be missed. It was built as a mausoleum for members of the Bowes family; evensong is held here on the first Sunday in each month, and there are annual programmes of concerts and guided walks.

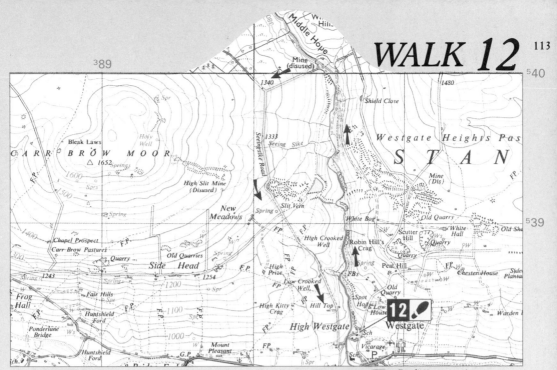

Millers, Miners and Farmers

The Cheviot – native to the Border country

Allow 1½ hours

A short circular walk alongside the Middlehope Burn, rich in natural beauty and wildlife, with fascinating glimpses of how man worked the land for its hidden wealth in past years. The path may be slippery and muddy in places, so stout footwear should be worn. A beck crossing has to be undertaken to complete the circular route. Alternatively there is an equally delightful and easier there and back walk.

Park in Westgate High Town; there is ample informal parking to the west of the moor road near the butcher's shop (NY907382). Walk up the narrow lane between the houses, and on through the gate past High Mill, respectful of the fact that you are walking through a private garden. High Mill is now simply a house, but once ground corn for the inhabitants of Westgate and surrounding parts, in an age when all scattered communities had to be largely self-sufficient. The large green pipe across the burn is a water main, taking drinking water from Burnhope reservoir to Wearside.

Walk on through the kissing gate beside the pretty little waterfalls, and follow the path over two wooden footbridges, as it criss-crosses the burn. The bank sides rise steeply from the rocky bed, and are covered with a typical north country scrub woodland mixture of hazel, blackthorn, alder and rowan – so hazelnuts and sloes may be found here in autumn. Dippers are busy up and down the burn all year, a sure sign of pure water — look for them bobbing and curtseying on any rock near the stream.

Pass through the handgate to Slit Mine. There are extensive industrial remains on either side of the path. The valley floor is narrow and tight, so the burn was covered to make more working space. Waterwheels and hydraulic engines worked here,

and the slit shaft was one of the deepest in the North Pennines lead industry – 585ft, which the miners negotiated by ladders. The shaft is safely capped, but all lead sites are dangerous, so explore with caution.

Follow the path beside the burn, by way of stiles over low walls, to Middlehope Shield Mine. The buildings have almost entirely disappeared, but retaining walls, dams, level mouths and bridge abutments all remain, a monument to the supreme skills of the masons. Some of the unfenced drops are hazardous; be careful where you stand.

Walk on up the path to the last gated mine opening on your right. The Middlehope Valley opens out here; there are no trees or scrub, and hill sheep and beef cattle graze contentedly among the lead mining remains. The sheep ensure that trees cannot colonise these rough pastures by nibbling any seedling that tries to establish itself.

You can choose either to retrace your steps from this point, or you can jump or ford the burn, go through the gate opposite, and join the Seeingsike Road, a green lane heading back down to Westgate. This is a road for tractors and landrovers, but it is ideal for walkers, with splendid panoramic views over Weardale on the descent.

Leave the road where it turns off to the right, and walk straight ahead through the field gate to follow the deteriorating track past High and Low Crooked Well. Here is an illustration of the results of upland depopulation — stoutly built long-founded dwellings falling into ruin. Gone are the large families raised here only a generation or two ago.

Follow the track down through the last farm gate, then turn left and then sharp left back over the footbridge to cross the Middlehope Burn for the last time. Take the left fork to Westgate High Town.

SCALE 1:25 000

WALK 13
Hill, Hall and Farm

Allow 2½ hours

The walk travels up and down the magnesian limestone ridge from which most of Durham County, the North Sea and the five adjoining counties can be seen. There are remarkable views over the industry and agriculture of the pleasant Durham landscape to the Cleveland Hills, the Pennines and the Cheviots.

Park beside the Duke of York public house at Littletown (NY340434) and walk between the houses of Plantation Avenue. Enter Dog Kennel Wood and the grounds of Elemore Hall by a stile. Cross the stream, go through the gate and take the path on the left. The Hall and its surrounding parkland was created by the Baker family, whose wealth came from the coal beneath. The house is now a special school; its pupils sleep and study beneath the marvellous stucco-work ceilings created by Guiseppe Cortese, an 18th-century Italian craftsman. The landscape gardens have gone and the park has been planted with conifers by British Coal to produce pit props.

Follow the track and a good way along meet the junction of three footpaths in the plantation of young trees, cross the stream and turn right on to a lesser footpath, keeping the stream on your right as you head for Low Haswell Farm. Surprisingly, Low Haswell is at the top of a hill. High Haswell is even higher and from the road which joins the two (a slight diversion) the North Sea can be seen sparkling in the east. The coastal collieries mine coal from as far as six miles out beneath the sea.

Turn left over the stile at Low Haswell and drop down to the Coldwell Burn. The valley of the Coldwell Burn is a perfect place to rest before the climb through East Wood to Hetton le Hill, a farm of almost village dimensions. The buildings are of local limestone, creamy yellow and known as dolomite. It weathers badly but almost shines in the sun. This stone was once the bed of a prehistoric sea. A massive distortion of the earth's crust many millions of years ago forced the rock to rise above the surrounding plain, bringing with it fossils of fish and insects.

Walk through the farm, cross the road, turn right and take the footpath to the left 50yds on. Penshaw Monument, ahead, looking from here like a giant television screen, was built to honour Radical Jack Lambton, the 1st Earl of Durham and first Governor of Canada. The Monument belongs to the National Trust and is open all year during daylight hours. From here, or at High Moorsley, a large proportion of industrial Tyneside, and land on both sides of the River Wear is visible.

The footpath leads to the road. Turn right, cross the road with care and take the path to the left. At the bottom of the hill turn left again to cross the road once more. Pittington Hill, like most of the limestone ridge, has been quarried in the past but has reverted to rough grazing.

The path circumnavigates the hill, along the contour. Follow the path until it meets the road; cross it 100yds ahead to join the wide path descending to Littletown. This final leg across the plain is over a reclaimed pit heap – for which Durham was infamous only 20 years ago – and a rubbish dump. The scars are not yet fully healed but the countryside is transformed. Such measures have ensured that pit heaps are now a rarity in this county.

Killhope and Carriers' Way

Jays move into conifer and birchwoods to breed

Allow 3 hours + 1 hour at the Lead Mining Centre

A vigorous hike over a lofty watershed, following in the hoofprints of pack horses carrying lead ore from the Weardale mines to the Allendale smelt mills. There are dark pine forests and heather-clad fells, the fascinating remains of a once vital industry, and a delightfully secluded up-country village. The moorland crossing requires navigational skills if there is hill mist or low cloud, and should only be undertaken if you have map and compass, and suitable footwear and clothing for adverse weather conditions.

Park at the Killhope Lead Mining Centre, which is open daily from Easter to the end of October (NY825431). The Centre covers all aspects of this fascinating industry, with expert staff on hand to explain the graphic displays, ingenious working models and impressive outdoor restorations. The great Killhope Wheel here is one of the marvels of our industrial heritage.

Cross the burn either at the ford or, if the water is too high, at the footbridge opposite the mine shop. Enter the forest through the gate beside the road bridge, and follow the track as it twists and climbs steeply up through the dark conifers. This is unnatural woodland, a dense single-species blanket planting for a timber crop, though you may glimpse roe deer and elusive jays which have moved in to take advantage of the

shelter. The afforestation is interesting because of the altitude – the top boundary fence is just above the tree line, the 1,800ft contour beyond which trees will not thrive. Experimental plots were established higher to the left of Carriers' Way; here the stunted wind-blasted trees are only waist-high, although planted at the same time as the main forest.

Go out through the forest gate and carefully follow the occasional 3ft-high wooden marker posts through moss and heather towards the skyline. Pick your route with care to avoid getting wet feet – never stand on anything bright green is a sound guide. The rounded summit to your left is Killhope Law, complete with a huge stone-built beacon mound. This dates from the Napoleonic Wars, and would have been lit as part of an early-warning system if the French had invaded.

Cross over the watershed to join the landrover track leading to a shooting cabin near the beacon. Turn right and head downhill towards the village of Allenheads. The view is breathtaking on a clear day – the distant hills to the north are the Cheviots, over 50 miles distant. The track which you are following down into Allendale is, in places, built on the collapsed ruins of the vaulted arch of the smelt mill flue, which carried deadly fumes away from the mill. Beside the track is a lovely horseshoe-shaped reservoir, another lead-mining relic.

Follow the road up into Allenheads, a 19th-century mining development with a big mine right in the centre of the village. Follow the walled lane round behind the hotel and past the old church, then take the track and footpaths linking former lead-miners' smallholdings to rejoin Carriers' Way. Turn left back uphill and retrace your steps to Killhope to complete the round trip undertaken by the carriers' ponies of a century ago.

SCALE 1:25 000

WALK 15
The Green Trod

Allow 4 hours + 30 minutes in Visitor Centre

A blood-stirring upland walk, with spectacular rocky river scenery and open windswept moorland. The circuit involves some bog and boulder hopping and should not be undertaken lightly – you will need boots, windproof and waterproof clothing, map, compass, and a small rucksack. Great care is needed on certain sections if children are present.

Park at Bowlees Picnic Area (NY907283). Follow the path across the beck and up the steps to the Visitor Centre (open daily from Easter to late autumn, with varied opening hours during the season). The Centre gives a fascinating account of the interaction of man, the elements and natural history in Upper Teesdale through the ages, and should not be missed – call now or on your return.

Go on past the Centre, down the narrow metalled lane and cross the road by the police box to the kissing gate diagonally opposite. Follow the path across two meadow fields to the pinch stile at the woodland edge. Low Force is a perfectly balanced mix of rushing peat-brown water, dark rock and handsome trees, and Wynch Bridge is as much a romantic landscape adornment as a river crossing. The bridge dates from 1830; it replaces an earlier structure with only one handrail, said to be the first suspension bridge in England. Low Force is known locally as Salmon Leap, and older folk hereabouts tell tales of pools being so crammed with the noble fish that they could be forked out by the barrow-load.

Cross the bridge, and turn right up the Pennine Way, following the clearly-defined riverside path to the Upper Teesdale National Nature Reserve. Walk on duckboards through the juniper forest to High Force. From the path there are spectacular views of the falls and the gorge below, **but the whinstone cliffs are sheer, slippery and unfenced, so take great care.**

Continue to the footbridge, with the delicate Flea Beck Force high up on your left. Pause here, and take account of modern-day upland economics. All the ingredients can be seen from this viewpoint: sheep, red grouse, nature conservation and recreation, and the extractive industries of water and minerals.

Walk on up Bracken Rigg, turn sharp left off the Pennine Way by the waymark post, and through the watergate to join the Green Trod near the NNR board. This is the ancient drovers' road linking Teesdale with the Eden Valley, a centuries-old route for livestock and humans, clearly defined by the passage of countless feet. It is still used by shepherds at dipping, clipping and gathering times, and you may be lucky enough to share the trod with a flock of hill sheep on the move, attended by border collies and men on dales ponies.

Turn left along the trod, with three becks to cross by fording or boulder-hopping, then join the Silver Bank track made by leadminers and now used only by shepherds and gamekeepers. Follow the track as it threads down between whinstone crags to the metalled road at the west end of Holwick, then turn sharp left along the road. The imposing mansion is Holwick Lodge, the Earl of Strathmore's shooting house.

When the road bears left follow the footpath straight ahead through meadows and pastures to Low Force and so back to Bowlees.

The River Tees

Allow 3 hours

A pastoral stroll along both banks of the Tees, a meandering mature river with the turbulent ways of a mountain torrent. Walking is largely on the level, apart from the occasional incline, and mainly on grassland which is often damp enough for stout footwear. At either end of the walk are castles and footbridges.

Park in Barnard Castle, either in Galgate, Horsemarket or the main car park (NZ049166). Barney, as it is familiarly known by all dalesfolk, is a perfect gem of a small North Pennines market town, handsome, friendly and full of character.

Go down the side road between the whitewashed Post Office and the large Methodist church at the bottom of Galgate; leave the castle on your left and follow the sign 'To the Woods'. Follow the track along the riverside when it reaches the footbridge. The woods beside the Tees Banks footpaths are varied, beautiful, and commercially managed; trees are felled and timber extracted. This can leave ugly scars briefly, but

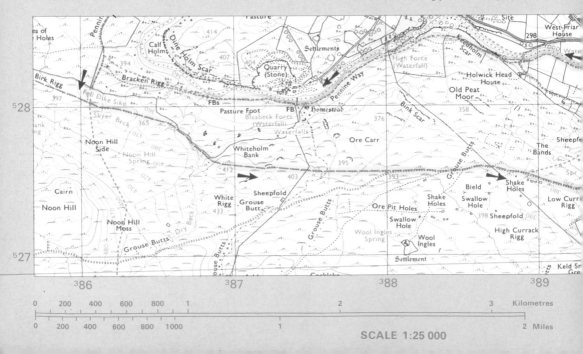

SCALE 1:25 000

replanting is part of the cycle, and nature is a great healer.

The path passes below another castle-like tower, with its double over the river – remnants of a railway viaduct. At a bend in the river, where steps were skilfully cut in the bedrock for access to a sulphur spring in Victorian times, look out for the dippers and kingfishers which haunt the waters here.

At the end of the woodland track go on through the field gate, then turn right almost immediately through a smaller handgate and climb up the steep bank, over the stile, and turn sharp left to walk alongside the fence. This is prime dairy land, the permanent meadows and pastures of the traditionally whitewashed Raby Estate farms.

Continue past West Holme House via gates and stiles, then where the fence curves look for the large waymarking arrow and follow the narrow path down to a slabstone footbridge. The path leads on by more gates and stiles and a sometimes slippery descent to the meeting of the waters of the rivers Balder and Tees, then by two substantial footbridges and a metalled lane steeply up to the delightful village of Cotherstone. A Norman castle once crowned the steep bank overlooking the waters' meeting point but all the stones are long gone into villagers' houses and barns. Cotherstone cheese is a local delicacy, still made by a few farmers' wives.

Continue down the village street, turn left down a narrow lane opposite the school, and follow its winding way past houses, gardens and allotments. Then turn left to follow Mill Hill Farm track back towards the Tees, and take the footpath off to the left before reaching the farmhouse.

The path now dips down twice to the riverside, by way of Cooper House Farm and a Klondike-like log cabin, then crosses Grise Beck and rises steeply up through Towlerhill Plantation (this section can be slippery). You are now in a different, arable world – the crop here is almost certain to be barley.

The right of way goes to the left round the margin between crop and fence to Towler Hill, but it may be better to take the path straight across the field towards the old railway bridge, then go by farm track left to Towler Hill – use whichever route seems most walked, subject to the dictates of common sense. Go on by way of stiles and steps to descend from the old viaduct, joining the farm road leading back to Barnard Castle. Pause on the waterbridge over the Tees to look at the castle. The oriel window overlooking the river was the vantage point of King Richard III.

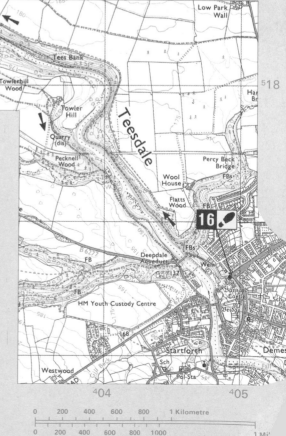

The ruins of Barnard Castle above the Tees

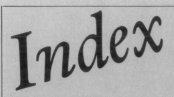

Page numbers in bold type
indicate main entries.

Acknowledgements

The publishers would like to thank the many individuals who helped in the preparation of this book. Special thanks are due to the Durham County Council Planning Department and the Northumberland National Park Authority.

The Automobile Association wishes to thank the following photographers, organisations and libraries. Many of the photographs reproduced are the copyright of the AA Picture Library.

Dean & Chapter Library Durham 11 Seal of Hugh de Puiset, 27 St Cuthbert's Pectoral Cross, 41 Conyers Falchion; *Folk Dance Society* 13 Rapier Dancing, 15 Clog Dancing (P J Power); *A J Hopkins* 22/23 Marsh Marigold, 22 Large Heath Butterfly, 24 Pinnacles Farne Isle, 42 Flodden Battlefield, 66 Simonside Hills, 67 Bloody Cranesbill, 99 Cawfields, 106 Cheviots, 110 East Allen River; *Houseteads Museum* 19 Sculpture from the Wall; *B Johnson* 73 Vindolanda Fort; *The Mansell Collection* Back Cover Newcastle upon Tyne, 9 Bamburgh Castle, 35 Lancelot Brown, 47 Dunstanburgh Castle, 48/49 Stockton & Darlington Railway, 52 Grace Darling, 117 Barnard Castle; *Mary Evans Picture Library* 48 George Stephenson; *S & O Mathews* 1 Alnwick Castle, 3 Cauldron Snout, 5 Smailholm Tower, 11 Flodden Field, 18/19 Houseteads Fort, 20 Vindolanda, 26 Saxon Horses Head, 28 Escomb, 33 Morpeth, 34 Alnmouth, 36 Amble Repairing Pots, 36 Bamburgh, 37 Barnard Castle, 37 Butter Market, 37 Seahouses, 38 Beamish Museum, 38 Co-op store, 38 The Street, 39 Berwick-upon-Tweed, 40 Bishop Auckland Castle, 40 Blanchland, 42 River Beamish, 44 Chesters Fort, 44 Chillingham Wild White Cattle, 45 Coldstream, 47 Craster, 47 Dunstanburgh Castle, 48 Darlington Railway Museum, 50 Durham Cathedral doorknocker, 50/51 Durham Cathedral, 52 Farne Islands, 53 Farne Island rocks, 54 Heighington, 55 Hexham Abbey Frith Stool, 55 Hexham, 56 Holy Island Lindisfarne Castle, 57 Hadrian's Wall, 58 Kelso, 58 Jedburgh Abbey, 59 Keilder Forest, 60 Mellerstain House, 60 Lanchester, 61 Low Force, 62 Newcastle, 64 Fish Stall North Shields, 64 Norham Castle, 65 Ovingham Churchyard, 65 Piercebridge Cottages, 66 Brinkham Priory, 68 Seaholm Houses, 68 Seaton Sluice, 69 Sedgefield Hardwick Hall C P, 70 Raby Castle, 73 Wallington Hall, 74 Wark, 75 Washington Old Hall, 76 Cullercoats, 77 Wylam, 94 Beadnell Lime Kiln, 94 Alnwick Castle, 99 St John's Chapel, 100 High Force, 101 Hamsterley Forest, 101 Stanhope, 102 Holy Island & Lindisfarne Castle, 115 Allendale; *Nature Photographs Ltd* 21 Grey Seal Calf (C H Gomersal), 22 Hen Harrier (F V Blackburn), 23 Puffin (P A Sterry), 24 Grey Seal (W Paton), 42 Grey Wagtail (P A Sterry); *Newcastle Upon Tyne City Libraries* 62/63 Newcastle, 63 SS Mauretania, 71 Ashington Colliery; *Northumberland County Record Office* 29 Haymaking at Mitford; *Northumberland National Park* 30 Ploughing stubble, 31 Sheep shearing, 95 & 97 Elsdon Pele Tower, 108 Hareshaw Linn; *Doc Rowe* 76 Whalton Baal Fire; *Sunderland Museum* 75 Lambton Worm; *R Surman* Cover Hadrian's Wall, 17 Hadrian's Wall, 46 Craigside; *University College Oxford* 25 Ornamental Initial, 25 St Cuthbert's Trial, 26 St Cuthbert's Body; *D Williams* 16 Allendale Fire Festival, 43 Chester-le-Street, Lumley Castle; *H Williams* 54 Allen Banks; *Tim Woodcock* 14 Northumbrian Pipes, 27 St Cuthbert's Cave, 35 Alnwick, 57 St Pauls Jarrow, 72 Tynemouth Priory, 74 Warkworth, 83 Penshaw Monument, 93 Jesmond Dene, 112 Gibside Chapel; *G N Wright* 6/7 River Coquet, 9 Bamburgh Castle, 10 Lindisfarne, 27 Holy Island Priory, 29 Hay Pikes, 30/31 Upper Teesdale, 32 Keilder Forest, 67 Killhope Wheel, 77 Glendale Show Wooler.

Other Ordnance Survey Maps of Northumbria

How to get there with Routemaster and Routeplanner Maps

Reach Northumbria from Edinburgh, Glasgow, York, Leeds, Manchester and Liverpool using Routemaster map sheets 4 and 5. Alternatively use the Ordnance Survey Great Britain Routeplanner Map which covers the whole country on one map sheet.

Exploring with Landranger Maps

Landranger Series
1¼ inches to one mile or 1:50,000 scale

These maps cover the whole of Britain and are good for local motoring and walking. Each contains tourist information such as parking, picnic places, viewpoints and rights of way. Sheets covering the Northumbria and The Borders are:

74 Kelso
75 Berwick-upon-Tweed
80 Cheviot Hills and Keilder Forest
81 Alnwick and Morpeth
87 Hexham and Haltwhistle
88 Tyneside and Durham

Other titles available in this series are: